Gallipoli Peninsula and the Troad

TAN Travel Guide

© Copyright 2019 by Izabela Miszczak

Technical editing: J&M

On the cover: Ottoman fortress in Kilitbahir

ISBN: 978-83-944269-9-6 (paperback)
ISBN: 978-83-953130-0-4 (ePub)
ISBN: 978-83-953130-1-1 (Kindle eBook)

Publisher: ASLAN Publishing House

Contact: contact@turkisharchaeonews.net
FaceBook: http://facebook.com/turkisharchaeonews
WWW: http://turkisharchaeonews.net/

Second Edition. February 2019.

Izabela Miszczak

Gallipoli Peninsula
and the Troad

TAN Travel Guide

Contents

Preface

Gallipoli Peninsula and the Troad. TAN Travel Guide has been prepared for the travellers who intend to spend active holidays exploring the northwestern part of Turkey, especially the Gallipoli Peninsula and the Troad. If you want not only to relax and sunbathe, but also to visit some historical buildings and archaeological sites, this is the book for you. It will help you to get acquainted with the most important information about Turkey and its northwestern part, to plan the entire trip and to select the places worth seeing. History lovers will be able to use it to locate rarely visited ruins of ancient cities, the seekers of beautiful landscapes will find tips on the most attractive viewpoints and the gourmets will get numerous suggestions for the best restaurants in the region.

The guidebook is divided into four main sections, organized geographically. They represent, respectively, the areas of the Gallipoli Peninsula, the Northern Troad, the Southern Troad, and the Turkish islands in the Aegean Sea. In each section, you will find in-depth descriptions of main cities, smaller towns, historical sites, and natural treasures located in the area. The descriptions these places provide their exact location, and, where it is essential, the opening hours, ticket prices, and other practical information. In the case of the cities, there are the sections outlining the accommodation options, including hotels and campsites, as well as restaurants, shops and malls, and the issues related to public transport. These places are also represented on maps and plans.

In addition to the main sections, the guidebook includes additional chapters, collected in the Appendices section. They are devoted to the most important issues related to travelling to Turkey.

You will find out what you need to do before visiting the country, learn the main facts concerning its inhabitants, the geography, and cuisine. You will find advice on souvenirs and methods of payment as well as weather information. There are also chapters devoted to the history of Greek settlements in this area and the Battle of Gallipoli. The final part of this guidebook is a bibliography that provides suggestions for further reading about the Troad and the Gallipoli Peninsula.

The second edition of this guidebook has been thoroughly revised and updated, including ticket prices and opening hours for 2019. Relevant information concerning renovations and reopenings has also been added. Moreover, this edition presents the newly opened Troy Museum and its fabulous collections.

In the book you will find:

- 30 maps and plans that facilitate orientation;
- detailed descriptions of 20 major cities and towns of the region plus numerous villages;
- descriptions of 10 ancient sites, along with their history and driving directions;
- descriptions of natural landmarks, islands, castles, fortresses, and museums;
- suggested tours around the Memorial Sites of the Gallipoli Peninsula and the sightseeing routes in the Northern and the Southern Troad;
- accurate information on regional bazaars.

About TAN

TAN stands for Turkish Archaeological News, a website

https://TurkishArchaeoNews.net/

created in 2013 with the aim of providing news about the latest archaeological discoveries in Turkey and neighbouring regions. The project has been developed into a travel portal, dedicated to history buffs who visit Turkey searching for historical buildings, ancient ruins, and fascinating museums. TAN website publishes the texts about such places as well as the news concerning archae-ological excavations and discoveries. All our texts are illustrated with original photos that TAN editorial team has taken during our travels around Turkey. We have been visiting this beautiful country regularly since 2004, and the website, as well as TAN Travel Guides, are the reflection of our ongoing fascination with Asia Minor.

About the Author

Izabela Miszczak is the editor of TurkishArchaeoNews.net website devoted to the cultural heritage of Asia Minor. She holds a Master diploma in social sciences, with the specialization in the sociology of culture. She has authored publications in the area of political studies and social science. She has also written several travel guides in Polish and English, and edits TurcjaWSandalach.pl portal for independent travelers. She lives in Poland with her husband, two kids, and two dogs.

Gallipoli Peninsula

The Gallipoli Peninsula, which belongs geographically to the Eastern Thrace, is a piece of land that defines the course of the Dardanelles. Its strategic location, on the sea route leading to Istanbul, was the reason of many bloody conflicts in the past. Currently, the majority of tourists arriving at the peninsula want to visit the places associated with an unusually fierce military campaign, which took place during the First World War. However, it is worth remembering that these areas also hide other impressive monuments, testifying to the rich past of the peninsula.

Do not miss

During your stay in the region of the Gallipoli Peninsula necessarily visit:

- the town of Gelibolu, especially the Piri Reis Museum and the prayer area known as Azebler Namazgah;
- the fortress and bunkers of Kilitbahir;
- several military cemeteries and memorial sites, especially the one called Abide, i.e. Çanakkale Martyrs' Memorial.

Short history

In ancient times, this geographical region was known as the Thracian Chersonesos. It was inhabited by the tribes of the Thracians. In the 7th century BCE, the Greeks began to settle here. They founded around a dozen cities on the peninsula. After a turbulent period of history associated with the Greek conflict with Persia, the Thracian Chersonesos finally got under the control of Macedonia. In the 2nd century CE, the Romans took it over and attached it to their province of Asia. The area was subsequently controlled by the Eastern Roman Empire, and was later conquered by the Ottoman Turks.

The Gallipoli Peninsula got into the Turkish hands gradually. The first attempts to gain a foothold in Europe were made in the 13th century. The peninsula became an important base for the conquest of Europe by the Ottomans from the year 1356. This fact means that the peninsula had already been controlled by the Ottomans for almost 100 years before the conquest of Constantinople by Mehmet the Conqueror. Within the peninsula, there are numerous reminders of the Turkish conquest of this strategic European foothold.

During the First World War, when the Ottoman Empire sided with the Central Powers, the Gallipoli Peninsula became the scene of ferocious fighting between the Turkish forces and the forces of the Entente. The control of the Ottoman capital city – Istanbul – was at stake. Initially, the Allied forces sought to break through to Istanbul by sea. In February 1915, in the waters of the Aegean Sea, 18 warships, under the British, French, and Russian banners arrived, just off the Gallipoli Peninsula. However, an attempt to move up through the strait failed, as there were numerous forts with gun batteries, diligently guarding the peninsula. Additionally, the strait was defended by minefields and anti-submarine nets. The Allies retreated after the loss of three ships and decided to start the overland campaign.

This campaign resulted in the Allied defeat and proved that the Gallipoli Peninsula was impossible to conquer. The balance of the struggle in the years 1915-1916 was tragic. According to various sources, from 120 to 130 thousand combatants were killed, and 2/3 of them were the soldiers of the Ottoman army so they paid for the victory with great losses. Among the fallen Allied soldiers, most were from the UK, France, Australia, New Zealand, and India.

You can find more information about the Gallipoli campaign during the First World War in the chapter devoted to this period of history, located in the Appendices section.

The geography of the Gallipoli Peninsula makes it a very scenic area. The landscape is dominated by high hills, with steep slopes descending directly into the Aegean Sea and the Dardanelles. The interior plains are now occupied by intensive agriculture, and the hills are the grazing land for cows and goats.

Planning a sightseeing tour around the Gallipoli Peninsula is relatively straightforward as just one main road – the route D550 – runs along its entire length. This road enters the peninsula from the north, near the town of Bolayır, heads in the south-westerly direction, and reaches its southernmost tip. It passes through the most important cities of the peninsula: Gelibolu and Eceabat. Both of them are good starting points for local tours, although the travellers who are mainly interested in the places connected with the military campaign of 1915-1916 are advised to start the tour from Eceabat.

Ferry crossings are the easiest way to travel from the Gallipoli Peninsula to Asia Minor. As there is no bridge over the Dardanelles yet, the land route follows a very circuitous road along the coast of the Marmara Sea, and then through Istanbul and across the Bosphorus strait. For this reason, the traffic on the route D550 is sometimes very heavy as it is used by the buses carrying passengers from Eastern Thrace to Asia.

Ferry terminals, serving both pedestrian and car traffic, are located in three cities of the peninsula. These are (from the north to the south): Gelibolu, Eceabat, and Kilitbahir. The ferry from Gelibolu travels to Lapseki, and you should use it when going on a trip along the southern shore of the Sea of Marmara. The ferry connection between Eceabat and Çanakkale is probably the most popular choice for travelers. You should take it when planning a trip along the coast of the Aegean Sea to the south, including the nearby ancient city of Troy. The connection from Kilitbahir to Çanakkale is an alternative option, recommended rather for the travelers without a car and with a lot of time, because the ferries

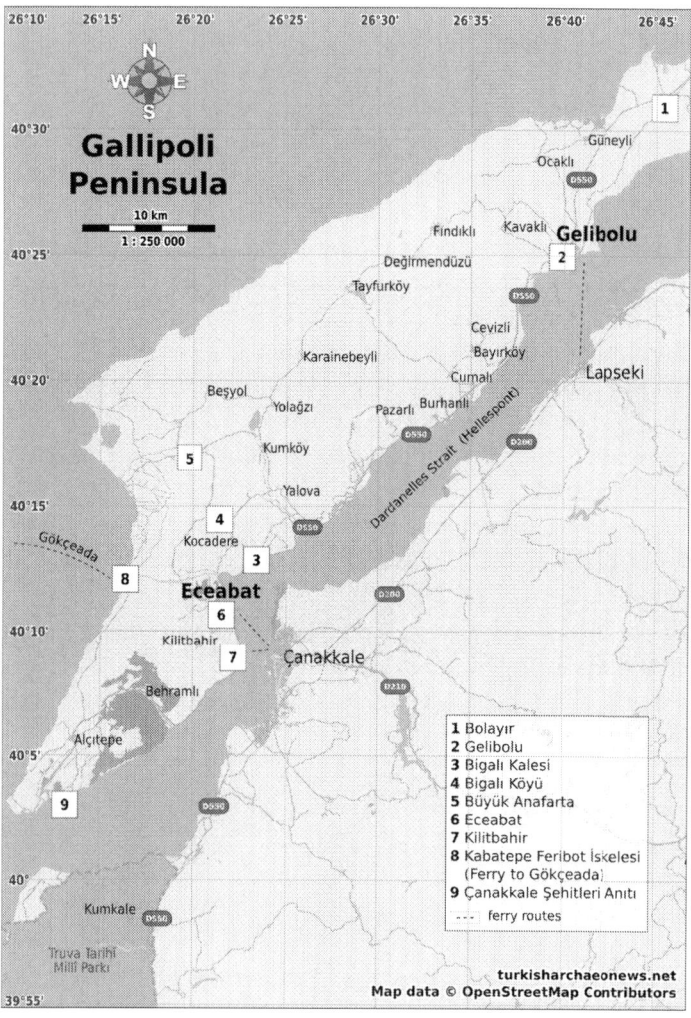

Gallipoli
Peninsula

10 km
1 : 250 000

Güneyli
Ocaklı
Findıklı   Kavaklı **Gelibolu**
Değirmendüzü
Tayfurköy
Cevizli
Karainebeyli   Bayırköy
Cumalı   **Lapseki**
Beşyol
Yolağzı   Pazarlı Burhanlı
Kumköy
Yalova
Kocadere
Eceabat
Kilitbahir
Çanakkale
Behramlı
Alçıtepe
Gökçeada
Dardanelles Strait (Hellespont)
Kumkale
Truva Tarihî
Milli Parkı

1 Bolayır
2 Gelibolu
3 Bigalı Kalesi
4 Bigalı Köyü
5 Büyük Anafarta
6 Eceabat
7 Kilitbahir
8 Kabatepe Feribot İskelesi
  (Ferry to Gökçeada)
9 Çanakkale Şehitleri Anıtı
--- ferry routes

turkisharchaeonews.net
Map data © OpenStreetMap Contributors

4

run less frequently, and are considerably smaller.

SUGGESTED SIGHTSEEING ROUTE

The most convenient way of visiting the Gallipoli Peninsula is by car. If you choose public transport, you will able to visit the largest cities of the peninsula, but reaching smaller villages and distant war memorials might be nearly impossible.

Tourists without their own transportation can use the services of local travel agencies, operating mainly in Eceabat, and in Çanakkale on the Asian shore. Among the most popular and highly recommended are Crowded House Tours and TJs Tours. Please note that the tours offered by these agencies are mainly focused on the locations significant for the visitors from Australia and New Zealand, not on the memorials associated with the Turkish side of the conflict. The route suggested here offers a more balanced point of view, and involves visiting some less-known, but noteworthy places.

The route D550 (E87) is the main axis of communication in the region. The trip starts in Bolayır, located in the northern part of the peninsula, and leads to the south. After driving 17 km, you reach Gelibolu, where it is worth stopping at least for a few hours. From Gelibolu, the route leads further to the south, to Eceabat, 44 km away. Before you reach this town, consider taking one of the side roads leading deeper into the interior of the peninsula, to the villages of Büyük Anafarta and Bigalı Köyü. Near one of the turnoffs, 7 km north of Eceabat, stand the remains of the Bigalı Castle. Near Eceabat, there is an important crossroad with the local roads leading to the most significant war memorials and military cemeteries.

The town of Eceabat is not really a fascinating place, but it is a convenient starting point and accommodation base for the explorers of the southern part of the Gallipoli Peninsula. Going further to the south, along the route D550, after just 4 km you reach Kilitbahir, and after another 19 km, the village of Alçıtepe, where the road forks off in two directions. Its western branch takes you to Seddülbahir and the eastern one to the monument of Abide.

After visiting the Gallipoli Peninsula, you can cross the Dardanelles to Asia Minor, using the ferry connections available in Gelibolu, Eceabat, and Kilitbahir. Detailed information about these connections can be found in the chapters devoted to these towns.

Another interesting option is a sea voyage to the Turkish island known as Gökçeada in the Aegean Sea. The ferries to the island depart from the harbour of Kabatepe (tr. *Kabatepe Feribot İskelesi*), on the western shore of the peninsula.

ACCOMMODATION

Important note! When planning your sightseeing tour of the Gallipoli Peninsula, take into account the dates of the Anzac Day (the 25th of April) and the Çanakkale Naval Victory Day (tr. *Çanakkale Deniz Zaferi*) – the 18th of March. During these periods the peninsula is crowded with tourists and finding a bed in a hotel is a minor miracle. Moreover, the journey is significantly hindered by the crowds of tourists from Australia, New Zealand, and Turkey. Suffice it to say that on the 90-th anniversary of the Allied landing at Gallipoli more than 20,000 visitors from the Antipodes visited the region. On the 18th of March, during the celebrations of the Turkish holiday, up to 50,000 domestic visitors arrive to the Gallipoli Peninsula every year.

The largest hotel base on the Gallipoli Peninsula is available in Eceabat and Gelibolu. The chapters devoted to these cities offer suggestions for available hotels and B&Bs. In smaller towns, there are also some accommodation options available, and they are described in the guidebook. However, if you plan only a quick trip across the peninsula, combined with visits to some of the biggest tourist attractions, you should consider staying in a hotel on the other shore of the Dardanelles, in Çanakkale, which has a much wider range of accommodation options.

VIEWPOINTS AND BEACHES

Driving along the Gallipoli Peninsula offers you magnificent vistas and many attractive photo opportunities. If you reach the penin-

Landscape of the Gallipoli Peninsula

sula from the north, before you get to Bolayır, you will be able to admire the Aegean Sea. Further to the south, between Gelibolu and Kilitbahir, the D550 route runs along the Dardanelles, offering views of ships and ferries crossing the strait, and the panoramas of the Asian shore.

To observe the interior of the peninsula, go up one of the hills that offer panoramic views of farmland, lakes, and forests. We recommend the vistas from the hill in Bolayır, where you can also visit the tombs of Suleiman Pasha and Namık Kemal. Also, the hill of Ecebey Mausoleum provides an excellent opportunity to admire the peninsula from above.

You can enjoy the views of the Aegean Sea and two nearby islands – Turkish Gökçeada and Greek Samothrace – from the memorial sites located on the western shore of the Gallipoli Peninsula, for example from the North Beach Anzac Commemorative Site.

When visiting the Gallipoli Peninsula in summer, you might use the opportunity to swim in the Aegean Sea or the Dardanelles. The best place to bathe in the waters of the Dardanelles is the town of Gelibolu, which has a beach district Hamzaköy. Small beaches are also situated near Eceabat and Kilitbahir. To swim in the Aegean Sea, head to the summer resort of Güneyli, which administratively belongs to Bolayır.

Bolayır

COORDINATES: 40.5147° N, 26.7567° E

BRIEF HISTORY

During the First Balkan War, in January 1913, an major battle was fought between Turkish and Bulgarian forces near Bolayır. The event went down in history as the Battle of Bulair. From the beginning of the war, the Ottoman fortress in Edirne was blocked by the Bulgarian army. To break this blockade, the command of the Turkish army prepared a campaign in a westerly direction. The offensive started at dawn on January 26th, and the Ottoman army enjoyed favorable weather conditions. Thick fog gave them an advantage as the element of surprise because the Bulgarians saw the approach of the 27th Infantry Division Myuretebi only tens of meters in front of their positions. An exchange of artillery fire started, slowing down the progress of the Turks.

The Turkish forces were initially successful, concentrating on the coast of the Sea of Marmara and slowly encircling the left wing of the 22nd Bulgarian infantry regiment. Recognizing the threat, the Bulgarian commander decided to counter-attack. In the face of the offensive, Turkish soldiers panicked and started running away from the battlefield. Many of them died during the retreat, killed by the Bulgarian artillery. In the afternoon, there was a second attempt at the Turkish offensive, but it was also stopped by the Bulgarian army. In total, the Ottoman forces lost half of their soldiers involved in the initial attack, and almost all equipment, abandoned during the retreat. A military march was later composed to commemorate the Bulgarian victory, and the village in Varna district was named Bulair.

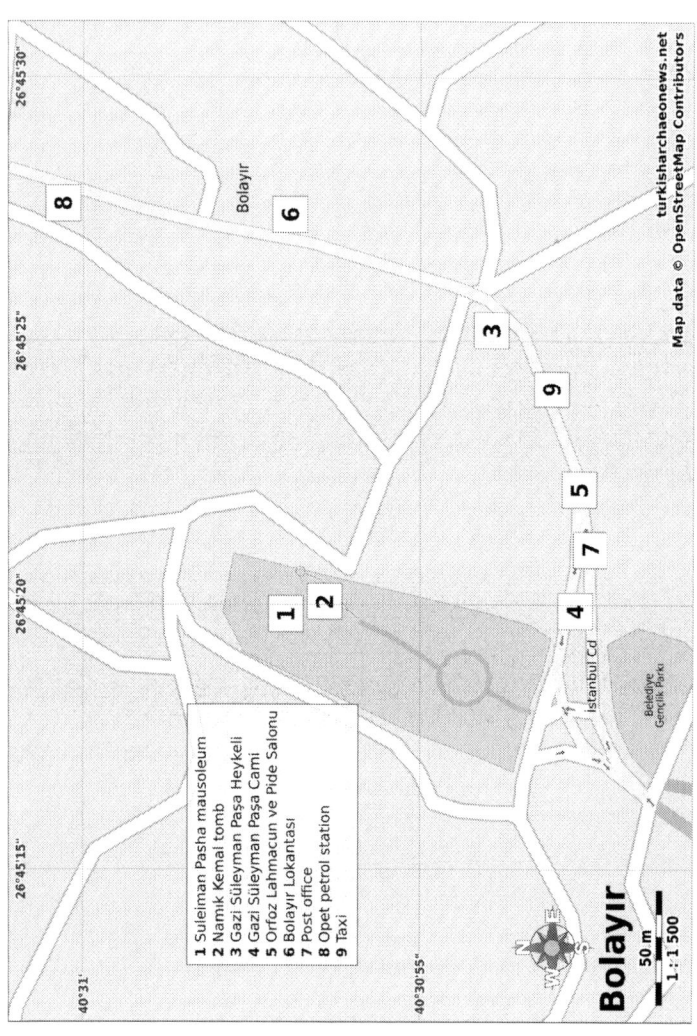

1 Suleiman Pasha mausoleum
2 Namik Kemal tomb
3 Gazi Süleyman Paşa Heykeli
4 Gazi Süleyman Paşa Cami
5 Orfoz Lahmacun ve Pide Salonu
6 Bolayir Lokantasi
7 Post office
8 Opet petrol station
9 Taxi

Bolayır

50 m
1 : 1 500

turkisharchaeonews.net
Map data © OpenStreetMap Contributors

Plan of Bolayır

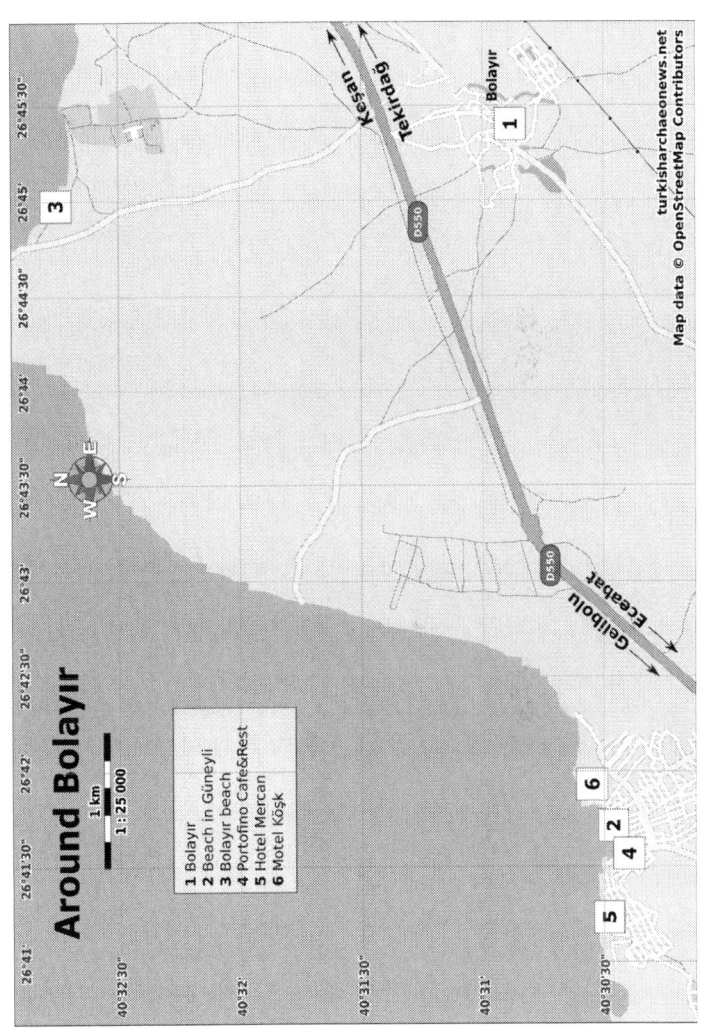

Bolayır and its surroundings

SIGHTSEEING

There are two important tombs in Bolayır, perched on a hill overlooking the plains of Eastern Thrace. The first one is the Mausoleum of Suleyman Pasha (tr. *Gazi Süleyman Paşa Türbesi*). The second bey of the Ottoman Empire, Suleyman, the eldest son of Sultan Orhan I, was buried in this traditional brick tomb. In the early days of the Ottoman Empire, the title of the bey was granted to the administrators of Ottoman capital cities. The first Ottoman capital was in Bursa, and the second one – in Edirne.

Suleyman Pasha is best remembered as the military commander who first controlled the areas located in Europe, on the Gallipoli Peninsula. This conquest contributed to the strengthening of the position of the Ottoman Empire and its expansion into Europe. The famous commander was seen as the natural successor to Sultan Orhan. Unfortunately, he died before his father, in 1357, as a result of injuries sustained after falling from a horse while hunting with falcons.

At the behest of his father, he was not buried in Bursa, where his grandfather, Osman, had been interred, but on the shore of the Dardanelles. This choice was to symbolise the recognition of his merit in controlling the areas of Eastern Thrace. His teacher and mentor, bearing the title of lala was buried in the same tomb. More surprisingly, the third sarcophagus in the mausoleum belongs to his horse.

The Tomb of Namık Kemal (tr. *Namık Kemal Mezarı*), the nineteenth-century poet, stands on the same hill. Namık Kemal was an advocate of two innovative (in the Ottoman Empire) slogans: freedom and homeland. Namık Kemal died in 1888 on the island of Chios, where he served as a governor. However, his wish was to be buried in Bolayır, alongside Suleyman Pasha, and his will was carried out to the letter.

In addition, there are two other places connected with the figure of Suleyman Pasha to be seen in Bolayır. The first one is the mosque that bears his name (tr. *Gazi Süleyman Paşa Cami*). Its origins date back to 1356, but the building was later completely redesigned,

Tomb of Namık Kemal in Bolayır

with very disappointing results. The second sight is his statue (tr. *Gazi Süleyman Paşa Heykeli*), standing near the entrance to the park where the discussed tombs are situated.

VISITOR TIPS

Orientation

Bolayır is located right on E87 route which connects the towns of the Gallipoli Peninsula. The town is situated at a distance from the coasts of the Aegean Sea and the Dardanelles. Travellers enter Bolayır driving along İstanbul Caddesi, which runs through the center of the town, and then goes further to the south-west, running parallel to E87 route, up to Gelibolu. All important buildings and service points in Bolayır are located along this street, and because the town is tiny, it is practically impossible to get lost.

The municipality of Bolayır also includes Güneyli village which is situated 10 km to the west of the center, on the Aegean coast. There you can find hotels and guesthouses, as well as several bars and restaurants, aimed at customers who come there for sunbathing and swimming in the sea.

Another lovely sandy beach in the area, called simply Bolayır

Beach (tr. Bolayır Plajı), lies 4 km to the north of the city center, in a pretty cove. There are numerous summer cottages there, and a couple of food courts.

Accommodation and restaurants

It is possible to dine in the center Bolayır at several simple restaurants offering traditional pastries (Orfoz Lahmacun ve Pide Salonu) and dinners (Bolayır Lokantası). The beach district of Güneyli offers a wider range of dining options, at slightly higher prices. Among these venues, Portofino Restaurant&Café enjoys the best reputation among customers.

The best idea for finding accommodation is also in Güneyli, where you can stay at luxurious Mercan Hotel, with its restaurant, a swimming pool, and rooms with sea views. Köşk Motel, situated in the same area,is a cheaper option, but of far lower quality.

Shopping and services

Bolayır is not a shopping paradise, but there are many shops selling basic groceries in the town centre. Several service points are located on İstanbul Caddesi, including Opet petrol station, a taxi stop, and a post office. In Güneyli, there is a discount shop that belongs to A101 network.

GETTING THERE

BY CAR: if you come from the direction of Istanbul (260 km) or Edirne (165 km), turn off E80 highway in the direction of Keşan (through Havsa and Uzunköprü), by taking D550/E87 route. Bolayır is situated on this road, 18 km to the north of Gelibolu. The right exit is marked with brown signposts that direct the travellers to the famous tombs on the hill.

Gelibolu

COORDINATES: 40.4054° N, 26.6701° E

The town, known internationally as Gallipoli, is located on a peninsula that bears the same name. Administratively it belongs to Çanakkale Province, although it is situated in Europe, and the capital of the province – in Asia. Gelibolu is the largest town of the Gallipoli Peninsula, with the Aegean Sea to the west and the Dardanelles Strait to the east.

BRIEF HISTORY

From Greek colonization to the Crusades

Gelibolu was founded by the Greeks in the 5th century BCE, as Kallipolis ('Beautiful City' in Greek). The modern name is the distortion of its original name. From the beginning, the town played an important role, firstly because of its proximity to Constantinople, and secondly – as a naval base, because of its location at the Dardanelles Strait, leading to the Sea of Marmara.

The Byzantine Emperor Justinian I fortified Gelibolu. On his orders, military warehouses storing grain and wine were built. After the conquest of Constantinople by the knights of the Fourth Crusade in 1204, and the formation of the Latin Empire, Gelibolu was controlled by the Venetians.

In 1306, the town was conquered by Almogavars – special forces of the Kingdom of Aragon, serving as mercenaries under the command of the famous adventurer, Roger de Flor of Sicily. After the death of their leader, the soldiers murdered almost all inhabitants of Gelibolu, and then withdrew from the city, previously destroying its fortifications.

15

Ottoman conquest

In March 1354, a strong earthquake caused the almost complete destruction of Gelibolu, and, as a result, the town was abandoned by its Greek inhabitants. The opportunity was seized by Suleyman Pasha, the son of the Ottoman sultan Orhan I. He quickly occupied the town, fortified it, and settled with Turkish families, brought in from Anatolia. Byzantine Emperor John VI, eager to regain the town, offered a significant amount of money to the Turks for returning Gelibolu, but his offer was declined. The sultan said that the city had not been occupied by force, and thus, as a gift from Allah, could not be abandoned.

At the news of the loss of Gelibolu, Constantinople was gripped by terror, and Emperor John VI was overthrown. It was believed that soon the capital of Byzantium would also get into the Turkish hands. In fact, 99 years passed before the final destruction of the Byzantine Empire. However, gaining a foothold in Europe made the conquest of Eastern Thrace much easier for the Ottoman forces. Within less than ten years this territory, including Adrianople (currently Edirne), was under the Ottoman rule.

Piri Reis – Gelibolu's most famous son

Piri Reis (literally Captain Piri), whose full name was Ahmed Muhiddin Piri, was born in Gelibolu in the middle of the 15th century. He was an admiral, but his major achievements were in the disciplines of geography and cartography.

His maps were collected in the form of the Book of Navigation (tr. *Kitab-ı Bahriye*), the atlas combined with detailed information for navigators. Interestingly, it contained not only the maps of the Mediterranean region but also some parts of the American coast. It is worth mentioning that this particular map dates back to 1513, and it means that it was made just 21 years after the discovery of this continent. Moreover, in 1929, in the archives of the Topkapı Palace in Istanbul, the map of the world made by Piri Reis was discovered. It is the oldest Turkish map showing the coast of the New World, but also one of the oldest of its kind in the world.

Crimean War and the First World War

During the Crimean War, French and British troops were stationed in Gelibolu, where they strengthened the 600-year-old fortifications. Their task was to defend Istanbul from the occupation by the Russians.

Soon, the situation changed dramatically. During the First World War, the city of Gelibolu and the entire Gallipoli Peninsula was defended by the Turkish forces against the Allies, who were trying to seize Istanbul. During the bloody battles fought to keep the peninsula under Turkish control, a young commander – Kemal Pasha, later known as Atatürk – became famous for his achievements and bravery. The fame of the 'Gallipoli defender' significantly facilitated his subsequent actions as the commander during the Turkish War of Independence.

Although most residents of Gelibolu were Greek, they were not resettled to Greece under the provisions of the Convention on the Exchange of Greek and Turkish population in 1923. They were protected from this necessity as Gelibolu belonged to the prefecture of Istanbul, whose Greek population was exempted from the resettlement.

Gelibolu today

Currently, Gelibolu is a small town, with a population of about 30,000 inhabitants, famous for its canned sardines. It is also an important port for the ferries connecting Europe and Asia. Gelibolu is a picturesque location where most of interesting places are concentrated in the vicinity of the harbour, and along the road leading to Hamzaköy beach district.

Gelibolu comes alive every year for about one week when crowds of tourists from Australia and New Zealand arrive to commemorate Anzac Day on the 25th of April. This day is celebrated in memory of the soldiers of the Australian and the New Zealand Corps (ANZAC) who died fighting on the Gallipoli Peninsula, during the First World War. If you are not particularly interested in these celebrations, visit Gelibolu in another time of the year as

Waterfront in Gelibolu

all hotels are full, and ferries and buses – booked well in advance.

SIGHTSEEING

The ferry harbour (tr. *Gelibolu Feribot Iskelesi*) is the best point where you can start a sightseeing tour of Gelibolu. It is located in the southern part of the city, near a characteristic roundabout formed by the Old Post Office Street (tr. *Eski PTT Caddesi). If you head left (to the west)* at the roundabout, then after 200 meters you will get to Gallipoli War Museum (tr. *Gelibolu Savaş Müzesi*), on Korean Heroes Street (tr. *Kore Kahramanlar*). Even from outside it is clear what the mission of this museum is – to commemorate incredibly bloody battles fought on the Gallipoli Peninsula. The building is surrounded by barbed wire and sandbags designed to evoke the trenches of the First World War. Inside you will find a collection of commemorative items from this period, including letters written by soldiers to their families, as well as photos from the excavations carried out in the areas of fighting. The most notable exhibits are a cartridge from the French ship Bouvet that sank during the naval operations of the Allies and an identification label of a downed French airplane. The museum is closed on

Mondays and Thursdays, and on other days of the week it is open from 8:00 am to 5:00 pm. The admission is symbolically paid.

The statue of the Ottoman Admiral Piri Reis, standing on the quay near the Gallipoli War Museum, suggests another point of interest in Gelibolu. This statue stands on the eastern side of the roundabout, next to the Piri Reis Museum (tr. *Piri Reis Müzesi*). This exhibition has been organized in a stone tower, which is a remnant of the Byzantine fortress, expanded in the 14th century, in the early Ottoman era. The building is the only preserved memorial of the Greco-Byzantine city of Kallipolis. The museum, opened in 1991, boasts an impressive collection of sundries related to the life and work of Piri Reis, a famous cartographer and admiral. He was the author of The Book of Navigation (tr. *Kitab-ı Bahriye*) that presented detailed information on sea travel, along with the maps showing the location of cities and ports of the Mediterranean Sea.

Piri Reis has recently become the object of great interest to the media after the Turkish President Recep Tayyip Erdoğan announced to the world that Muslim sailors discovered America before Christopher Columbus. One piece of evidence for this claim was a map, drawn in 1513 by Piri Reis, which shows a part of the American continent. It was discovered accidentally, during an inventory conducted in 1929 in Istanbul's Topkapı Palace, and is considered one of the oldest surviving maps of America. This map is currently stored in Topkapı Palace and is rarely shown to the public.

Tourists visiting the Piri Reis Museum in Gelibolu have to settle for much more modest exhibits, arranged on two floors of the fortress. On the ground floor, at the entrance, there is a well, where the visitors throw coins. Steep stairs lead to the upper level of the building. Among the displayed items, the engravings depicting the ships from the Ottoman era and the port in Gelibolu attract most attention. Moreover, there are some reproductions of Piri Reis maps, including a map of the Dardanelles, several mannequins dressed in sailor outfits from the times of Piri Reis, as well as navigation instruments and cartographer tools of his era. The museum

Piri Reis Museum in Gelibolu

also has a collection of oil paintings, including the portraits of Piri Reis, showing him during the preparation for a sea voyage, at work on the creation of a map, and writing a book. The collection of exhibits also includes a gun and some weapons from the days of the admiral. Piri Reis Museum is open daily except Mondays and Thursdays, from 9:00 am to 5:00 pm. Admission is free. Taking photos is allowed, and we recommend taking a photograph of the city of Gelibolu from the windows of the tower.

The most attractive mosque in the center of Gelibolu is the Mosque of Suleyman Pasha (tr. *Gazi Süleyman Paşa Cami*), located 350 meters to the north of the roundabout at the marina. To get there, walk uphill, along İbni Hasancik Street. The mosque was built in 1385, and its name commemorates the Ottoman conqueror of the city and the sultan's son, Suleyman Pasha. In the 19th century, the building underwent a complete renovation, and its present appearance is far from the fourteenth-century design. Look carefully at the columns outside the building, as the mosque was constructed from the fragments of ancient structures of Kallipolis. The interior of the mosque is spacious, elegantly decorated, and extremely well lit, because of numerous windows and a roof opening.

Other points of interest in Gelibolu are situated along the route leading from the harbour to Hamzaköy beach district, located in the bay on the eastern side of the city. If you have just visited the Mosque of Suleyman Pasha, then go straight to the east, along Big Mosque Street (tr. *Büyük Cami Sokak*) and General Dursun Street (tr. *Dursun Bak Caddesi*). Just 450 meters away from the Mosque of Suleyman you get to a large roundabout where Tuğsavul and Muhittin Reis streets start. The same point can also be easily reached from the ferry terminal (900 meters), by walking down Tuğsavul Street, first to the east, and then, still following the same street, to the north. To the north of the roundabout, there is a bazaar area, and the streets are closed on market days.

On Muhittin Reis Street, just 100 meters from the roundabout, there are the tombs (tr. *türbe*) of two Ottoman clergymen, bearing the names of Ahmet-i Bican Efendi and Mehmed-i Bican Efendi, as well as a mosque bearing the name of the second one. Mehmed-i Bican Efendi, who died in 1453, is a figure virtually unknown outside Turkey, but in this country his name is mentioned with reverence and respect, as the author of the famous commentary on the Qur'an, entitled Muhammadiye.

If you choose to follow Tuğsavul Street, going from the roundabout to the north, after 200 meters you come to the Tomb of Mansur Al-Hallaj (tr. *Hallaca-ı Mansur Türbesi*). He was a Persian mystic, writer, and teacher, who lived at the turn of the 9th and the 10th centuries. He became famous when he coined a phrase 'I am the Truth', by which he expressed his full communion with God. After many years of imprisonment, he was sentenced to death as a heretic, but many Muslims still consider him as a saint. The tomb in Gelibolu was built in 1407 by Iskender Bey, and it is only a symbolic resting place of Mansur Al-Hallaj, whose body was burned after the execution. This stone and brick building, standing in a small garden, has impressive dimensions, and is mistakenly taken for a mosque by many tourists. You can enter the carpeted interior and see the symbolic sarcophagus of Mansur Al-Hallaj.

From the Tomb of Mansur Al-Hallaj the tour of the city takes you to the right (to the east), along Lighthouse Street (tr. *Fener Yolu*). On a hillside, on the north side of the street, there is one of the most amazing tombs in Turkey. This is the grave of Flag Father (tr. *Bayraklı Baba Türbesi*), thoroughly covered with Turkish flags. Here, a soldier bearing the name Karaca is buried. He was serving in the Ottoman army as a standard bearer. In 1410, his squad was surrounded by enemies. Karaca did not want the banner to fall into the hands of the enemy, so he cut the flag into small pieces and ate it. It is not the end of this incredible story – when his squad was finally victorious, the companions of Karaca doubted the truth of his story, so to convince them, this crazy soldier cut his stomach and showed them the pieces of the standard inside. Visiting the tomb is free of charge, but you can spend some money to buy a Turkish flag and put it on the grave.

Lighthouse Street continues towards a hill rising on the seashore where, naturally, there is a lighthouse (tr. *Gelibolu Deniz Feneri*). It was built by the French during the Crimean War, and its task was to facilitate the navigation through the Dardanelles Strait. It stands on a 50-meter-high cliff, and is 25 meters high. Apparently, its light can be seen at night from a distance of 30 kilometers. The lighthouse, still operational, is currently managed by the Turkish Coast Guard.

If you turn back towards the Tomb of Mansur Al-Hallaj, the most attractive walking route takes you further to the north, down Muhittin Reis Street. After 200 meters, turn right (to the east), to reach the Tomb of Sarıca Pasha (tr. *Sarıca Paşa Türbesi*), just 50 meters down the road. Sarıca Pasha was the founder of the first Ottoman shipyard in Gelibolu, built in 1391.

Right next to the tomb there is a magnificent military cemetery, known as the French Cemetery (tr. *Fransiz Ölüklüğü*). You can see it from afar, thanks to a high, snow-white belfry. The soldiers buried there were the members of the troops fighting during the Crimean War (1853-1856) and the First World War. During the Crimean conflict, France, along with Britain and Sardinia, were on the side of the Ottoman Empire, fighting against Russia. The

French Cemetery in Gelibolu

soldiers who died in the First World War came to this area from Senegal, then a French colony in Africa. During the First World War, these troops fought against the Turks. Now the soldiers who died in both military conflicts rest in a cemetery in Gelibolu. It is worth visiting this neighborhood and ponder over the volatile political alliances and the fate of ordinary conscripts, thrown to distant lands to fight bloody battles.

From the French Cemetery, it is possible to descend to the coast, following Muhittin Reis Street. Hamzaköy beach district stretches in the northern direction, along Kemal Reis Street. If you go all the way to its northern end, over a distance of 1 kilometer, you reach the two-story tomb of Sinan Pasha (tr. *Sinan Paşa Türbesi*), a son in law of Sultan Bayezid II.

The tomb of Emir Ali Baba (tr. *Emir Ali Baba Türbesi*) is also located nearby. Ali Baba was an admiral of the Ottoman fleet in the 14th century. His main achievement was the conquest of Imralı Island on the Marmara Sea. This island, formerly known as Kalolimnos, now serves as a prison and a military base. Billy Hayes was serving a life sentence in this prison, after getting caught as a drug smuggler. After a daring escape from the island in 1975,

Hayes fled from Turkey, and then wrote a book 'Midnight Express.' Later, a famous film was produced with the same title.

If you choose to go to the north instead, along the inland Muhittin Reis Street, and then turn left (to the west), after 500 meters you get to the impressive edifice housing the Mevlevihane, i.e. the lodge of whirling dervishes from Gelibolu (tr. *Gelibolu Mevlevihane*). In this building so-called sema ceremonies take place regularly. These ceremonies are a characteristic form of a prayer, during which the dervishes rotate in a trance. The building draws attention to its unusual exterior, especially the double staircase leading directly from the street on the upper floor. Some experts argue that this is the biggest dervish lodge in the world.

You can also shorten a walk around the city, by going down to the coast from the French Cemetery, and then turning to the south along the coastal Ahmet Başyurt Sahil Street. It goes around the promontory jutting out into the waters of the Dardanelles. On the northern side of this promontory, there is a pier where you can take lovely photos of Gelibolu, the local bay, and the entire strait. Cormorants usually sit on the rocks protruding from the water. On the promontory, there is the Naval Heritage Park (tr. *Deniz Kuvvetleri Kültür Parkı*), with an exhibition of underwater mines, torpedoes, and even a submarine.

The road running along the coast changes its name to Ordu Evi Altı Sahil Yolu. After walking 250 meters from the Naval Heritage Park take a turn to the right, into Fener Altı Street. At the junction, a small plaque announces the location of the so-called House of Experiences (tr. *Çilehane*). In reality, this 'house' consists of two tiny rooms, carved in the rock, for prayer and meditation. You can go inside and check how the claustrophobic conditions influence your mood. Older residents of the city still benefit from this hermitage. The place and its garden are cared for by an attentive guardian, who can show you around for a small donation.

A path leads from Fener Altı Street to a park located on a hill, where the already mentioned lighthouse is situated. At the entrance to the park there is the tomb of Kalafat Mehmed Pasha (tr.

Azebler Namazgah in Gelibolu

Kalafat Mehmet Paşa Türbesi), who served as grand vizier at the court of Sultan Abdulhamid I in the years 1778-1779.

The last point of the walking tour is an impressive structure called Azebler Namazgah, located next to the tomb of Kalafat Mehmed Pasha. It is a rare example of an open-air Muslim prayer space in Turkey. The second one in this region can be seen in Kilitbahir but it is in much worse condition. The highlight of this venue is an unroofed building erected from marble blocks in 1407. It resembles the interior of a mosque, along with two pulpits (tr. *mimber*) and a niche indicating the direction to Mecca (tr. *mihrab*).

VISITOR TIPS

Orientation

Gelibolu is located on the eastern coast of the Gallipoli Peninsula, on route E87 (D550) that connects the area of northern Thrace with the town of Kilitbahir in the south of the peninsula. There are two access roads to Gelibolu from E87 route, of which the main, southern one, leads along Korean Heroes Street (tr. *Kore Kahramanlar*), straight to the harbour. In this harbour, you can embark on a ferry that will take you to the Asian part of Turkey.

The second access road to Gelibolu, the northern one, takes you to the city center along November Street (tr. *Kasım Caddesi*). It finishes at Gazi Suleyman Pasha roundabout (tr. *Gazi Süleyman Paşa*), which is adorned with the statue of this commander. From this roundabout, the streets lead to various districts of the city. In the vicinity of the roundabout, there are many service outlets, hotels, banks, restaurants, and grocery stores.

The city center is located on the tip of a promontory jutting out into the waters of the Dardanelles. The ferry harbour is on its southern side, and Hamzaköy beach district – on the northeastern side. The promontory is in the very center of the city, and the best way of getting around it is on foot. The streets are narrow and crowded, often blocked, or one-way only.

Restaurants

The gastronomic scene in Gelibolu is well developed, but the premises are aimed mainly at the Turkish clientele, so do not expect menus in foreign languages or English-speaking staff. Among several restaurants that are situated near Gazi Suleyman Pasha roundabout, we particularly recommend an eatery (tr. *lokanta*) known as Köfte Koca Usta. In addition to the specialty of this venue – meatballs (tr. *köfte*) – you can order several kinds of soups, salads, rice, and chicken kebab.

Other notable restaurants are located near the ferry terminal. The bakeries in the area specialize in the preparation of the so-called Turkish pizza (tr. *pide*). You can also enjoy a cup of tea in the family tea garden Nezih Aile Çay Bahcesi, or try roasted sheep intestines in Fotörlü Kokoreçci restaurant.

The most exclusive fish restaurants in the city are located just next to the harbour. Among them, the most highly recommended is Ilhan, which serves sardines (tr. *sardalya*), baked in a clay pot, a specialty of Gelibolu.

Several restaurants and bars operate in Hamzaköy district, along Kemal Reis Street. These venues are mainly ice cream parlours, pastry shops, and bars, but their activity is often seasonal.

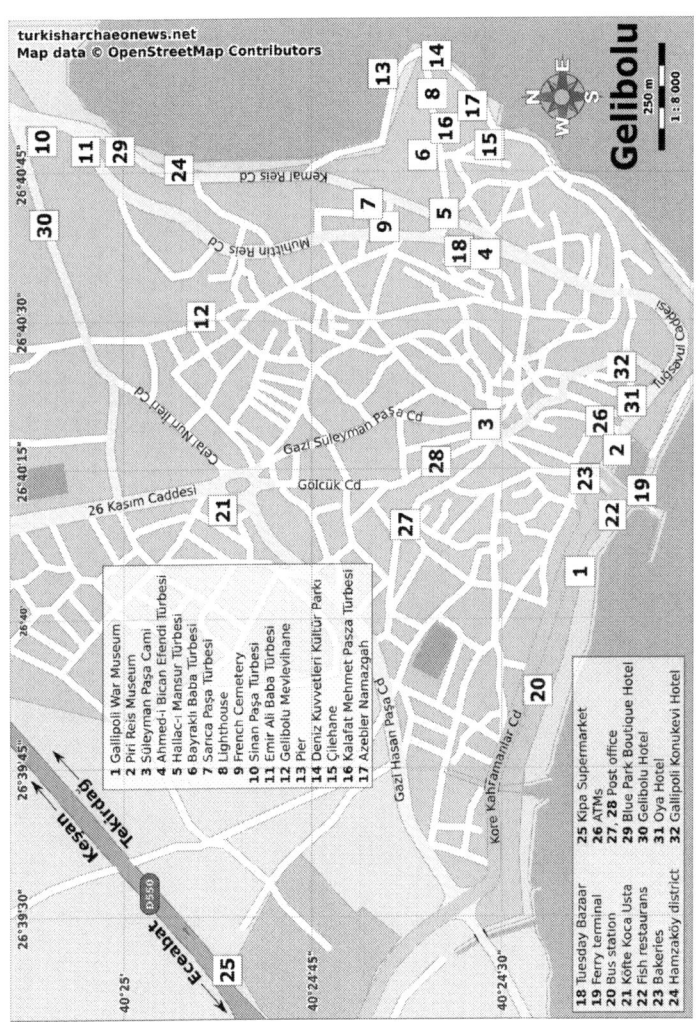

turkisharchaeonews.net
Map data © OpenStreetMap Contributors

Gelibolu

1 Gallipoli War Museum
2 Piri Reis Museum
3 Süleyman Paşa Cami
4 Ahmed-i Bican Efendi Türbesi
5 Hallac-ı Mansur Türbesi
6 Bayraklı Baba Türbesi
7 Sarıca Paşa Türbesi
8 Lighthouse
9 French Cemetery
10 Sinan Paşa Türbesi
11 Emir Ali Baba Türbesi
12 Gelibolu Mevlevihane
13 Pier
14 Deniz Kuvvetleri Kültür Parkı
15 Çilehane
16 Kalafat Mehmet Pasza Türbesi
17 Azebler Namazgah

18 Tuesday Bazaar
19 Ferry terminal
20 Bus station
21 Köfte Koca Usta
22 Fish restaurans
23 Bakeries
24 Hamzaköy district
25 Kipa Supermarket
26 ATMs
27, 28 Post office
29 Blue Park Boutique Hotel
30 Gelibolu Hotel
31 Oya Hotel
32 Gallipoli Konukevi Hotel

Plan of Gelibolu

Accommodation

Accommodation options are not particularly abundant in Gelibolu because most of the tourists coming to the Gallipoli Peninsula choose to stop in Çanakkale, located on the Asian shore of the Dardanelles. Çanakkale is selected due to its proximity to the battlefields and military cemeteries on the peninsula, but also to the ruins of the famous ancient city of Troy. If you plan to stop for a night in Gelibolu, remember the dates of the anniversaries of the battles of Gallipoli, and book your accommodation well in advance if you plan a stay in March or April. In other months of a year, it often turns out that the prices offered via online booking platforms are much higher than the ones offered if you go directly to the selected hotel and ask for a room.

If you decide to stay in Gelibolu, you can choose from the following options:

- Hamzaköy Blue Park Boutique Hotel – best-rated hotel in the city, located on Kemal Reis Street No. 41, in Hamzaköy district. The hotel has a restaurant and offers spacious rooms with the views of the Dardanelles Strait.
- Gelibolu Hotel – in the same area as the previous one, but a little further from the coast, on Celal Nuri İleri Street No. 41. The hotel does not have a restaurant, but the price includes an open buffet breakfast.
- Oya Hotel – conveniently located near the ferry docks, on Miralay Şefik Aker Street No.7.
- Gallipoli Konukevi – a little further away from the harbour, on Miralay Şefik Aker Street No. 27. This is probably the most expensive lodging option in town.

An interesting idea for accommodation near Gelibolu is Kalanora Resort Hotel, located in the village of Sütlüce, about 7 km to the south of Gelibolu. It is a holiday complex situated in a quiet area, consisting of bungalows that surround a swimming pool. The on-site restaurant serves superb dinners.

Shopping

In Gelibolu, there are many shops, supermarkets, and discount stores. The largest supermarket, a branch of Kipa chain (Tesco), is located on D550 road, on the western side of the city. The largest bazaar is held on Tuesdays, near Muhittin Reis Street.

Services

Many banks have their branches and ATMs in the vicinity of the ferry terminal, on Zübeyde Hanım, Belediye, and Atatürk streets.

The post office operates on Cumhuriyet Okulu Street, about 650 meters to the north of the ferry terminal, and on Gölcük Street, 500 meters to the north.

Gelibolu is often treated by travellers only as a transit point on their sightseeing route. It is connected by the ferries to the town of Lapseki, on the Asian shore of the Dardanelles. Many people start a tour of the memorial sites on the Gallipoli Peninsula from Gelibolu, but they do not spend much time in the city. However, if the circumstances allow you spending a few hours there, for example, waiting for a ferry, you can find some interesting places and buildings. However, do not expect too much as there are no world-class museums or monuments in the town.

GETTING THERE

BY COACH: Gelibolu coach terminal is situated 500 meters to the west from the ferry terminal, on Korean Heroes Street (tr. *Kore Kahramanlar*). There are frequent connections to Istanbul (5 hours), Edirne (3 hours), and Tekirdağ (3 hours).

BY MINIBUS: minibuses wait just outside the ferry terminal. They can take you to the southern part of the Gallipoli Peninsula: to Eceabat (1 hour) and Kilitbahir (1 hour and 15 minutes).

BY FERRY: every hour a ferry departs from Gelibolu to Lapseki, on the Asian shore of the Dardanelles (30 minutes). If you pay per vehilce, the transport of its all passengers is included in the price.

BY CAR: Gelibolu is located on E87 (D550) route that connects this town with Edirne (180 km), Uzunköprü (111 km), Keşan (70 km), and Bolayır (14 km) – in the northern direction. E87 (D550) route goes further to the south, to Eceabat (53 km) and Kilitbahir (57 km). To continue the journey to Asia Minor you can take a ferry, from Gelibolu, Eceabat, or Kilitbahir. It is also possible to get to Asia via Istanbul (300 km), first going to Keşan and then taking D110 route via Malkara (95 km) and Tekirdağ (155 km).

Ecebey Mausoleum

COORDINATES: 40.3515° N, 26.4395° E

Ecebey Mausoleum (tr. *Ecebey Türbesi*) is a memorial tomb of the Ottoman statesman and commander Ecebey. It is situated on a hill overlooking the Gallipoli Peninsula, near the village of Karainbeyli. Ecebey became famous as the commander of Ottoman forces that won a foothold on the peninsula in the 14th century.

BRIEF HISTORY

The village Karainbeyli is considered to be the first Turkish settlement on the Gallipoli Peninsula. Ecebey is revered by the local Turks as their spiritual father. Some even say that the name of the city Eceabat derives directly from his name, although there are also other theories in this respect.

Ecebey served under the command of Suleyman Pasha, who is buried in the north of the Gallipoli Peninsula, in Bolayır. Both mausoleums are regularly visited, especially during annual celebrations of the anniversary of the conquest of the peninsula by the Ottoman forces.

During other times of the year, Ecebey Mausoleum is a place rarely visited, as it is located off the beaten tourist trails of the peninsula. Most of the travellers arrive at the Gallipoli Peninsula to see the places associated with events in the history of the 20th century.

Ecebey Mausoleum, renovated in 1989, is worth a visit mainly because of the wonderful views that extend from the hill out to the countryside. Unfortunately, getting up the hill is only possible with your transport, and the road to the summit is winding and rocky.

Ecebey Mausoleum

GETTING THERE

The access to Ecebey Mausoleum is only possible by car, as there are no public transport options. To get to Karainbeyli from Eceabat, follow the inland road through Bigali and Kumköy. From the village of Karainbeyli, follow white signposts with the inscription 'Ecebey Türbesi' to the top of the hill. The road is quite steep and its surface is in poor condition. The total length of the route from Eceabat is 24 km.

Büyük Anafarta

COORDINATES: 40.2817° N, 26.3285° E

A small village bearing the name of Large Anafarta (tr. *Büyük Anafarta*) will always be associated with the events of the First World War. In its vicinity, one of the decisive battles of the campaign of the Gallipoli Peninsula was fought. Currently, the village is inhabited by around 400 people, living from livestock husbandry and the cultivation of cotton and tomatoes. The turbulent past is recalled by the billboards with wartime photos, and the monument of Atatürk in a pose of a thoughtful commander, standing at the central square of the village.

BRIEF HISTORY

The village suffered great human losses during the First World War. In August 1914, many of its inhabitants were called to military service in the 27. Infantry Regiment. The regiment was one of the first units which clashed in a battle with soldiers from Australia and New Zealand, on the 25th of April, 1915.

In August 1915, the remaining population of the village was forced to evacuate after the landing of the British troops in its neighborhood. In the next five months, most buildings of the village were destroyed by artillery fire. Mustafa Kemal Atatürk had his field headquarters there.

The landing of the Allies in the Suvla Bay (as the Allies described the area of Anafarta) turned out to be the last, unsuccessful, attempt to conquer the Gallipoli Peninsula. The attacking forces failed to break through to the sector controlled by the Allies, located 8 km to the south. The British commander Frederick Stop-

33

ford, responsible for many of the mistakes made during the attack, was dismissed.

The commanding officer of the Turkish forces in Anafarta battles, Atatürk, later summed up the campaign of the Gallipoli Peninsula, saying that the most important battles took place at Chunuk Bair and Anafarta. When asked why there are no great monuments commemorating the sacrifice of Turkish soldiers, he replied that the biggest monument of all is the 'Small Mehmet' (tr. *Mehmetçik*). In Turkey, this phrase means the collective body of all anonymous soldiers of the Ottoman army, whose courage decided the fate of the campaign. According to Atatürk, the sacrifice of the lives of the thousands of Mehmetçiks allowed Turkey to keep the area of the Gallipoli Peninsula within the borders of the country.

SIGHTSEEING

The most important institution in Büyük Anafarta is the Museum of War (tr. *Anafartalar Savaş Müzesi*). It is the largest private facility of this kind on the Gallipoli Peninsula. The collected memorabilia of the hostilities in the region include weapons, soldiers' equipment, uniforms, maps, documents, and photographs. The exhibits have been collected from all fronts of fighting on the peninsula, but particular emphasis is placed on the objects related to the fighting in and around Büyük Anafarta. The museum is the work of life of Özay Gündoğan, whose family has lived in the village for many generations. Many members of this family served in the Ottoman army during the First World War. The museum is open daily, from March to September from 9:00 am to 6:00 pm, and in other months – from 9:00 am to 5:00 pm. Admission fee is paid in the form of a donation for the upkeep of the museum.

Also, the Museum of Peace (tr. *Büyük Anafarta Köyü Barış Müzesi*) was opened in the village in 2007. In a small building, there are collected memorabilia from many battles. The exhibition includes pieces of missiles and equipment of soldiers, such as shovels, bottles, cutlery, and coins. The admission to the facility is free of charge.

In Büyük Anafarta, you can see traditional stone buildings, and

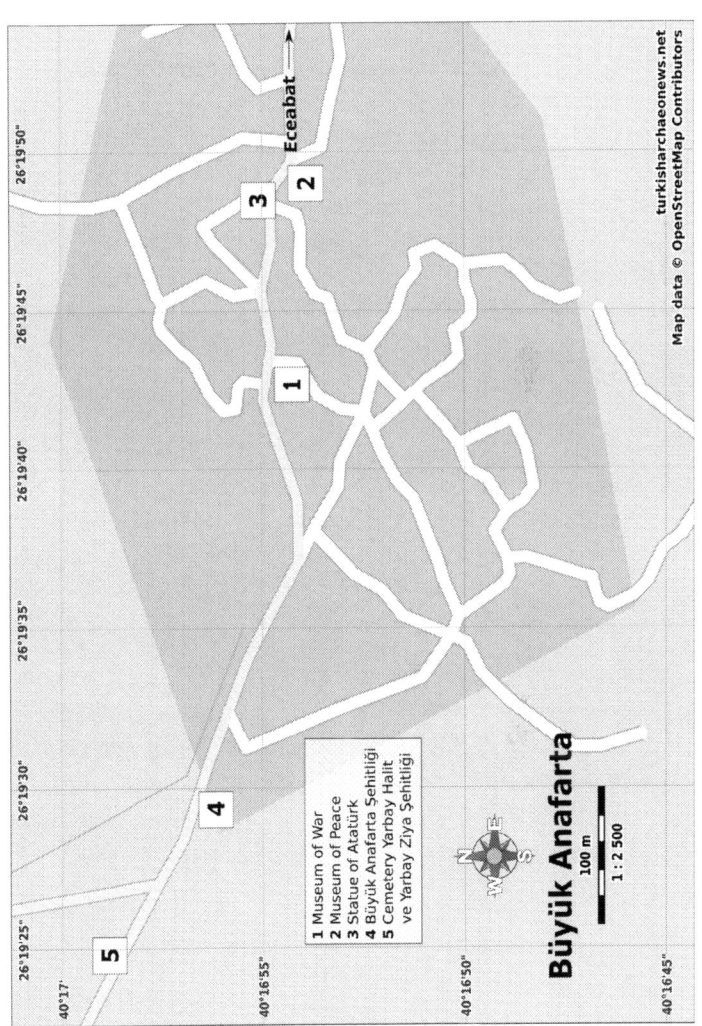

Plan of Büyük Anafarta

some of them have been carefully restored. There are also ruins of an old bath from the Ottoman era, and a historical fountain.

A military cemetery (tr. *Büyük Anafarta Şehitliği*) lies on the west side of the village. It was created in 2005 to commemorate the soldiers from the village who died during the First World War.

Another memorial military cemetery (tr. *Yarbay ve Halit Ziya Yarbay Şehitliği*) is located at a distance of half a kilometer from the village center, on the road to the west, on the coast of the Aegean Sea. Two Turkish commanders who died on the 11th of August, 1915, are buried there. Colonel Ziya Bey commanded the 21. Infantry Regiment, and Colonel Halit Bey – the 20. Infantry Regiment.

VISITOR TIPS

There are no hotels or B&Bs in Büyük Anafarta, but you can spend some time in one of two cafes: on the main square of the village, i.e. the Republic Square (tr. *Cumhuriyet Meydani*), and in the War Museum. You can order a simple meal as well as hot or cold drinks.

GETTING THERE

BY CAR: if you drive from Eceabat, take D550 road to the north, along the coast. After about 2.5 km turn left into a side road, to the village of Bigalı. From Bigalı continue to follow the bronze signposts to Büyük Anafarta. The total distance from Eceabat is only 17 km, but the roads are narrow and poorly maintened.

Bigalı Köyü

COORDINATES: 40.2368° N, 26.3588° E

Bigalı is a tiny village, located in the province of Çanakkale, on the Gallipoli Peninsula. During the First World War, is became an important strategic point. Colonel Mustafa Kemal selected this place as his headquarters. This heroic commander, later known as Atatürk, largely contributed to the Turkish victory on the Gallipoli Peninsula, and the salvation of Istanbul against the attack of the Allied forces.

Today, long after the roar of cannons was silenced, and the smoke of gunfire disappeared, Bigalı has a feel of somewhat unreal place. In the summer, the men sit in a shaded tea garden under ripe grapes, idly sipping tea, engaged in endless discussions. Low buildings surrounding the central square of the village, built of gray stone, seem to doze under the scorching sun. By the main (and only street), old Turkish women trade in various goods, to earn a few extra liras. This scenery is carefully observed by the great leader – Atatürk – immortalised in the form of a monument standing in the place of honour. Everything seems to be almost identical to the scenes well known from thousands of Turkish villages, scattered from Thrace in Europe to the foot of Mount Ararat far in the east of the country.

Yet something disturbs the newcomers, and soon you feel like trying to solve a puzzle of finding the differences in two pictures. All the houses seem to have been built in the same moment, when the time suddenly stopped. Their facades shine in unnatural purity, and window frames and doors seem to come from the workshop of one carpenter. There are also signboards, in Turkish and English,

37

hanging on these houses. They show black and white reproductions of faded photos depicting serious men in old-fashioned uniforms. Moreover, the main square of the village has street lamps powered by solar panels, funded by the Australian government. All these signs point out to what Bigalı Köyü actually is: a village museum, prepared for those travelers who are looking for the traces of the military campaign on the Gallipoli Peninsula.

BRIEF HISTORY

The most important moment in the history of Bigalı village is associated with the times of the First World War. At the time of its beginning, Colonel Mustafa Kemal served as a military attaché in Sofia. Anticipating the imminent involvement of the Ottoman Empire in the war, he filed a request to allocate him to active duty in the country. On the 20th of January 1915, he was appointed the commander of the 19th Division, which had just been formed. He was personally responsible for the hasty completion of its preparations for the fight at the front. On the 25th of February, he was stationed in Eceabat with his forces, and after less than two months they were transferred to Bigalı. In this location he lived in a small house, which also served as his headquarters. During the battles on the Gallipoli Peninsula, he commanded the troops from this location. In this modest yellow house the plans for the Turkish offensive were drafted, and Mustafa Kemal set off every day on a tour of the front lines.

SIGHTSEEING

There are two museums in Bigalı. Both venues attract mainly Turkish families with children, as not many foreigners show up in the village. The travellers from Austalia and New Zeland choose to visit the military cemeteries of the Allied forces, but going to Bigalı offers a wider perspective on the events of First World War.

The first museum in Bigalı is the so-called House of Atatürk (tr. *Atatürk Evi*), already mentioned above. This building functioned as Atatürk's headquarters during the campaign on the Gallipoli Peninsula. After the war, it served its owners as a private house.

However, everyone in the neighbourhood knew its history. Finally, the local community established a committee with the goal to create a museum. The house was bought from its owners, restored in 1973, and opened to the public as a museum. On the ground floor, there is a kitchen and a living room. Upstairs, it is possible to visit the office of Mustafa Kemal, his bedroom, and a bedroom of his aide. However, only a desk in the office remained of the original furnishings and other pieces of furniture date back to a later period. The walls are decorated with the portraits of the leader, reproductions of photographs, and information boards, unfortunately in Turkish only.

A part of the exhibition is located outside the building, in a small inner courtyard, surrounded by bushes and trees that cast cool shadows. There are information boards as well, the first one – with the text of the March of Independence (tr. *İstiklâl Marşı*) – the song which has been the national anthem of the Republic of Turkey since 1921. The second one presents the text of the speech which Atatürk addressed to the Turkish youth. Both texts are written in Turkish and translated into English. In addition, there are numerous reproductions of photographs from the times of the Battle of Gallipoli, as well as maps and charts explaining the history of the fight. The price of a regular ticket to the House of Atatürk is 2 TL, and a discounted ticket (for students) 1 TL. Taking photos is allowed, with no additional fee.

The exhibition at the Museum of the 19th Division (tr. *19. Tümen Müzesi*) is small, but absorbing. It consists of the mannequins dressed in costumes of the First World War period. These mannequins demonstrate the scenes of a family farewell to a soldier leaving to the battlefront, and the interior of the field hospital. Next, there are showcases that display the letters written from the front, and documents related to the military operations.

In other cabinets there are weapons and ammunition used during the First World War, as well as everyday items, including spoons, forks, and canteens. There is also information about the soldiers' diet, based on bean dishes. Throughout the museum there are

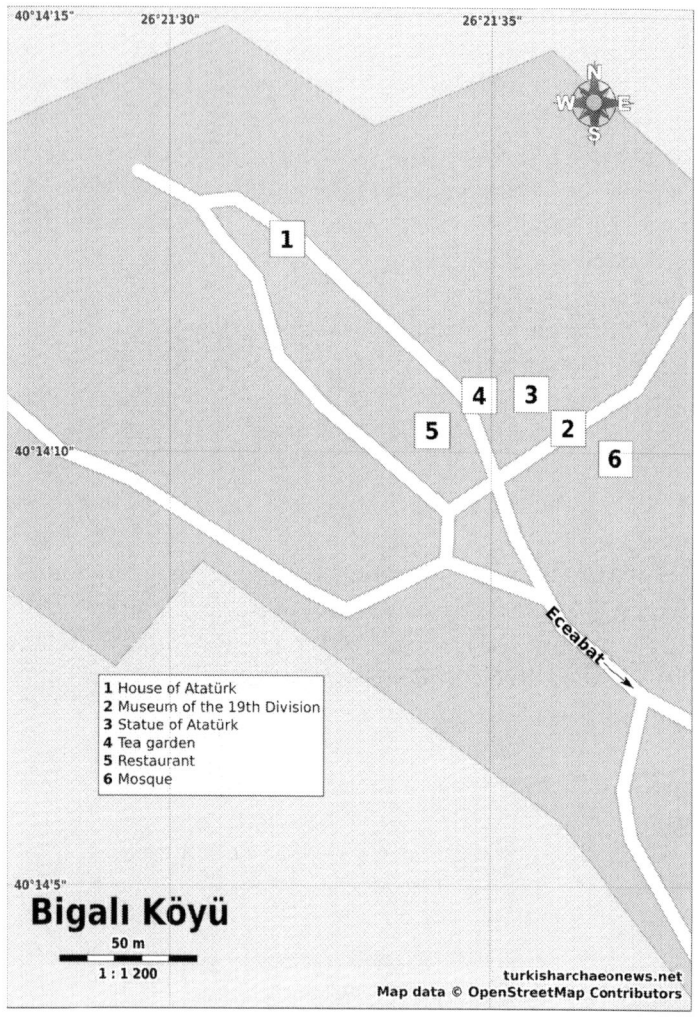

1 House of Atatürk
2 Museum of the 19th Division
3 Statue of Atatürk
4 Tea garden
5 Restaurant
6 Mosque

Bigalı Köyü
50 m
1 : 1 200

turkisharchaeonews.net
Map data © OpenStreetMap Contributors

Plan of Bigalı Köyü

many information boards and photo reproductions of times of the fight. Unfortunately, there is no information in English – all texts are in Turkish only – and that makes it difficult to fully understand the significance of the exhibition. The museum is housed in a small building located in the central square of the village. The regular ticket costs 2 TL, and a discounted one (for students) 1 TL. You can take photos in the museum, with no additional fee.

VISITOR TIPS

Orientation

Bigalı is a tiny village where the buildings are located along one street – Bigalı Köyü Yolu. At the entrance to Bigali, on the right side of the road, there is a square with parking places. At this square stands a statue of Atatürk (tr. *Atatürk Anıtı*), the only mosque in the village (tr. *Bigalı Köyü Cami*), and the Museum of the 19th Division. The House of Atatürk is located about 100 meters away, at the end of the road, at number 126.

Restaurants

The most pleasant place to rest during the exploration of Bigalı is a tea garden, operating on the main (and only) square in the village. There is also a small eatery (tr. *büfe*), where you can buy toasts and gözleme (Turkish pancakes).

GETTING THERE

BY CAR: take D550 road from Eceabat to the south-west. After 36 km, turn right and drive further 7 km. The roads to Bigalı are clearly signposted.

Bigalı Fortress

COORDINATES: 40.2134° N, 26.3891° E

The ruins of Bigalı Fortress (tr. *Bigalı Kalesi*) are visible just off the Gelibolu-Eceabat road, about 6 km to the north of Eceabat. The Turkish Ministry of Culture inscribed Bigalı Fortress on the list of archaeological sites in 1980. When looking for the information about Bigalı Fortress, it isimportant to remember that it has several alternative names: Bogali Kalesi, Bokali Kalessi, and Boğalı Kalesi.

BRIEF HISTORY

The construction of Bigalı Fortress began in the late 18th century, during the reign of Sultan Selim III, and ended at the beginning of the 19th century, during the reign of Sultan Mahmud II. The fortress was founded as an artillery outpost, with the task to protect the Dardanelles Strait from the threat of the British Navy. At the same time, Nara Fortress was built opposite Bigalı Fortress, on the Asian shore of the strait.

Building materials obtained from the nearby ancient Sestos Castle were used for the construction of Bigalı Fortress. Therefore, not much of Sestos Castle has been preserved to our times. Nevertheless, it is worth mentioning the mythological tale of tragic lovers: Hero of Sestos, the priestess of the goddess Aphrodite, and Leander from Abydos. Every night, Leander swam across the Dardanelles to his beloved Hero, led by the light of a lamp placed in the window. One night, when the light was extinguished during a storm, Leander got lost in the waters of the Dardanelles and drowned. On hearing the news of his fate, Hero killed herself by jumping from a tower. In 1810, Lord Byron recreated Leander's

Bigalı Fortress

feat by swimming from Sestos to Abydos, and it took him four hours to complete this challenge.

Visitor tips

Although the walls of Bigalı Fortress were relatively well preserved, in 2017 the authorities of Çanakkale Province decided to launch an extensive reconstruction programme. As a result, the castle is temporarily closed to visitors. Despite the promise that the works will be finished in 500 days, the reopening date remains unknown.

Getting there

By car: Bigalı Fortress is located just off D550 route, 6 km north of Eceabat. Its location is marked with a brown signpost Bigalı Kalesi, which is visible only for the travellers coming from the direction of Eceabat.

Eceabat

COORDINATES: 40.1841° N, 26.3597° E

Eceabat is a town situated on the eastern side of the Gallipoli Peninsula, on the shore of the Dardanelles. Its current importance for tourism in the region results from the proximity of the most important places associated with the military campaign during the First World War, including battlefields and cemeteries of the fallen soldiers. In addition, Eceabat is an important ferry port which enables crossing the Dardanelles Strait to the city of Çanakkale, located on the Asian shore of the strait.

BRIEF HISTORY

Eceabat was formerly known as Maydos (Madytos), and its current name is probably a distorted Arabic word from the military dictionary – Hijabat – which means the furthest point of command on the battlefield.

The city was founded as a Greek colony, in the 7th century BCE. The settlers were the Greeks from the Aeolian tribe, living on the island of Lesbos in the Aegean Sea. Later, Maydos was also settled by the Greeks from the cities of Miletus and Klazomenai in Asia Minor. Maydos is mentioned by the historian Herodotus in the context of the wars against the Persians, and by Thucydides, in reference to the battle of Eurymedon, fought between the member states of the Ionian League and the Persian Empire in 466 BCE.

In the Byzantine period, Maydos was a famous trading port. In the 15th century, the Turks conquered it, but until the 20-ies of the 20th century, the city was inhabited mainly by the Greek population. As a result of population exchange established by the

Respect for History Park in Eceabat

Treaty of Lausanne in 1923, most of the inhabitants were resettled to the present-day Greece.

SIGHTSEEING

While walking along the promenade or waiting for the ferry to Asia, you can take an opportunity of visiting the Respect for History Park (tr. *Tarihe Saygı Parkı*), established in 2008. This is an outdoor exhibition, where several battle scenes of the First World War have been recreated. There are also some exhibits from this period of history. Admission to the park is free of charge.

There are two mosques in the center of Eceabat: the Mosque of the Fallen (tr. *Şehitler Camii*), built in 1984, with a terrace overlooking the Dardanelles Strait, and utterly uninteresting City Mosque (tr. *Merkez Cami*).

Seyit Ali Çabuk Monument (tr. *Seyit Onbaşı Anıtı*) stands near Liman Balık Restaurant. It shows the heroic soldier of the Ottoman army, who became famous for having carried three artillery shells, each weighing 275 kg, during the Allied attempt to force the Dardanelles on the 18th of March 1915. His deed enabled the bombardment of the Allied fleet despite the broken shell crane.

To the south of the city, there is a narrow pebble beach where you can seize the opportunity to swim in the Dardanelles Strait.

Even further to the south, 1.5 km from the city center, you can find Çamburnu Information Center (tr. *Çamburnu Ziyaretçi Merkezi*). In this facility, you can get information about the Battle of Gallipoli and the most important sites commemorating the events of the First World War. A small museum operates onsite.

The Ottoman fortress in Kilitbahir is located just 5 km to the south of Eceabat. Eceabat is also the most convenient base for visiting the battlefields and cemeteries from the times of the First World War.

VISITOR TIPS

Orientation

Eceabat is located on the western shore of the Dardanelles. D550 (E87) route, connecting the most important cities of the Gallipoli

Waterfront in Eceabat

Peninsula, runs through the town. This road goes in an arc around the center of Eceabat, skirting it from the west, and serving as a ring road known as Atatürk Street (tr. *Atatürk Caddesi*).

Two main streets in the centre of Eceabat are: Republic Street (tr. *Cumhuriyet Caddesi*) and Independence Street (tr. *İstiklal Caddesi*). These streets go along the shore of the Dardanelles and join next to the ferry terminal where they widen to form the Square of the Republic (tr. *Cumhuriyet Meydanı*). Independence Street continues further in the southerly direction, with a parallel Zubeyde Hanım Square (tr. *Zubeyde Hanım Meydanı*). In this area, you can find hotels, shops, restaurants, and service points.

The beach district of the city is located on the southern side of Eceabat, beyond the junction of the ring road and Independence Street. There you can also find several hotels and B&Bs, of a higher standard than in the city center.

Accommodation

If you plan to stop for a night in Eceabat, remember the dates of the anniversaries of the battles of Gallipoli, and book your accommodation well in advance if you plan a stay in March or April. In

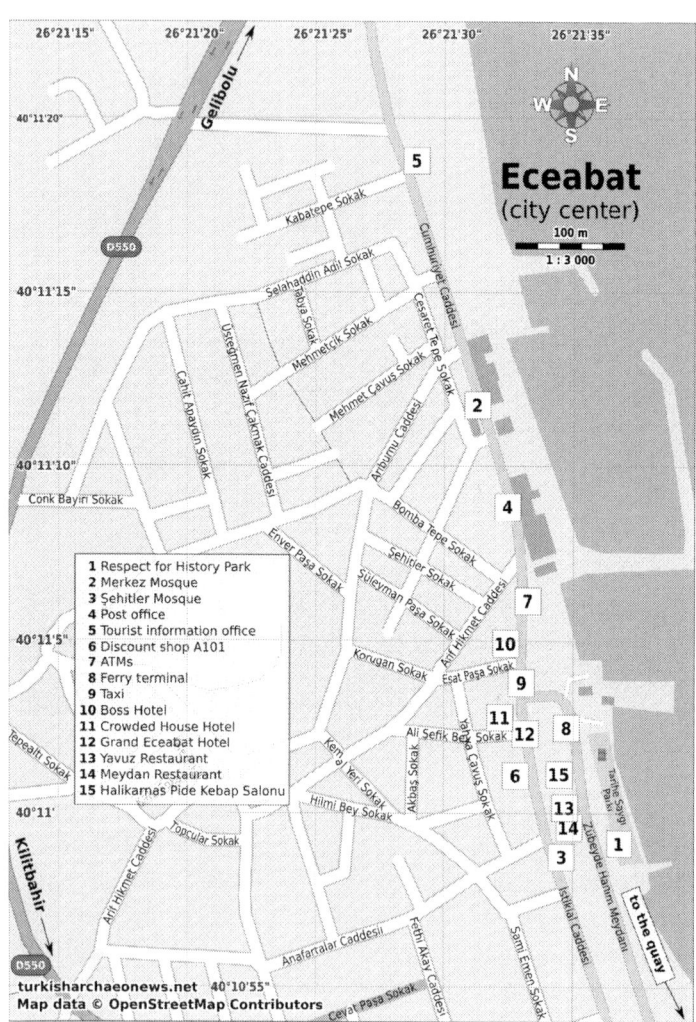

Eceabat
(city center)
100 m
1 : 3 000

1 Respect for History Park
2 Merkez Mosque
3 Şehitler Mosque
4 Post office
5 Tourist information office
6 Discount shop A101
7 ATMs
8 Ferry terminal
9 Taxi
10 Boss Hotel
11 Crowded House Hotel
12 Grand Eceabat Hotel
13 Yavuz Restaurant
14 Meydan Restaurant
15 Halikarnas Pide Kebap Salonu

turkisharchaeonews.net 40°10'55"
Map data © OpenStreetMap Contributors

Plan of Eceabat – city center

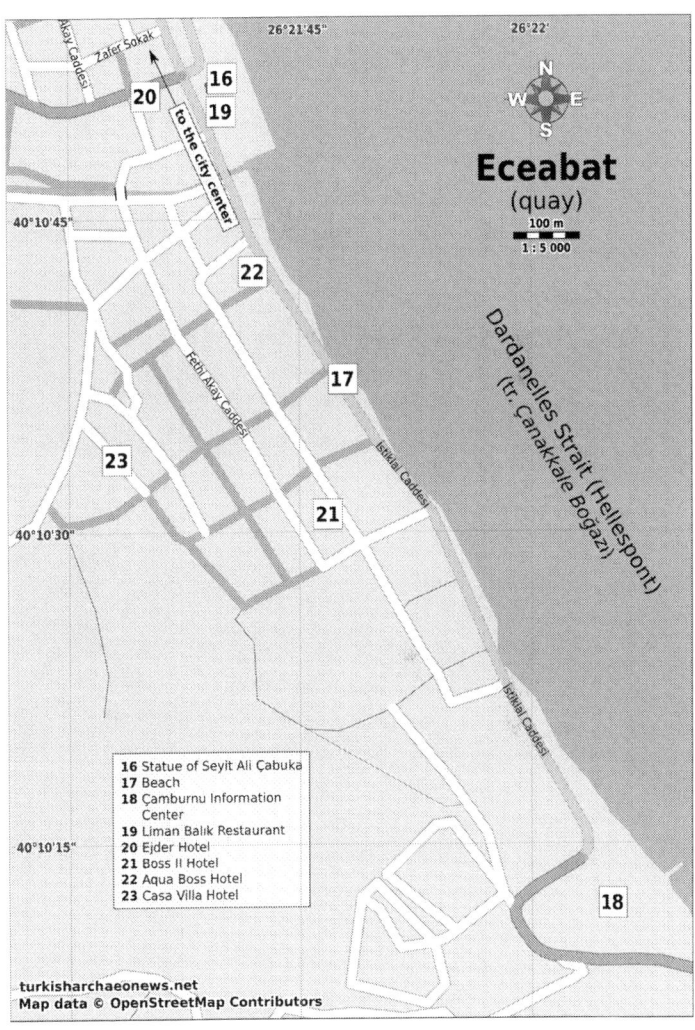

Plan of Eceabat – quay

other months of a year finding accommodation in Eceabat is not a problem. Several hotels are situated opposite the ferry terminal and along the coast, along Republic Street and Independence Street.

Boss is the largest network of hotels in Eceabat with the following accommodation options:

- Boss Hotel – the flagship of the Boss hotel chain is located right next to the ferry terminal, at the Square of the Republic. Hotel guests can take advantage of free parking in the city center, and wi-fi.
- Boss II Hotel – away from the center, to the south, on Mehmet Akif Street. The rooms are small and modestly furnished but clean and renovated. The price includes a typical Turkish breakfast.
- Aqua Boss Hotel – the most interesting of the group, located on Independence Street No. 91. It is situated on the waterfront, in a renovated stone building of a former tomato canning factory. It has a restaurant, private parking places, and a fitness center. The breakfast, included in the price, is plentiful and delicious.

Also, the following hotels are noteworthy in Eceabat:

- Casa Villa Hotel – located on the southern side of the city, on Camburnu Street No. 75. This is the most elegant and best-rated hotel in Eceabat. It has a garden, where rich, village-style breakfasts are served. Dinners are also prepared for the guests upon request.
- Crowded House Hotel – located in the city center, on Hüseyin Avni Street No. 4. This is the most popular place among foreign tourists visiting Eceabat. In addition to standard single, double, and triple rooms, it offers accommodation in a dormitory.
- Ejder Hotel – on Atatürk Street No. 5, near Seyit Ali Çabuk Monument. This highly rated new hotel offers clean, but small rooms and breakfast included in the price.

- Grand Eceabat Hotel – situated in the city center, at the Square of the Republic, near the ferry terminal. It offers spacious, elegantly furnished rooms with breakfast included.

Restaurants

Cheaper restaurants are located around Zubeyde Hanım Square, opposite the ferry terminal. More expensive venues that serve fish and seafood are situated a little further to the south.

If you choose to dine in a cheaper restaurant, go to Yavuz Lokantasi near the ferry terminal. It offers several kinds of soups, kebabs, and a bistro menu of meat, vegetables, and salads. Nearby eateries offer similar menus and prices – Meydan Lokantasi specializes in chicken kebab, and Halicarnassus Pide Kebap Salonu serves Turkish pizza (tr. *pide*).

Liman Balık restaurant, located at the end of the promenade, serves fish dishes and traditional Turkish snacks (tr. *meze*) as well as Turkish breakfasts and soups. Expect to pay a premium price for the pleasure of consumption of grilled fish on a pleasantly shaded terrace.

Shopping

In Eceabat, there are numerous groceries, as well as discount shops of BIM (on Arif Hikmet Street) and A101 (on Independence Street) networks.

You can also buy typical souvenirs of the Gallipoli Peninsula, commemorating the battles of the First World War. The stands on the promenade are dominated by shoddy pictures and miniatures of Seyit Ali Çabuk Monument.

Services

Banks, ATMs, and a post office are all located at the Square of the Republic, right next to the ferry terminal. In this location, you can also find the offices of coach companies, while the taxi stand and minibus stop are nearby.

Tourist Information Office is located on Republic Street No. 72. It is open on weekdays, from 8:00 am to 5:00 pm, but, unfortunately, its employees do not speak foreign languages very well.

GETTING THERE

BY COACH: there are numerous coach connections from Eceabat, for example to Istanbul (6 hours) and Izmir (7 hours).

BY MINIBUS: local minibuses go from Eceabat to Gelibolu (1 hour) and Kilitbahir (10 minutes). Additionally, there is a connection to the ferry terminal in Kabatepe (15 minutes), on the western side of the Gallipoli Peninsula. There you can catch a ferry to the Aegean island known as Gökçeada.

BY CAR: Eceabat is situated on D550 route, from Istanbul to Çanakkale (by ferry). The distance from Gelibolu is 45 km, and the road offers beautiful vistas of the Dardanelles and its Asian shore. If you drive from Eceabat further to the south, you will get to Kilitbahir, just 4 km away.

BY FERRY: as there is no bridge over the Dardanelles yet, the only way of crossing the strait to its Asian shore is by a ferry. The ferries connect Eceabat with Çanakkale. The ferry terminal in Eceabat is the main one on the Gallipoli Peninsula.

The ferries offer regular connections, at all times of day and night. At night, they depart every two hours, and during the day – every hour. In summer, the frequency rises to two ferries per hour. The crossing takes approximately 25 minutes. If you pay per vehilce, the transport of its all passengers is included in the price.

Because of heavy traffic on this route, there are frequent traffic jams in Eceabat, created by cars and buses that await the boarding. The best idea is to avoid the crossing in the afternoons, especially on Sundays.

Kilitbahir

Coordinates: 40.1478° N, 26.3796° E

Kilitbahir is a small town and fishing harbour in the southern part of the Gallipoli Peninsula. Its importance for tourism is due to the presence of the vast Ottoman fortress and the existence of the ferry terminal that enables crossing the Dardanelles to the Asian shore.

Brief history

The word 'Kilitbahir' means 'Key to the Sea.' It reflects the critical role of the fortress built here to defend the Dardanelles Strait and the entire Ottoman Empire. During the siege of Constantinople by the Ottomans in 1453, the Genoese fleet managed to get through the Dardanelles in an unsuccessful attempt to save the capital of the Byzantine Empire. Mehmed the Conqueror drew the right conclusions from this situation and decided to strengthen the Dardanelles with a chain of strategically placed fortifications. The immediate reason for the construction of fortresses on both shores of the Dardanelles were the fears of the sultan that the Venetians would attempt to wrestle Constantinople from the Ottoman control. The Italians spoke of these fortresses simply as *i Castelli*, i.e. the castles.

The Ottoman fortress in Kilitbahir was strengthened and renovated over the centuries. During the war with Italy in 1911, the entrance to the strait had been mined. In 1914, the fortress became one of the key points of defense against the Allied troops, and a torpedo base was set up near Kilitbahir. The preparations to repel the attack turned out to be a good strategic move when, in Febru-

Kilitbahir Fortress

ary 1915, the Allied fleet of British and French ships launched an attack on the Dardanelles. Their primary goal was the elimination of artillery batteries positioned in Kilitbahir. The fleet suffered a great defeat, especially after the ships encountered naval mines. As a result, the decision of the Allies was not to repeat the attack by sea and to launch the land campaign. Its bloody history is described in the chapter devoted to the Battle of Gallipoli.

Even today, Kilitbahir is the place firmly protected by the Turkish army, and the soldiers can be observed during maneuvers in the neighbourhood.

SIGHTSEEING

Kilitbahir Fortress (tr. *Kilitbahir Kalesi*) dominates the European shore of the Dardanelles at its narrowest point. The fortress is located opposite the city of Çanakkale, on the Asian shore of the Dardanelles. Its twin in Çanakkale – Çimenlik Fortress (tr. *Kale-i Sultaniye*) – is clearly visible across the water. Both castles were built on the orders of the Ottoman Sultan Mehmet the Conqueror in the years 1462-1463. Their aim was to ensure the control of the Ottoman Empire over the strait which was the most important

Museum of Naval Battles in Kilitbahir

sea passage to the new Ottoman capital – Istanbul.

Kilitbahir Fortress is characterized by an unusual architectural plan. It was built on the plan of a five-leaf clover, obtained by the demarcation of three partially overlapping circles. Perhaps this plan was to symbolize the shape of a key, which would explain the origins of its name. Because it was built on such a plan, the walls do not run in straight lines, but in arches that were marked by the principal architect with a compass. Apparently the passion that Sultan Mehmet felt for geometry inspired the creation of such an unusual shape of the fortress.

A sever-storied tower rises over the castle. It was built later, during the reign of Sultan Suleyman the Magnificent. In the old days, it provided the vantage point for the continuous observation of the waters of the Dardanelles, aimed at early detection of approaching enemy ships. A full garrison of Ottoman troops was stationed in the fortress at all times, just in case of an unexpected attack.

Kilitbahir Fortress underwent a restoration in the years 2011-2013, and reopened to the public in 2015. It is available to visitors daily, from 8:00 am to 7:00 pm (in winter months to 5:30 pm). The ticket costs 15 TL.

The castle is surrounded by an additional line of the outer fortifications with three bastions: Sarıkule, Mecidiye, and Namazgah. Namazgah redoubt (tr. *Namazgah Tabyası*) is the complex of massive bunkers built in the 19th century, during the reign of Sultan Abdülaziz. The Museum of Naval Battles (tr. *Kilitbahir Namazgah Tabyası Müzesi*) operates inside this bastion.

Namazgah was designed to strengthen the defense of the Dardanelles at its narrowest point. In the 19th century, it was the greatest bastion of the entire Dardanelles region. A complex of artillery batteries was installed here, and it was only removed in the 50s of the 20th century. In 2006, the bastion underwent a complete renovation, in 1980 the Turkish Ministry of Culture recognized it as a protected historic building, and in 2006 the museum was organised inside.

The interior of the Museum of Naval Battles, located in one of the bunkers, displays the exhibits related to the military history of the Dardanelles. There are paintings, sketches, and photographs illustrating the state of the fortifications and the weapons over many centuries. You can also see the photos of warships from the times of the First World War.

In the display cases, there are items of soldiers' equipment, including stationery, shoes, and keys as well as guns, bullets, and cannonballs. An unexpected addition to this collection are the examples of antique ceramics from Çanakkale. There is also a gap in the bunker – a reminder of shelling during the First World War. Today it is glazed, so it is possible to look into the museum from the outside.

Within the bastion, there is a large mock-up showing its plan. It is worth to climb the stairs onto the walls towering over the Dardanelles to see the views of the Asian shore and the city of Çanakkale.

Admission to the bastion is free of charge, but to get to the bunker with the museum exhibitions, you have to buy a ticket, for a symbolic price. Information boards, not only in Turkish but also in English, are a great asset of the museum.

Opposite the compound of bunkers, on the other side of the D550 route, there is a severely ruined building that was a place of prayer for the Ottoman soldiers. It is called namazgah (an open-air prayer area) and it gave the name to the whole bastion. A much better-preserved example of such a structure can be seen in Gelibolu.

On the street leading from the fortress uphill, in a nicely renovated house, operates the local Center for Culture and Arts (tr. *Kültür ve Sanat Merkezi*). In its interior, there is an exhibition displaying the relics of the First World War and ethnographic exhibits from Kilitbahir region.

The district of the town situated away from the coast is a maze of narrow cobbled streets, where one can find several historic houses from the Ottoman period. You can also locate a fountain built at the turn of the 17th and 18th centuries, on the orders of Damat Ibrahim Pasha, Grand Vizier, and a son in law of Sultan Ahmed III.

The mosque and tomb of Cahidi Ahmed Efendi (tr. *Cahidi Sultan Ahmet Türbesi ve Camisi*), restored in 2014, is another local curiosity. Cahidi Ahmed Efendi, born in Edirne, was the founder of a powerful Sufi sect known as Halvetiyye. He died in Kilitbahir in 1642, and his tomb was erected here.

Very close to Kilitbahir, to the south, on the D550 road, there is a monument of Seyit Onbaşı (tr. *Seyit Onbaşı Anıtı*), similar to the one which stands in the center of Eceabat. It is a favorite stop for organised tours that take tourists to the battlefields located on the southern tip of the Gallipoli Peninsula. Kilitbahir is a good starting point for the exploration of the memorials from the times of the First World War.

VISITOR TIPS

Orientation

The people who visit Kilitbahir for the first time might get a false impression that this town is made up only of one street (D550 route), fortifications on the coast, and the ferry terminal. Meanwhile, there is yet another face of Kilitbahir – an old quarter sit-

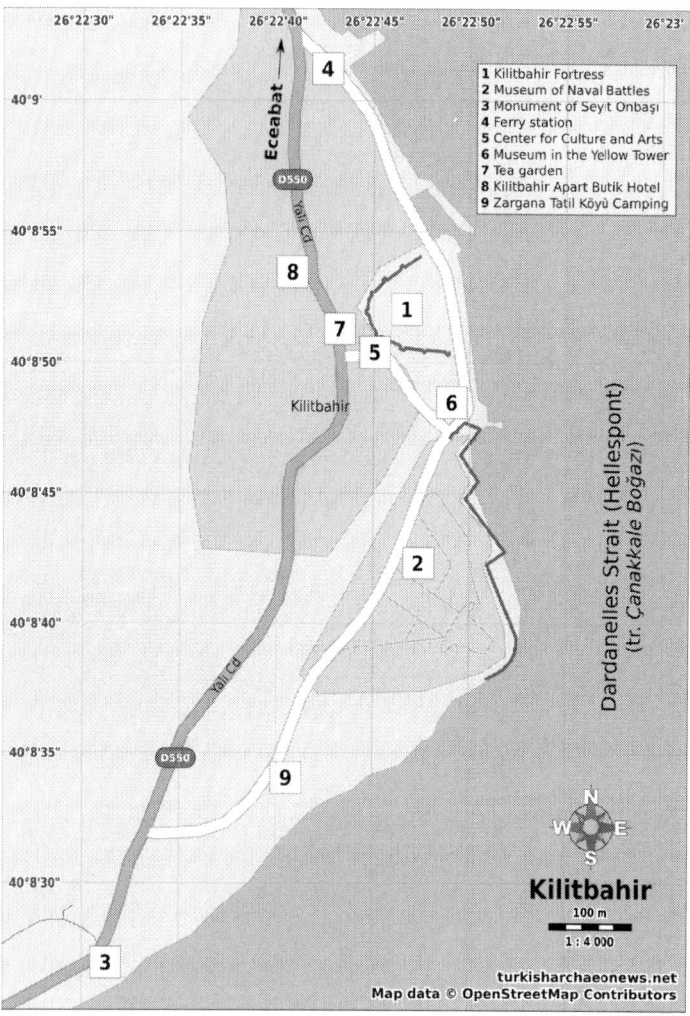

1 Kilitbahir Fortress
2 Museum of Naval Battles
3 Monument of Seyit Onbaşı
4 Ferry station
5 Center for Culture and Arts
6 Museum in the Yellow Tower
7 Tea garden
8 Kilitbahir Apart Butik Hotel
9 Zargana Tatil Köyü Camping

Plan of Kilitbahir

uated on the hills above the fortress, with its narrow streets and charming old buildings.

D550 route runs along the coast, and in Kilitbahir it is known as Wharf Street (tr. *Yalı Caddesi*). Just at the northern entrance to Kilitbahir, there is a ferry terminal, some restaurants and shops. Kilitbahir Fortress and the bastions stand a little further to the south.

Right at the entrance to Kilitbahir, Wharf Street forks off, and its western branch – Market Street (tr. *Çarşı Caddesi*) – takes you to the old district of the town. Both roads converge again to the south of Kilitbahir.

Accommodation and restaurants

In Kilitbahir, there are several restaurants specializing in fish and seafood. They are located near the ferry terminal, along D550 route. In addition, just over the fortress, there is a local tea garden (tr. *Park Çay Bahçesi*), where you can relax in the shade of trees and sip hot tea while children enjoy a little playground.

Accommodation options in Kilitbahir are very limited, and it is much easier to find a place to stay in Eceabat. If you are determined to spend the night in the town, Kilitbahir Apart Butik Otel is the most attractive option. It is located on a hill, on a side street just off Market Street. The hotel offers both simple rooms with shared bathrooms, as well as larger suites with a kitchenette.

On the southern side of the town, just off the coast, there is a beach club and a camping ground called Zargana Tatil Köyü. There you can relax, swim in the Dardanelles, and spend the night in a rented tent. There is an on-site café, and a restaurant. This holiday village operates only during the summer season, from May to October.

GETTING THERE

BY MINIBUS: there are regular minibuses from Eceabat (10 minutes) and Gelibolu (1 hour 15 minutes).

BY CAR: from the northern direction take D550 route, from Keşan

(114 km), through Gelibolu (49 km), and Eceabat (4 km).

BY FERRY: as the Dardanelles Strait is narrowest at this point, the ferry crossing takes only 15-20 minutes, depending on weather conditions. The connection is provided by a private shipping company, and the ferries can take only several passenger cars aboard. The ferries depart several times a day but often it is necessary to wait for the departure as they set off when they are full.

Seddülbahir

COORDINATES: 40.0426° N, 26.1881° E

Seddülbahir is a village situated on the southern tip of the Gallipoli Peninsula, in the place where the waters of the Aegean Sea enter the narrow isthmus between the peninsula and the north-western Anatolia, demarcating the starting point of the Dardanelles Strait. The strategic location of Seddülbahir, at the entrance to the strait, means that this place has witnessed numerous struggles for control of the water corridor, opening the waterway to Istanbul for the fleet. The name of Seddülbahir means 'the Walls of the Sea' in the Ottoman dialect of Turkish, and it perfectly captures the role of this beachhead. Anglo-Saxon historians often use the name Cape Helles, derived from the ancient name of the Dardanelles, i.e. the Hellespont.

BRIEF HISTORY

In the mid-seventeenth century, the Ottoman Empire fought a long and bloody war with the Republic of Venice. This war was known as the War of Candia because the bone of contention was the island of Crete, along with its main Venetian harbour city – Candia (now Heraklion). The Venetians planned an offensive assuming the destruction of the Ottoman fleet and threatening the imperial capital – Istanbul. The implementation of this plan required the control of the Dardanelles by the Venetian fleet. The initial successes of Venice – blocking the mouth of the strait into the Aegean Sea – caused panic among the Turks. Sultan Ibrahim I was ousted from power, and his place was taken by his six-year-old son, Mehmet IV. The changes at the highest level of authority of the Ottoman Empire did not stop the Venetian fleet, which attacked the villages located along the shores of the strait over the next nine years.

In 1656, the Ottoman fleet attempted to remove the Venetians. As a result of the failed offensive it suffered huge losses, compared to the defeat of Lepanto in 1571. This time, the personal changes made at the Ottoman court proved to have serious consequences. The position of the Grand Vizier was appointed to Mehmed Köprülü, the patriarch of the family, which included successive viziers, statesmen, and military commanders. Köprülü family directed the policy of the Ottoman Empire for the next half of the century. However, the beginnings of Mehmed Köprülü rule were not easy, as a new offensive of the Ottoman fleet ended in another failure. It resulted in the death sentence for the great admiral who commanded the Ottoman warships. On the other hand, the Venetian admiral Mocenigo was killed during the sea battle, the Venetian fleet lost momentum, and eventually withdrew from the zone of the Black Sea Straits.

The Grand Vizier drew vital conclusions from the events of the War of Candia. One of them was understanding the need to build the second line of defenses in the Dardanelles Strait. Until then, the most important defenses of the Dardanelles were two castles, standing on its opposite shores: Kilitbahir Fortress and Kale-i Sultaniye Castle in Çanakkale. However, they were situated too deeply into the Dardanelles. Mehmed Köprülü ordered the construction of two other fortresses, which were to guard the entrance to the strait from the south. One of them was Seddülbahir Fortress at Cape Helles, and the second one – Kumkale Castle on the Asian shore.

The twin fortresses built by Mehmed Köprülü protected the Dardanelles until the First World War. During the Allied offensive on the Gallipoli Peninsula in 1915, Seddülbahir Fortress became the target of the British artillery and was seriously damaged as the result of bombardment. At the same time, the French forces destroyed Kumkale Castle.

SIGHTSEEING

Impressive ruins of Seddülbahir Fortress (tr. *Seddülbahir Kalesi*) are the most important monument in the village. There are pre-served fragments of the defensive wall, a tower, and the northern gate. The castle has been renovated for the last few years, and there are promises that it will reopen in 2019.

In addition, around Seddülbahir, there are several important monuments. It is possible to visit the Allied cemetery at V Beach and the Monument of the First Martyrs (tr. *İlk Şehitler Anıtı*). A tomb and a monument of Sergeant Yahya (tr. *Yahya Çavuş Şehitliği Ve Anıtı*) commemorate the heroic soldier who com-manded the Turkish troops during the Allied landing. The British Memorial of Cape Helles (tr. *Cape Helles Anıtı*) is the monument erected to commemorate more than twenty thousand British and Australian soldiers, who died during the First World War in this area.

VISITOR TIPS

Currently, Seddülbahir is a tiny village with only about 300 in-habitants. Because Cape Helles is often visited by tourists, both domestic and foreign, in the area there are several B&Bs and restau-rants. The most popular accommodation option is Seddülbahir Helles Panorama Guesthouse. It is located on a hill with a stunning view of the most important places commemorating the battles of the First World War. At the coast, there is also a camping site, and a grocery store operates in the village.

D550 route, which runs through the entire Gallipoli Peninsula, ends in Seddülbahir. At the beginning of the village, this road runs in an arc, turning to the west and leads along the west coast of the peninsula, joining with the main route, situated to the north of the village of Alçıtepe. In Seddülbahir, this road is simply called the Road of Seddülbahir Village (tr. *Seddülbahir Köyü Yolu*). It takes the travellers directly to the ruins of Seddülbahir Fortress.

GETTING THERE

BY CAR: take D550 route from the northern part of the Gallipoli Peninsula, and drive through Gelibolu (70 km), Eceabat (30 km), and Kilitbahir (26 km). About 2 km to the north of Seddülbahir this road forks off and its western branch goes to the biggest monument commemorating the First World War battles on the Gallipoli Peninsula, known as Çanakkale Martyrs' Memorial (tr. *Çanakkale Şehitleri Anıtı*).

Memorial Sites on the Gallipoli Peninsula

For hundreds of years, a narrow strip of land, now known as the Gallipoli Peninsula, has been the key to the conquest of Constantinople. The fleet that would have been able to break through the narrow Dardanelles Strait, had an excellent chance to capture this great capital of many empires. The last such attempt was made during the First World War by the Allied forces that suffered a crushing defeat.

BRIEF HISTORY

The balance of the struggles in 1915-1916 was tragic. From 120 to 130 thousand combatants were killed, according to various sources. Ottoman victory was paid for with massive losses as 2/3 of the fallen were the soldiers of the Ottoman army. Among the fallen Allied soldiers, most victims were from the UK, France, Australia, New Zealand, and India.

Since 1973, the southern part of the peninsula has been protected as the National Historical Park of Gallipoli Peninsula (tr. *Gelibolu Yarımadası Tarihî Millî Parkı*). On its territory there are military cemeteries, monuments commemorating the fallen, including the soldiers buried at sea, and battlegrounds. All these tragic reminders of the turbulent past of the Gallipoli Peninsula are located among pine forests and thickets, rising above the blue waters of the Dardanelles and the Aegean Sea.

VISITOR TIPS

The tour of the Memorial Sites of the Gallipoli Peninsula is considered to be a kind of 'a rite of passage' into adulthood among young

Australians and New Zealanders. Particularly in the second half of April, when the Anzac Day is celebrated on the 25th of April, the peninsula is crowded with coaches filled with the visitors from the Antipodes.

However, for the tourists from other regions of the world, visiting all cemeteries and monuments can become a tedious task. It is enough to realise that there are more than 30 Allied cemeteries on the peninsula, not to mention 20 cemeteries of Turkish soldiers, numerous memorial sites, tombs of lone soldiers, and battlefields. It is sufficient to visit just a few of them to gain some understanding of the importance of the events of the First World War.

Therefore, below you will find only some selection of cemeteries and memorial sites on the Gallipoli Peninsula. Moreover, we recommend visiting two villages – Bigali Köyü and Büyük Anafarta – presented in separate chapters. In these villages, there are museums, monuments and military cemeteries. More memorial sites and monuments are described in the chapters devoted to Gelibolu, Eceabat, Kilitbahir, and Seddülbahir.

The suggested starting point for the memorial sites tour is Eceabat. You can also start from the town of Gelibolu, located to the north, or cross the Dardanelles for one day from Çanakkale, situated on the Asian shore of the strait.

TURKISH CEMENTARIES

Akbaş Şehitliği

COORDINATES: 40.2333° N, 26.4374° E

Akbaş Bay was one of the most important places of supplies delivery during the campaign on the Gallipoli Peninsula. The Turkish forces controlling it were targeted by the Allies from the water and the air. In the nearby valley, there was a large field hospital. The soldiers who died as a result of wounds were buried in a cemetery on the north side of the harbour.

Currently, there is a cemetery surrounded by a wall. In front of one of the entrances to the cemetery stands a statue of a soldier carrying a wounded comrade. A 5-meter stone obelisk, erected

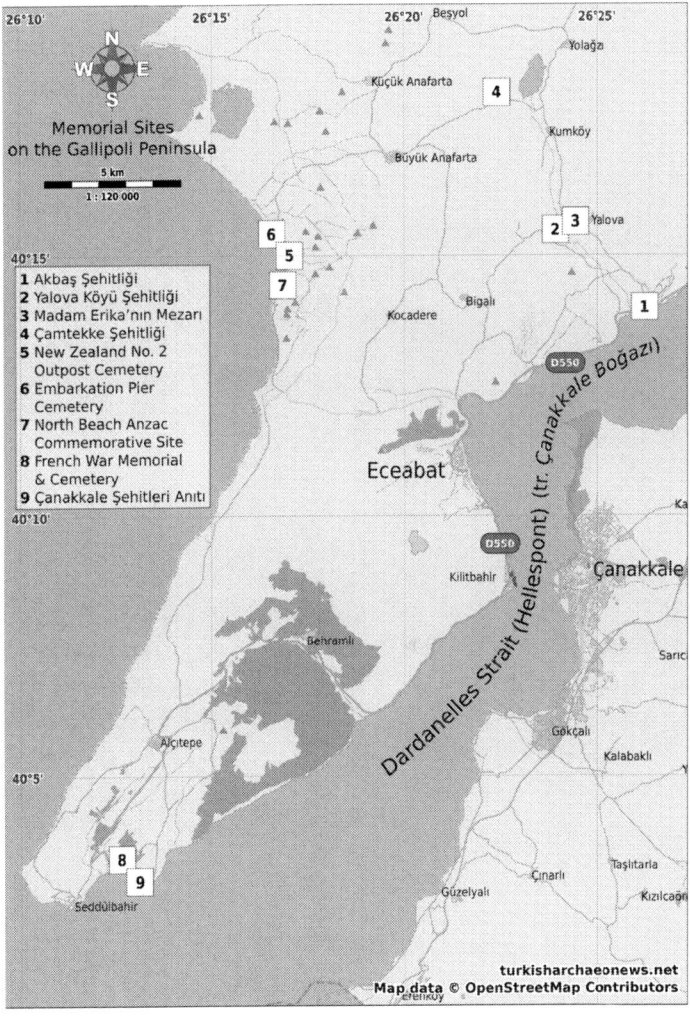

Memorial Sites on the Gallipoli Peninsula

to honour the fallen, stands in the cemetery. The cemetery was opened to the public in 1999, but it is visited almost exclusively by Turkish groups. Near the cemetery, there are several souvenir stalls. Akbaş Navy Cemetery is located just off D550 route from Gelibolu to Eceabat, about 12 km to the north of Eceabat.

Yalova Köyü Şehitliği
COORDINATES: 40.2607° N, 26.4073° E

Yalova Village Cemetery is also the burial place of the fallen in the First World War, including major Çırpanlı Zeynel Abidin Ali Bey. Unlike Akbaş Cemetery, this rural burial place has a more casual atmosphere, and as such it may be better placed for peaceful reflections than the more well-known and popular memorial sites.

Madam Erika'nın Mezarı
COORDINATES: 26.4073° N, 26.4052° E

This lonely tomb is located on a hill just outside the village of Yalova. Madam Erika was a German wife of Ragip Bey – a military doctor. During the war, she worked as a nurse and was killed during the bombing of the field hospital, where she had assisted the wounded Turkish soldiers. The village of Yalova and the tomb of Madam Erika are located 17 km to the north of Eceabat. You can reach them by driving along D550 route in the direction of Gelibolu and turning left at Akbaş Şehitliği cemetery.

Çamtekke Şehitliği
COORDINATES: 40.3019° N, 26.3730° E

This tomb, nestled among fields between the villages of Büyük Anafarta and Kumköy, is a mystery to many travellers. According to the information engraved on the gravestone, 71 soldiers are buried here. In the nearby Kumköy, there were military warehouses, guarded by these soldiers. Apparently they were killed by the bombing during an air raid, when they gathered around the well, washing their clothes. The mass grave is surrounded by

New Zealand No. 2 Outpost Cemetery

beautiful cypresses. It is located on a dirt road about 18 km north of Eceabat.

ALLIED CEMENTARIES

New Zealand No. 2 Outpost Cemetery

COORDINATES: 40.2522° N, 26.2815° E

New Zealand No. 2 Outpost Cemetery is located near the defensive positions occupied by troops from New Zealand, on the left flank of Anzac troops. 183 soldiers are buried in the cemetery, but only 33 of them could be identified. They came from New Zealand, the UK, and Australia. They were killed during the offensive in August of 1915.

The cemetery is located just off the road leading along the west coast of the Gallipoli Peninsula, on the coast of the Aegean Sea. Eceabat is about 23 km away.

Embarkation Pier Cemetery

COORDINATES: 40.2547° N, 26.2797° E

The cemetery is adjacent to the evacuation station for wounded allies, who were transported to the ships from hills and valleys of the Gallipoli Peninsula. The cemetery was established after the end of hostilities, by the transfer of previously buried soldiers from smaller cemeteries and hills.

Out of 944 soldiers buried here, only 282 have been identified. For those that could not be identified, a special commemorative monument has been erected. This cemetery is located just 200 meters from the New Zealand No. 2 Outpost Cemetery.

French War Memorial & Cemetery

COORDINATES: 40.0569° N, 26.2106° E

Located on the tip of the Gallipoli Peninsula, at Morto Bay, French War Memorial & Cemetery is a memorial site for the valiant troops from France and its African colonies. French troops first attacked and captured Kumkale Castle, located on the Asian side of the Dardanelles, and were then transferred to the European shore. They were there to support the British forces during the Battle of Cape Helles (tr. *Seddülbahir*). During this campaign, the French troops were virtually wiped out.

On this relatively rarely visited cemetery, 18 thousand soldiers were buried. The identified bodies lie in 2,240 graves with iron crosses. The others were buried in five concrete mass graves, one of which is in the shape of a 15-meter high lighthouse that also serves as a memorial to the fallen.

MEMORIAL SITES

North Beach Anzac Commemorative Site

COORDINATES: 40.2406° N, 26.2809° E

North Beach Anzac Commemorative Site has been designed to meet the needs of the growing masses by visitors to the Gallipoli

Peninsula. Since 2000, this is the place where the Holy Mass is celebrated at dawn on the 25th of April in memory of the fallen. The site was prepared in cooperation with the governments of New Zealand, Australia, and Turkey. Its commissioning was attended by the Prime Ministers of the Australia and New Zealand, and the Turkish Minister of Forestry. They officially uncovered the panel stating that the Gallipoli Peninsula Peace Park is dedicated to peace, harmony, freedom, and mutual understanding.

On the days when no official ceremonies are held, it is a peaceful place, conducive to contemplation of the past and the bloodshed of the First World Was. In the distance, visible on the horizon, you can admire the Turkish island of Gökçeada and the Greek island of Samothrace.

Çanakkale Martyrs' Memorial
COORDINATES: 40.0498° N, 26.2184° E

Çanakkale Martyrs' Memorial, also known as Abide, is the largest memorial on the Gallipoli Peninsula. It stands on the southern tip of the peninsula, near the Gulf of Morto, on Hisarlık Hill. At the monument, there is a museum with souvenirs of war, and to the north of the monument there is a cemetery where 600 Turkish soldiers were buried.

This monument, commemorating the service of 253,000 Turkish soldiers who took part in the fighting on the Gallipoli Peninsula, has a height of over 41 meters. It is well visible from the Asian shore of the Dardanelles. It has the shape of four columns with a square base, covered with a concrete slab measuring 25 to 25 meters. Its design was created by three Turks: Doğan Erginbaş, Ismail Utkular, and Ertuğrul Barla, who won the official competition. The construction began in 1954, but due to financial problems it was only finished in 1958. In the meantime, a nationwide fundraiser was conducted to complete the work.

Çanakkale Martyrs' Memorial

Dardanelles Strait

The Dardanelles (tr. *Çanakkale Boğazı*) is a water passage connecting the Aegean Sea to the Sea of Marmara. Together with the Bosporus it is collectively referred to as the Turkish Straits (tr. *Türk Boğazları*) or the Black Sea Straits.

GEOGRAPHY

The Dardanelles Strait is 61 km long, and its width varies from 1.2 to 6 kilometers. The average depth of the strait is 55 meters, with the deepest point of 103 meters. Interestingly enough the water in the strait flows in both directions: from the Sea of Marmara to the Aegean Sea with the surface current, and inversely with the deep-sea current.

Because the strait is very narrow and long, it is often compared to a river. It is considered one of the most hazardous and crowded waterways in the world.

NAME

Turkish name of the Dardanelles – Canakkale Boğazı – comes from the largest city and the capital of the whole region. Its internationally used name – Dardanelles – derives from the ancient land of Dardania, which lay on the Asian shore of the strait. The main town of Dardania was situated on the slopes of Mount Ida. The most interesting archaeological site associated with Dardania is Dardanos Tumulus.

The Greek name of the strait – Hellespont – means 'Sea of Helle' and comes from the mythological figure of Helle, the daughter of King Atamas. According to Greek myth, Helle and her brother

Dardanelles Strait

Phrixus were persecuted by the evil stepmother, who wanted to kill them. They fled from her on the back of a flying ram with the golden fleece, but during the flight over the strait, Helle fell into the water and drowned. There is also an alternate version of this story, in which Helle was rescued by Poseidon, who fell in love with her. Another story connected to the Dardanelles is the one about the tragic lovers, Hero and Leander, which is related in the chapter devoted to Bigali Fortress.

HISTORY

The strategic importance of the Dardanelles is related to its location – on the sea route connecting the Mediterranean Sea to Istanbul, and further to the Black Sea. One might say that the earliest military conflict, which was associated with the Dardanelles Strait, was the Trojan War. It took place near the entrance to the strait from the Aegean Sea. Naturally, there is a dispute as to whether the legendary events described in the Iliad are related to the actual history of the region, but there are many indications of the historical background that inspired Homer to create this epic tale.

The Dardanelles has been a convenient place to control the trade and reap the benefits since the ancient times. Numerous Greek colonies were founded on both shores of the strait. Ancient historian Herodotus reported that the first attempt to construct a bridge over the strait was made during the second Persian invasion of Greece, in 480 BCE. The Persian army, led by Xerxes I, created pontoon bridges to get from Asia to Thrace. The construction of a pontoon bridge is based on boats and barges, linked together. The first attempt failed because the bridges were destroyed by the storm. During the second, successful, approach, two bridges were constructed in the vicinity of Abydos: the northeastern one was made from 360 ships, and the southwestern one – from 314 ships.

From the 5th century BCE, the power of Athens was based on the corn imported from Asia, transported from the harbours on the shores of the Black Sea, through the Dardanelles Strait, to Greece. All ships from other fleets had to pay a duty of 10% of the value of goods if they wanted to sail through the straits. The swift payment was guaranteed by the Athenian navy, stationed at Sestos.

In the days of the Byzantine Empire, the Dardanelles played a key role in the defense of Constantinople and as a source of revenue for the state. A marble plaque dated to the beginning of the 6th century CE with the customs regulations for ships passing through the strait has been discovered. It is now in the collections of the Archaeological Museum in Istanbul.

In 1354, the Ottomans crossed the Dardanelles Strait and captured the city now known as Gelibolu. This city became the first European foothold for the Turkish army, from which the Ottoman dynasty set off to conquer the lands of Europe. Within less than a decade, nearly all the territories belonging to Byzantium in Thrace were captured by the Turks.

In later times, when the Byzantine Empire disappeared from the maps, the so-called matter of the Black Sea Straits became a pressing issue, involving all the European powers. In 1833, the Ottoman Empire signed a secret treaty with Russia in Hünkâr

İskelesi. Under this pact, Russia was obliged to assist the Ottoman Empire during a war. In return, the Russians got the promise of closing the strait in the case of any threat of attack from the sea. This treaty alarmed Britain and France as the potential Russian expansionism in the Black Sea and Mediterranean regions would conflict with their economic interests.

Russia lost the benefits of the Treaty of Hünkâr İskelesi in 1841 when the London Straits Convention was signed between Russia, Great Britain, France, Austria, and Prussia. This agreement resulted in closing of the Turkish straits to all warships. Such a solution favored Great Britain at the expense of Russia, for which a corridor through the straits was the only access to the Mediterranean Sea.

During the First World War, the Dardanelles became one of the main stages of the drama that took place on the Gallipoli Peninsula. Thousands of soldiers and sailors lost their lives when the Allied forces attempted to reach Istanbul. After the end of the war, the Treaty of Lausanne from 1923 restored the Dardanelles to Turkish territory, on the condition that Turkey would keep them demilitarized and allow all foreign ships to traverse the strait.

Currently, the situation of the Bosporus and Dardanelles straits is regulated by the Montreux Convention of 1936. This international agreement states that the straits are an international shipping lane. However, Turkey is allowed to restrict the warship traffic of non-Black Sea states.

CITIES AND FORTRESSES

There are three towns worth visiting on the European shore of the Dardanelles, i.e. on the Gallipoli Peninsula. These towns are (from north to south): Gelibolu, Eceabat, and Kilitbahir. On the Asian shore of the Dardanelles, the major city is Çanakkale while Lapseki is a convenient alternative for crossing the strait by ferry.

Numerous fortifications were erected on both shores of the Dardanelles, due to the strategic importance of the strait. They were built in pairs on both shores, to guard the strait more effectively. The most famous pair is Kilitbahir Fortress on the European side and Çimenlik Castle in Asia. They are located at the narrowest point of the strait. The second line of fortifications is formed by Seddülbahir and Kumkale strongholds that guarded the entrance to the strait from the Aegean Sea.

FERRY CROSSINGS

While the idea of building a bridge over the Dardanelles dates back to the times of Xerxes, the only way to cross the strait until today has been by ferry. The three main ferry routes across the strait are: from Gelibolu to Lapseki, from Eceabat to Çanakkale, and from Kilitbahir to Çanakkale. More detailed information about these connections can be found in the chapters devoted to these cities.

There are plans to build a suspension bridge in the place where the strait is narrowest, i.e. between Kilitbahir and Sarıçay district of Çanakkale. The proposed bridge would have a length of about 2,200 meters, with 1,400 meters over the waters of the strait.

Northern Troad

The word 'Troad' describes an ancient land, located between the Aegean Sea, the Dardanelles Strait, and the Sea of Marmara, separated from the south-east areas by the massif of Ida (Kazdağı) Mountain. This region of Turkey is now called the Biga Peninsula. The main river of the Troad is Scamander (tr. *Karamenderes*). In ancient times, the major cities of the region were Troy and Lampsakos.

Currently, the area of the Troad corresponds fairly accurately to the Asian part of the Çanakkale Province. The European part of this province is the Gallipoli Peninsula. Below, the term 'Northern Troad' will describe the northern part of the Biga Peninsula, divided arbitrarily in such a way that the southernmost point of it are the ruins of Troy.

Do not miss

During your stay in the region of Northern Troad necessarily visit:

- the ruins of famous city of Troy;
- the city of Çanakkale;
- at least one of the ancient cities of the region, with Priapos ruins near Karabiga being the most spectacular.

Short history

The oldest historical references to the region of the Troad date back to the times of the Hittite Empire. According to a widely accepted interpretation of the cuneiform inscriptions, it was then known as Wilusa. In the thirteenth century BCE, Wilusa was continuously attacked by the Ahhiyawā tribe, often identified with the Achaeans from the book by Homer, i.e. the ancient Greeks.

The most famous city of the Northern Troad is the ancient Troy, whose spectacular collapse was described by Homer. Its ruins are now one of the biggest attractions of this region of Turkey. The exact history of this unique place and its discovery are described in the chapter devoted to Troy.

In the area of the Troad, another significant event in the history of Asia Minor took place. It was the Battle of the Granicus in 334 BCE. This battle was fought by the Macedonian troops led by Alexander the Great against the Persian army. It was the first victory of the Macedonian leader in Asia Minor. It opened for him the way to the conquest of extensive territories in the east. The famous river Granicus is, in fact, a large stream, now bearing the name of the Biga Çayı and flowing into the Sea of Marmara near the town of Karabiga.

GEOGRAPHY AND TRANSPORTATION

The Northern Troad, bordered on the west by the waters of the Dardanelles, and from the north – by the Sea of Marmara, is a hilly and heavily forested land. The largest cities of the region are located on the coast, and its interior is sparsely populated and seldom visited by tourists. In this interior, where quiet towns of Çan and Yenice are hidden, vegetables, especially tomatoes and peppers, are grown on an industrial scale, and wild animals still roam vast forests.

The most important communication routes of the Northern Troad run along the coasts. Çanakkale, the capital city of the province, is the point from which land and sea routes radiate. The southbound route E87 (D550) runs from Çanakkale to Edremit (128 km) through Ayvacık (70 km) and continues further to Izmir (325 km). The route E90 (D200) leads from Canakkale to the north-east, via Lapseki (35 km) and Biga (95 km) to Bandırma (167 km). The inland route D220 goes from Çanakkale straight to the west, to Çan (72 km) and Yenice (90 km).

Çanakkale is an important ferry terminal as ferries set out from here to the cities located on the Gallipoli Peninsula – to Eceabat

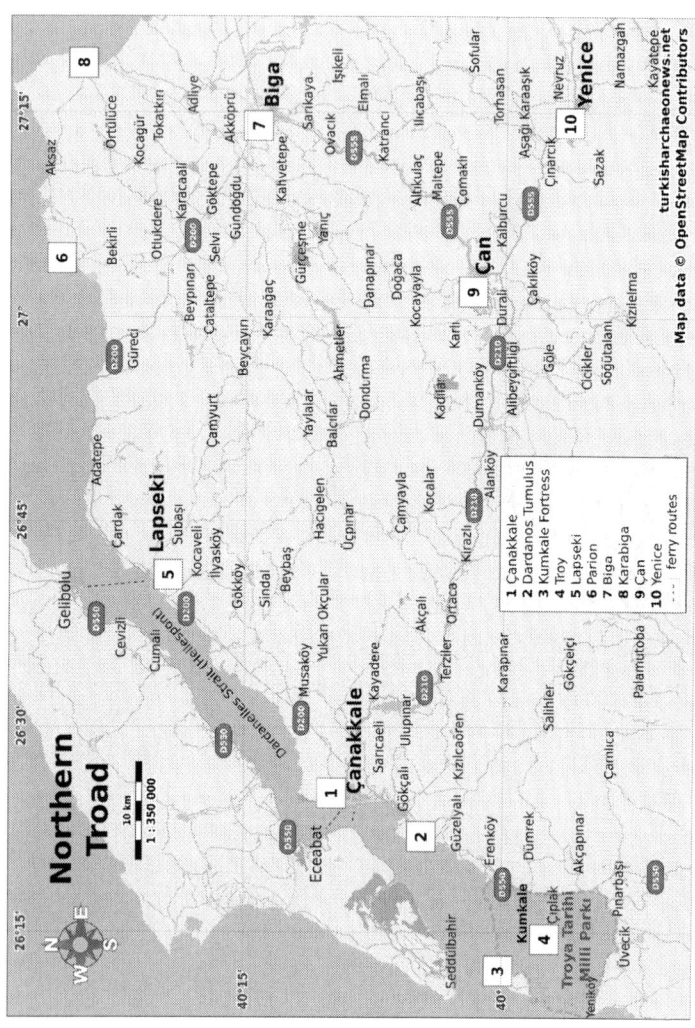

Map of the Northern Troad

and Kilitbahir, as well as to the Turkish islands in the Aegean Sea. Detailed ferry connections from Çanakkale are described in the chapters on Eceabat, Kilitbahir, and the Aegean islands – Gökçeada and Bozcaada.

SUGGESTED SIGHTSEEING ROUTE

The largest city of the Northern Troad is Çanakkale, an important ferry hub. It is an excellent starting point for travellers arriving from the Gallipoli Peninsula located on the European shore of the Dardanelles, who are planning to visit Troy. If your itinerary includes extra visits to the ruins of ancient cities of Parion and Priapos, situated further to the north, consider choosing a smaller port town of Lapseki as a base for further travel.

Most travel destinations in the Northern Troad are located along the coast. The key transport routes in the region are: the route E90 leading to the north-east of Çanakkale, running through Lapseki and Biga farther to the east of the country, and the southbound route E87, which runs along the Aegean coast to the region of Kuşadası. Ferry connections between the Northern Troad and the Gallipoli Peninsula are presented in the Gallipoli Peninsula section of this book. There are also irregular ferry connections between the town of Karabiga and Barbaros harbour, situated across the Sea of Marmara, in Thrace, 9 km south-west of Tekirdağ.

At least three days are necessary to visit the main tourist attractions of the Northern Troad. We suggest spending the first day in Çanakkale. On the second day, take a trip to the north-west: through Lapseki to the city of Biga, with a detour to the ruins of Parion and Priapos. On the way back, you can also choose the inland route – from Biga through Çan to Çanakkale. The total distance of this trip is 240 km. Alternatively, the travellers heading farther to the east can head directly from Biga to Bandırma.

Another trip from Çanakkale takes you to the south – to the famous city of Troy, through Dardanos Tumulus and Kumkale village. Since the distance between Troy and Çanakkale is just 30 km, there is still plenty of time to explore the ruins of the city of King Priam. Instead of returning for the night to Çanakkale you can stay in one of the hotels in Tevfikiye village, near Troy or continue the journey to the Southern Troad, according to the plan outlined in the next section of this guidebook.

Accommodation

The largest selection of accommodation options in the Northern Troad is available in Çanakkale. Several hotels and guesthouses can also be found in other towns of the region, including – Lapseki, Biga, Çan, Karabiga, and Tevfikiye village near Troy. However, due to the convenient location near the ferry terminal, at the crossroads of major transport routes, Çanakkale remains the best choice as a base for exploring this part of the Troad.

Viewpoints and beaches

The roads from Çanakkale are very scenic, especially the one running to the north-west, to the town of Biga. It takes you first along the coast of the Dardanelles, and then – along the coast of the Sea of Marmara. The most beautiful vistas in the region are: the panoramic view of the Dardanelles seen from the waterfront in Çanakkale, and the Sea of Marmara seen from the hill where the ruins of the fortress in Priapos dominate the landscape.

It is difficult to find attractive beaches in this region, although there are some charming coves near Lapseki and Parion. However, in terms of seaside relaxation, the Southern Troad is much more convenient, as discussed in the section devoted to this area.

Çanakkale

COORDINATES: 40.1499° N, 26.4025° E

Çanakkale, a city situated on the eastern shore of the Dardanelles, is the most popular base for the travellers sightseeing this region of Turkey. It is visited by the tourists seeking the traces of ancient settlements in the Troad, and the travellers who follow the traces of the military campaign on the nearby Gallipoli Peninsula. However, Çanakkale is not just a convenient starting point for further journeys, as it is also an absorbing city, where it is worth to stay for at least one day. In addition to local museums, the fortress, and some other historical buildings, it is a pleasant city with a European atmosphere. A broad waterfront promenade is a great place for an evening stroll, and numerous bars and restaurants are visited by students from the local university (tr. *Çanakkale Onsekiz Mart Üniversitesi*). After all, the city has about 120 thousand inhabitants, with as many as 35 thousand students who significantly contribute to its relaxed and lively ambience.

SHORT HISTORY

For the city which is located in a region with such an eventful past, the history of Çanakkale is surprisingly brief. This settlement was established when Sultan Mehmed the Conqueror ordered the construction of Çimenlik Castle in 1461. The building materials for its construction were obtained mainly from the nearby ancient city of Abydos. At the same time, Kilitbahir Fortress was erected on the European shore of the Dardanelles. These sister fortifications were built at the narrowest point of the strait, with the aim to protect the waterway leading to Istanbul.

Initially, the settlement was known as Kale-i Sultaniye, from the Sultan's fortress rising on the coast. As the time passed, the settlement grew and took on the name of Çanakkale or 'Bowl Fortress' – çanak in Turkish means a bowl. The origin of this name is explained in two ways. Some people derive it from the appearance of the fortress, apparently reminiscent of a bowl. Others link it to ceramics, produced in the city and throughout the Çanakkale Province.

In the 18th century, Çanakkale was already an important harbour city, and its wealth was due to its strategic position at the Dardanelles. There are numerous historical buildings is the city that testify to its multicultural character. In the 18th and the 19th centuries, the city was inhabited not only by the Turks but also the Greeks, the Jews, and the Armenians. In 1914, just before the First World War, the Muslims constituted about 64% of the population of the city, and the rest of its population consisted of the Orthodox Greeks (20%), the Jews (10%), and the Armenians (6%). In Çanakkale, there was also a large Roma community, settled here in the 15th century, to work on the construction of the Çimenlik Castle.

The outbreak of the First World War was the turning point in the history of the city. In March 1915, the Allied fleet, composed of British and French warships, attacked the Dardanelles. Their goal was to master the sea route to Istanbul. The failure of this operation resulted in long-lasting and extremely debilitating overland campaign, which was fought mainly on the opposite shore of the strait. The campaign, known in the West as the Battle of Gallipoli, is often referred to as the Battle of Çanakkale (tr. *Çanakkale Savaşı*) by the Turks.

In the years that followed the creation of the Turkish Republic, the multicultural ethnic composition of Çanakkale community underwent some drastic changes. Most of the Greeks were resettled to the lands belonging to Greece, the Jews, discouraged by the hostile atmosphere and the outbursts of violence, emigrated to Istanbul, Izmir, and Israel, while the Roma community remained on the margins of the cultural life of the city.

Old buildings adorning the city are the most visible remembrance of the people who used to live in Çanakkale. They include Greek houses and schools on the waterfront, the synagogue in the bazaar, which was once the Jewish quarter, and the former Armenian church, transformed into a cultural center, in the atmosphere of the protests of the Christian community.

SIGHTSEEING

Clock Tower Area

The best starting point for Çanakkale walking tour is the ferry terminal. If you go to the south, just 50 meters away, on the square formed between Eski Balıkhane and Yalı streets, you will find the most famous symbol of the city – the Clock Tower (tr. *Saat Kulesi*). This five-storey building dates back to the Ottoman era, or more precisely – to 1897. Its construction was sponsored by an Italian consul, who was also a wealthy local merchant. In his testament, he dedicated 100,000 gold francs for the purpose of building the tower. Today it serves as a distinctive landmark in the vicinity of Çanakkale harbour.

Yalı Hanı Caravanserai, built in the same period, stands a little further, on Fetvane Street. Until the 70s of the 20th century, this building served its original function of an inn for travellers. It has now been restored and transformed into a cultural center, which regularly hosts art exhibitions, seminars, and music competitions. In the courtyard of the caravanserai, there is a tea garden (tr. *çay bahçesi*) that also offers alcoholic drinks.

Yalı Hamam, a historical Turkish bath, operates in the neighbourhood, on Çarşı Street No. 5. It was built in the 17th century and is still open for customers. Women and men are provided with separate entrances and different opening hours. Women can take advantage of the bath from 8:00 am to 6:00 pm, and men – from 6:00 am to 11:00 pm. The price depends on the selected range of treatments.

Clock Tower in Çanakkale

Nearby, at the intersection of Çarşı, Fetvane, and Hapishane streets, you can find the Çanakkale City Museum and Archive (tr. *Çanakkale Kent Müzesi*). This is a relatively new institution in the city, established in 2006. Its mission is to bridge the time gap between the exhibitions of Troy Museum that focus on the ancient history of the region, and the exhibitions at the Military Museum, devoted mainly to the events of the First World War. City Museum focuses on presenting the history of Çanakkale and its inhabitants from the Ottoman era to the present times. It includes photographs, newspaper clippings, and everyday objects. The visitors can obtain information about religious minorities that used to live in the city. A separate section is devoted to the Roma community. The museum is open daily except Mondays, from 9:00 am to 5:00 pm (in the summer, from April to August, to 7:00 pm).

Military Museum and Çimenlik Castle

If you follow Yalı Street from the Clock Tower, after about 250 meters you will reach the entrance to the Military Museum (tr. *Çanakkale Deniz Müzesi*). The facility is also known under a much longer name as the Museum of the Navy Command of the Dardanelles Strait (tr. *Çanakkale Boğaz Komutanliği Deniz Müzesi*) but here we will use the shorter version. The museum was founded on the 67th anniversary of the naval victory of the Ottoman fleet (the 18th of March, 1915).

Admission to the open-air area of the museum, where there is a large part of the exhibition, is free of charge. The purchase of a ticket is required to see the exhibitions in Çimenlik Castle, to board a replica of Nusret minelayer, and to visit a library. A ticket costs 8.50 TL for adults, while children and teenagers can visit for free. Additionally, it is necessary to pay for the permission to make photos (17 TL) and videos (34 TL). However, you can take photos and videos of the exhibition in the park free of charge. It is prohibited to take photos during the multimedia presentations on the castle grounds and on the Nusret minelayer.

The open-air section of the museum is open to visitors every

Çimenlik Castle in Çanakkale

day, but the castle and the minelayer are closed on Mondays, and on the other days of the week they are open from 9:00 am to noon, and from 1:30 pm to 5:00 pm. Therefore, it is a good idea to avoid visiting these venues around 1:30 pm, as a long queue of visitors usually waits for the opening.

Many exhibits from the First World War have been displayed on the extensive grounds, along tree-shaded alleys. You can see naval mines, produced in Turkey, Russia, and the USA, as well as cannons and anchors. The biggest, literally and figuratively, attraction of this part of the museum is the UB-46 submarine. This submarine was built in Bremen (Germany) and launched in 1915. During the First World War, Germany and the Ottoman Empire were allies, and this submarine was tasked with patrolling the waters around Istanbul. During the six-month service, it sank four ships, including the British steamer Huntaral, and the Russian warship Melenia. In December 1916, during the fifth patrol, UB-46 hit a mine in the Black Sea, near the entrance to the Bosphorus and sank. The remains of the ship were discovered in 1933 in the waters near the village of Akpinar. Currently, they are exhibited in the Military Museum.

Minelayer Nusret in Tarsus Çanakkale Park

The most interesting exhibit of the Military Museum is a replica of the warship – minelayer Nusret (tr. *Nusret Mayın Gemisi*). Minelayer Nusret was constructed at a shipyard in Kiel (Germany) in 1912. It was acquired by the Ottoman fleet three years later. During the First World War, it played a key role in the defense of the Gallipoli Peninsula against the Allied fleet. In short, its history during this campaign is as follows: at night on the 8th of March, 1915, the commander of Nusret, Captain Hakki Bey, secretly steered the ship into the waters of Erenköy Bay. There, 26 sea mines were positioned, parallelly to the shoreline. The Allies had known of the other mines in the area of the Dardanelles, but Erenköy Bay was considered to be safe for the maneuvers. In this way, a trap was prepared to catch the French and British flotillas.

On the 18th of March, massive Allied flotilla began a concentrated attack, intending to gain a sea route to Istanbul through the Dardanelles Strait. During the maneuvers in Erenköy Bay, French battleship Bouvet hit a mine and sank, taking 639 sailors to the bottom of the bay. This event significantly raised the morale of Turkish troops that were operating the cannons located on the shores of the strait. Soon afterward, two British ships, HMS Irresistible and HMS Ocean, also hit the mines during their maneuvers and sank. As a result of the tragic balance of just one day of warfare, the command of the Allied forces decided to discontinue the maritime campaign and start overland campaign instead.

After these events, Nusret was hailed a hero of the campaign for the defense of the Dardanelles. However, its fame did not result in early retirement as it served the Turkish Navy for 42 years, until 1955. In 1982, the shipyard in Istanbul built an exact replica of Nusret in 1 to 1 scale, which is now exhibited at the Military Museum in Çanakkale. On board of this replica, you can see the photos and plans depicting the history of the warship.

You may be wondering why the museum does not display the original Nusret. After the minelayer had been retired from the military service, it was bought by private entrepreneurs and transformed into a civilian freighter. The ship served from 1966 as Kaptan Nusret, and, in 1989, it sank near the port of Mersin. But this is not the end of its story – after ten years under water, Nusret was extracted from the seabed and purchased by the city of Tarsus. In 2008, it was converted into a museum ship that can be visited in the area known as Tarsus Çanakkale Park. Therefore, to visit the original ship, you need to go to the south of Turkey, to the Mediterranean Coast. The more detailed history of Nusret is presented in a separate chapter.

The Gallery of Photos and Paintings (tr. *Resim ve Fotoğraf Galerisi*) operates in the building erected in 1927, in the early-republican style. Originally, it housed the headquarters of the fortress and was converted into the gallery building in 1982. Today, on the ground floor there is an exhibition of sea mines, on the first floor – photos, uniforms, weapons, and flags from the First World War, as well as a mock-up of the Dardanelles. On the second floor, the sketches and paintings by military painter Mehmet Ali Laga are on display.

In the same building, there is a specialized Library of the Gallipoli Campaign (tr. *Çanakkale Savaşları İhtisas Kütüphanesi*), that was established in 2002. According to the orders from the

Naval Museum in Çanakkale

Dardanelles Strait Command, this institution collects the documents related to the naval battles of 1915, as well as the entire military campaign of the Gallipoli Peninsula.

Çimenlik Castle – the Meadow Castle – also known as Kale-i Sultaniye, was built in the 15th century on the orders of Sultan Mehmet the Conqueror. The construction of the fortress on the Asian shore of the Dardanelles took two years to complete, from 1461 to 1462. Building materials were obtained from the ancient city of Abydos and other sites. At the same time, Kilitbahir Fortress was erected on the European shore of the strait.

The outer walls of the fortress make up a roughly rectangular shape with the sides 100 meters and 150 meters long. The height of the external walls is 11 meters, with a thickness 5 to 7 meters. Inside these walls, there is a courtyard, where the inner fortress (tr. *İç Kale*) stands. It is also rectangular, with the sides measuring 44 and 29 meters. Its walls have a height of 25 meters and are 9.5 meters thick. The interior of the fortress has three floors, of which only the lowest one was built of stone, and the others – of wood. The fortifications are strengthened by nine towers, located along the outer walls and inside the fortress.

Two mosques – Fatih Camii and Abdulaziz Camii – stand in the inner courtyard of the fortress. They bear the names of the Ottoman sultans who ordered their construction. Fatih Mosque was built simultaneously with the fortress. This rectangular building has two floors. On the ground floor there are living rooms, and on the first floor – a prayer room. One minaret rises above the mosque. Abdulaziz Mosque has no minaret at all. It was built at the end of the 19th century, on a rectangular plan with a semicircular niche.

The creation of Çimenlik Castle was also the moment of founding the town of Çanakkale, which has grown in the following centuries, from the village at the foot of the castle to the sizable city it is now. It is said that the famous Ottoman cartographer – Piri Reis – finished the most important work of his life, the Book of Navigation (tr. *Kitab-ı Bahriye*), in his room in this fortress.

During its existence, Çimenlik Castle has repeatedly been repaired and expanded. Its major reconstruction was carried out in 1551, during the reign of Sultan Suleyman the Magnificent. In the 19th century, new artillery units were installed in the castle. During the sea battle of the Dardanelles, in 1915, the fortress was used as the command and administration headquarters.

Today, the fortress is located in the area of the Military Museum and it can be visited for a fee. Please note that the tour of the fortress is available in the company of a guide only. There is no possibility of individual exploration and taking photographs during the presentations is strictly prohibited.

The courtyard is surrounded by the cannons, made in English, French, and German foundries, which were used during the Battle of the Dardanelles. The big attraction for visitors is a crater in the defensive wall, with an unexploded shell which was launched from Queen Elizabeth warship on the 18th of March, 1915.

On the three floors inside the fortress, there is an exhibition (tr. *Sergi Salonu*) commemorating the Battle of the Dardanelles. On the ground floor, a guide tells the visitors about the battle, showing them the movies and specimens of weapons used during the fighting. Theatrical performances are held on the first floor;

there are also recreated scenes from the times of the war. On the second floor, there is an exhibition of oil paintings depicting the Battle of Gallipoli by F. Korkut Uluğ.

Bazaar District

After leaving the area of the Military Museum, go in the southeastern direction, along Çimenlik, Hanım, and Fatih streets. After walking about 300 meters, you reach the most important historical mosque in the city, that is Fatih Camii. It stands on the southern end of the bazaar area. The mosque was built in 1452 on the orders of Sultan Mehmed the Conqueror, whose nickname gave the building its name (fatih means a conqueror in Turkish). The mosque was renovated and rebuilt during the reign of Sultan Abdul Aziz, in the years 1862-1863.

The Bazaar District is a vast, pedestrianized area. The most impressive building here is the Mirror Bazaar (tr. *Aynalı Çarşı*). It was built in 1889 by a Jewish merchant İlia Halyo. The famous Spice Bazaar in Istanbul was used by the architects as a model. Above the main entrance, there was a bilingual inscription, in Turkish but written in the Arabic alphabet, and in Hebrew. The name of the bazaar was derived from the mirrors placed at the gate, but the bazaar was also known as Halyo Çarşısı. During the battle of the Dardanelles, the bazaar was severely damaged by artillery shells fired from the British warship Queen Elizabeth. After the end of the First World War, during the British occupation of Çanakkale, the ruined building served as stables, and then it was forgotten and abandoned until the beginning of the 21st century. The inscription above the entrance was damaged during the anti-Jewish riots in 1934, and then covered. In 2007, the Mirror Bazaar underwent a complete renovation, and since then it has been used by sellers of souvenirs, textiles, and spices.

The building of Children Mosque (tr. *Tıflı Cami*), erected in 1892, stands opposite the Mirror Bazaar. Its name indicates that it was constructed to serve the needs of a school, situated next door. Korfmann Library (tr. *Manfred Osman Korfmann Kütüphanesi*) operates now in the former school building. It is a relatively new institution, opened in 2007. It bears the name of one of the most important scholars of the history of ancient Troad and the long-term manager of the archaeological site of Troy – Manfred Korfmann. After his death, in 2005, his books and publications were given to the city of Çanakkale and soon presented to the public in the 19th-century building in the historical district of the city. The collection of the library consists of about 6,000 books and 10,000 documents, representing scientific achievements of Professor Korfmann. The library can be visited from Tuesday to Saturday, from 10:00 am to 6:00 pm.

Next to the Korfmann Library, from the side of Tıflı Street, you can find Helvacıoğlu Street, leading in the southern direction. It takes you to the Armenian church dedicated to St. George (tr. *Surp Kevork Kilisesi*). The last Armenians left Çanakkale in 1915, and their former church came under the management of the city authorities. Despite the protests of the local Christian community, the temple has recently been converted into the Museum of Ethnography. Currently, the famous sema (whirling dervishes) ceremonies are also held in this former church.

The building of Mekor Haim Synagogue (tr. *Mekor Hayim Sinagogu*) is another reminder of the multicultural past of Çanakkale. It is the last synagogue still standing in the city. It is located at the intersection of Old Synagogue (tr. *Eski Havra Sokak*) and Great Baths (tr. *Büyük Hamam Sokak*) streets, about 200 meters northeast of the Armenian Church. Its name means 'the Source of Life', and it was built in the late 19th century. The Jewish community in Çanakkale currently consists of only a few people, so the synagogue is not often used for religious purposes. However, it has been restored and is now open to visitors, also as a hall of classical music concerts.

Waterfront Promenade

The best place for the last leg of the walk through the center of Çanakkale is in the vicinity of the ferry terminal, where this walking route started. In the northern direction, there is a wide pedestrianized promenade, running parallel to Kayserili Ahmet Paşa Street.

Çanakkale waterfront

A stroll along this elegant promenade provides an excellent opportunity of watching the Dardanelles and its European shore, where the hills are covered with monumental patriotic slogans. From the promenade, you can also see Kilitbahir Fortress. There are several tourist attractions on the promenade. The most recognizable one is the model of the Trojan horse. However, in contrast to the similar construction standing in Troy, it is impossible to climb into this horse. It is mostly known for the role it played in the film 'Troy' from 2004, with Brad Pitt as Achilles.

Near the horse, there is a good-sized mock-up, which reproduces the appearance of Troy at the times of its glory. It is accompanied by numerous information boards and an exhibition of contemporary sculpture, referring to the theme of the Trojan War. In addition, on the promenade, there is an absorbing mosaic reproducing the famous map of Admiral Piri Reis, whose bust looks at passers-by. There is also a sundial, slides for children, smaller, colorful versions of 'Trojan Horses', and contemporary sculptures. Sightseeing tour of Çanakkale finishes in a tea garden, located at the northern end of the promenade, or in one of numerous restaurants operating in this area.

Archaeology Museum

After a refreshment break you might want to consider another place to visit in Çanakkale – the Archaeology Museum (tr. *Çanakkale Arkeoloji Müzesi*). Due to its distance from the ferry terminal, a visit to this facility is mainly recommended to the lovers of ancient history. The museum is situated in the direction which you should take if you are heading to the ruins of Troy, and further, to the south of the Troad region. The museum was founded in 1936. Initially, it operated in a former church, but in 1984, it was moved to a new building.

Until recently, the Archaeology Museum in Çanakkale collected the exhibits from the area of the ancient Troad, i.e. the Biga Peninsula. However, despite the enormous historical significance of the region and its incredibly rich history, the museum collections were quite disappointing. With the opening of the new Troy Museum, situated next to the ruins of the ancient city of Troy, many artefacts were transferred there, making a visit to the Çanakkale Archaeology Museum even less atractive.

The Archaeology Museum in Çanakkale is housed in a building on 100 Yil Caddesi. The distance to the city center is about 2.5 km. The museum is located on a side street, just off the main road from Çanakkale to Troy. It can be reached from the center by a minibus heading to Troy or Güzelyalı. The admission ticket to the museum costs 6 TL. The museum is open daily except Mondays, from 8:00 am to 7:00 pm (from April to October). From November to March it closes earlier, at 5:00 pm.

VISITOR TIPS

Orientation

The city of Çanakkale lies at the point where the Dardanelles Strait is narrowest, opposite the town of Kilitbahir, located on the European shore. Despite the fact that for many travelers Çanakkale is their first contact with Asia, the city definitely turns itself towards Europe. The center of Çanakkale, the most important monuments, and most of the service points, restaurants, and hotels are located in the immediate vicinity of the ferry terminal. The ferries that arrive here from Eceabat form a waterway that is a part of D550 route. This route leads from the city of Edirne, located on the border with Greece and Bulgaria, to Muğla, located in the southwest of Turkey.

To get to know Çanakkale just a little bit, it is necessary to take a walk around the area of less than 1 square kilometer that extends from the ferry terminal. The boundaries of this area are demarcated by the Dardanelles from the west, Sarıçay River from the south, Atatürk Street from the east, and Admiral Piri Reis Street from the north. This area is divided into northern and southern parts by the Boulevard of the Republic (tr. *Cumhuriyet Bulvarı*). A coastal promenade, parallel to Kayserili Ahmet Paşa Street is the most attractive area to the north of the ferry terminal.

To get to the most attractive historical district of Çanakkale, head to the south from the ferry terminal, along Seaside Street (tr. *Yalı Caddesi*). It takes you straight to Çimenlik Fortress and Military Museum. If you take a turning to the south, the Market Street (tr. *Çarşı Caddesi*) leads to the historic bazaar district.

The main street departing from the ferry terminal is the Boulevard of the Republic, going in an easterly direction. After 700 meters, the boulevard intersects Atatürk Street, extending from the north to the south. If you follow it to the south, after 4 km you reach the suburbs, where this street joins with D550 route that acts as the ring road of Çanakkale. In the city it is called Çanakkale-İzmir Asfaltı. Travelling along this route further to the south takes you straight to the most famous tourist attractions of the Troad, including Troy, 30 km away from Çanakkale.

However, if you turn to the north at the intersection of Boulevard of the Republic and Atatürk Street, after 900 meters you reach another junction, this time with Admiral Piri Reis Street. By turning here to the right (to the east), after 4 km you reach a major junction. This is a point where several important roads converge: the D550 mentioned above to the south and D200 route that runs along the shores of the Dardanelles to the north-east, to Lapseki,

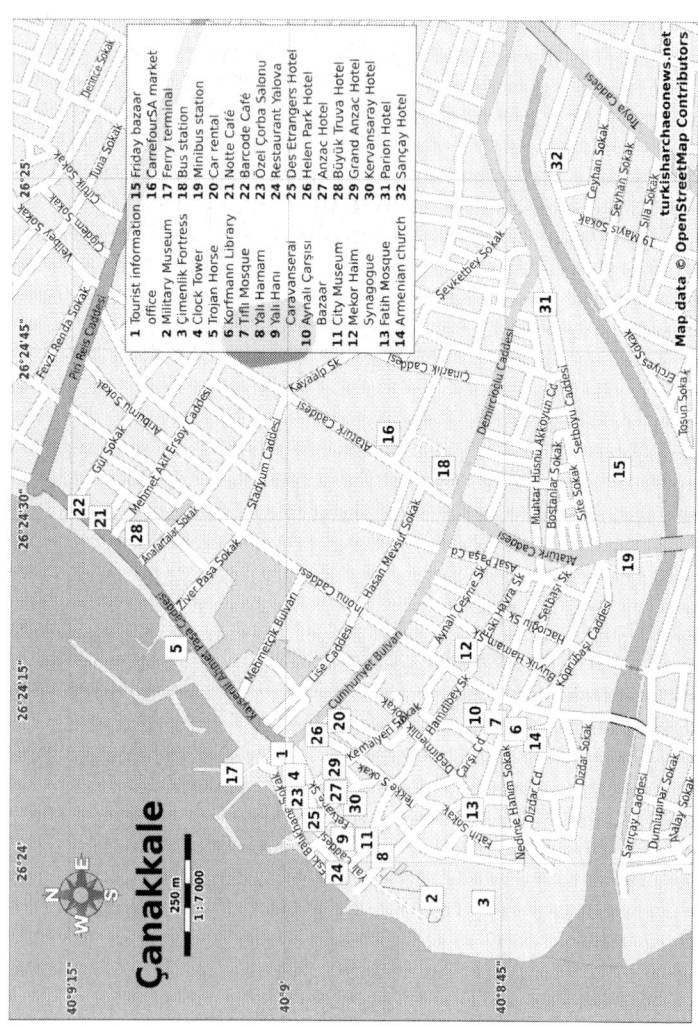

Key to map:

1 Tourist information office
2 Military Museum
3 Çimenlik Fortress
4 Clock Tower
5 Trojan Horse
6 Korfmann Library
7 Tifli Mosque
8 Yali Hamam
9 Yali Hani
10 Aynali Çarşisi Bazaar
11 City Museum
12 Mekor Haim Synagogue
13 Fatih Mosque
14 Armenian church
15 Friday bazaar
16 CarrefourSA market
17 Ferry terminal
18 Bus station
19 Minibus station
20 Car rental
21 Notte Café
22 Barcode Café
23 Özel Çorba Salonu
24 Restaurant Yalova
25 Des Etrangers Hotel
26 Helen Park Hotel
27 Anzac Hotel
28 Büyük Truva Hotel
29 Grand Anzac Hotel
30 Kervansaray Hotel
31 Parion Hotel
32 Sarıçay Hotel

Çanakkale
250 m
1 : 7 000

turkisharchaeonews.net
Map data © OpenStreetMap Contributors

Plan of Çanakkale city center

and further, along the shore of the Sea of Marmara to the east, to Bandırma. At the same intersection the route D210 starts, and by taking it you go straight to the east, to the town of Çan, deep in the interior of the Troad.

Restaurants

Finding a meal along the promenade and in the surrounding area is not a problem. The simplest snacks (pretzels, mussels, boiled corn) are sold by itinerant vendors. Local cafés enjoy good reputation, especially Notte Café and Café Barcode, that also serve salads and pasta dishes in addition to drinks. At the northern end of the promenade, there is a tea garden known as Golf Çay Bahçesi. It is a place frequented by Turkish families, with lovely views of the Strait and the opposite shore.

Clock Tower Square (tr. *Saat Kulesi Meydanı*) is a place where you can find several restaurants. We recommend so-called soup salon (tr. *Özel Çorba Salonu*), where it is possible to get a tasty lentil or tripe soup for a few liras. In the same area, there are numerous cheap eateries where you can fill your stomach at very modest prices.

Bars and pubs are concentrated in Çanakkale in a tangle of narrow streets between the Clock Tower and the Military Museum, for instance on Matbaa and Fetvane streets. These venues enjoy a good reputation among young Australians, so you should expect a rather international menu (pizza, sandwiches, toast), and not traditional Turkish fare.

The best fish restaurant in the city is called Yalova, and it is situated on Customs Street (tr. *Gümrük Sokak*). You can personally choose the fish that will be prepared for you.

Accommodation

If you plan to stop for a night in Çanakkale, remember the dates of the anniversaries of the battles of Gallipoli, and book your accommodation well in advance if you plan a stay in March or April. In other months of a year, it often turns out that the prices offered via online booking platforms are much higher than the ones obtained

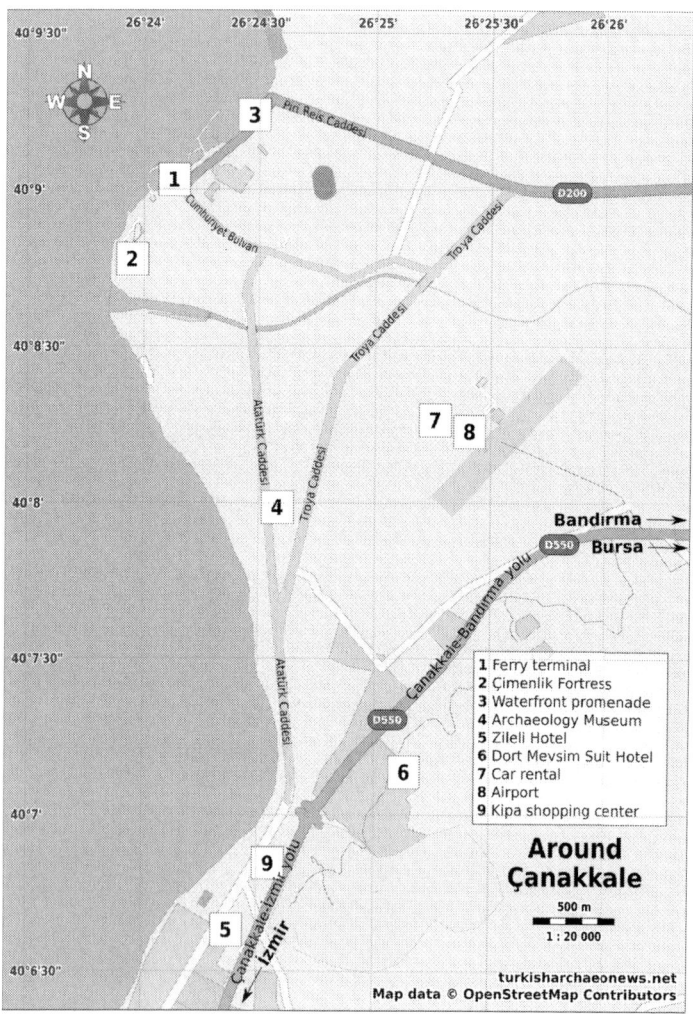

1 Ferry terminal
2 Çimenlik Fortress
3 Waterfront promenade
4 Archaeology Museum
5 Zileli Hotel
6 Dort Mevsim Suit Hotel
7 Car rental
8 Airport
9 Kipa shopping center

Around Çanakkale

500 m

1 : 20 000

turkisharchaeonews.net
Map data © OpenStreetMap Contributors

Çanakkale and its surroundings

by asking directly at the selected hotel.

Most hotels and B&Bs in Çanakkale are located close to the ferry terminal. On the one hand, it is a great facilitation for visitors, since many tourist attractions are situated nearby. On the other hand, if you come to Çanakkale by car you may have a problem with finding a parking place. Note that the information provided by hotels in this area states that the guests can use public parking lots nearby. However, in practice, it is hard to find free parking space in the center of Çanakkale and you may need to use paid private parking lots.

The following hotels in the center of Çanakkale enjoy the best opinion:

- Des Etrangers Hotel – housed in a historical building, on Yalı Caddesi No. 25/27. The hotel has a restaurant, and breakfast, included in the price, is served in the buffet form. This is one of the more expensive accommodation options in the city.
- Helen Park Hotel – located right next to the ferry terminal, on Tekke Caddesi No 10. This hotel is highly rated by its guests and much cheaper than Des Etrangers Hotel.
- Anzac Hotel – located near the famous Clock Tower. Its main advantage, in addition to the central location, are soundproofed rooms and a relatively low prices.
- Büyük Truva Hotel – located on the coast, next to the marina. It boasts stunning views of the Dardanelles and has two rooms adapted for people with disabilities.
- Grand Anzac Hotel – on Kemalyeri Caddesi No. 11. Guests are offered bicycle and car rental. The breakfasts are highly rated by the guests.
- Kervansaray Hotel – located on a side street, Fetvane Caddesi No. 13. The hotel is housed in a historical building, but in spite of being assigned to the category of boutique hotels, it offers a moderate standard and equally moderate prices.

If you are looking for accommodation outside the city center, take these hotels into account:

- Parion Hotel – 1 km away from the ferry terminal, on Demir-cioğlu Caddesi No. 130. This is the most luxurious lodging option in Çanakkale, as the hotel has an indoor swimming pool, a hammam (Turkish bath), and a spa center. The rooms are very spacious and there is also an extensive suite.
- Saricay Hotel – located slightly further from the center, on the banks of Sarıçay River, on Reşat Tabak Caddesi No. 18. In contrast to Parion Hotel, this hotel is a place to stay for a moderate price.

However, if you want to stay in a quieter area, on the coast, consider finding accommodation south of Çanakkale, on D550 road that leads in the direction of Troy and further, to the south of the Troad. Barbaros and Kepez districts are situated there, and the top-rated hotels in the area are:

- Dort Mevsim Suit Hotel – in the heart of Barbaros district, on Binboga Caddesi No. 1. This is an apartment hotel, which means that its guests enjoy fully equipped apartments with an area of 60 square meters each. Each apartment can accommodate up to 4 people, but the price depends on the number of guests.
- Zileli Hotel – in Kepez, on Ibrahim Terzioglu Caddesi No. 7. The hotel is located next to a big shopping center and only a short walk from the coast.

Shopping

The largest concentration of shops of all kinds in the center of Çanakkale is located in the bazaar district, with the historical Mirror Bazaar at its heart. If you are after fresh seasonal products, head to the Friday Market (tr. *Cuma Pazarı*) that takes place every Friday, in a specially designated area (tr. *Pazar Yeri*), on the east side of Atatürk Street. The largest shopping center in the city – Kipa AVM – is situated in Barbaros district, on the south side of the city, just off D550 route. There is a large CarrefourSA supermarket closer to the center of Çanakkale, on Atatürk Street, next to the coach terminal.

Services

Most of the service points needed by tourists are located in the immediate vicinity of Cumhuriyet Square, right next to the ferry terminal. There is a post office, ATMs, and telephone booths, as well as local tourist information office. This office provides helpful transportation advice, its staff speak English and have handouts in the form of brochures and maps. The office is open from 8:00 am to 7:00 pm during the summer season (July-September), and from 8:30 am to 5:30 pm during other months of the year.

In Çanakkale, you can easily rent a car, and this kind of transportation is extremely helpful when visiting this part of the Troad. Small vehicle rental agencies are located on Dibak Street, just off to the right from the ferry terminal and on Cumhuriyet Boulevard. You can also find car rental agencies at the local airport (tr. *Çanakkale Havaalanı*), located 3 km to the east of the city center.

GETTING THERE

BY FERRY: as there is no bridge over the Dardanelles yet, the only way of crossing the Strait to its Asian shore is by a ferry. The main ferry line connects Çanakkale with Eceabat. The ferries offer regular connections, at all times of day and night. At night, they depart every two hours, and during the day – every hour. In summer, the frequency rises to two ferries per hour. The crossing takes approximately 25 minutes. If you pay per vehilce, the transport of the passengers is included in the price.

Alternatively, it is possible to take a ferry to Çanakkale from Kilitbahir. The ferry crossing takes only 15-20 minutes, depending on weather conditions. The connection is provided by a private shipping company, and the ferries can take only several passenger cars aboard. The ferries depart several times a day but often it is necessary to wait for the departure as they set off when they are full.

Other ferry connections from Çanakkale include the cruises to the Turkish islands in the Aegean Sea. A ferry to Bozcaada departs several times a day; the crossing takes about 40 minutes. Once a day (around 5:00 pm) you can also get to the island of Gökçeada and the trip takes 2.5 hours.

BY COACH: Çanakkale coach terminal (tr. *Çanakkale Otogarı*) is located at the intersection of Atatürk and Demircioğlu streets, about 850 meters east from the ferry terminal. The coaches starting from this terminal provide connections with the major cities of Turkey, including Ankara (10 hours), Antalya (12 hours), Bursa (4.5 hours), Edirne (4.5 hours), Istanbul (6 hours), Izmir (6 hours), and Şanlıurfa (23 hours).

BY MINIBUS: Çanakkale minibus station (tr. *Minibüs Garajı*) is located near Sarıçay river, 1 km southeast from the ferry terminal, at the intersection of Köprübaşı and Atatürk streets. The most important connection (from a tourist's point of view) is the one to Troy. Minibuses depart in this direction every hour between 9:30 am and 4:30 pm (in summer till 7:00 pm). The ride takes 40 minutes. Please note the last return minibus from Troy to Çanakkale departs at 3:00 pm (5:00 pm in summer), which means that you might need to stay in Troy if you decide to visit this site in the afternoon as there are no other public transport options in the evenings.

Dardanos

COORDINATES: 40.0759° N, 26.3632° E

Dardanos Tumulus is considered to be one of the most important archaeological sites in the Troad. Despite the importance of this ancient burial place and its priceless contents, there are few systematic studies concerning this discovery. What is more, a visit to the site may also be quite disappointing and the golden treasures of Dardanos exhibited in the Troy Museum may prove to be much more attractive.

BRIEF HISTORY

Not much is known about the ancient city of Dardanos. No systematic excavations have been conducted so far to uncover the remains of municipal buildings. Judging from the fragments of pottery, the settlement was founded in the 7th or the 6th century BCE, that is, in the time of the Greek colonization of the Troad from the island of Lesbos. It is also known that in times of the domination of Athens, Dardanos paid a tribute of one talent to the Delian League.

The inscriptions on the walls of the tomb indicate that it was built in the late 6th century BCE by a wealthy citizen of Dardanos called Skamandrios or on his behalf. The tumulus was the burial place for an extended period, until the 1st or the 2nd century CE. When it ceased to be used for this purpose, the entrance to the hall was closed by boulders, and its exterior masked by mud and debris.

The discovery of Dardanos Tumulus occurred by accident, during construction works for a nearby cement factory, conducted in 1959. When the burial chamber was found, archaeological research

Dardanos Tumulus

was undertaken by a team composed of employees of museums from Istanbul and Çanakkale, under the leadership of Rüstem Duyuran. After a long break, the next series of excavations was conducted in 1989. The motivation for the second round of research was a detected attempt of robbery of the tomb. The finds discovered during these excavations can be seen in the Troy Museum.

SIGHTSEEING

The contrast between the ideas concerning the tumulus acquired during a visit to the museum and the reality of the site, is tremendous. Dardanos Tumulus is an inconspicuous hill overgrown with weeds, hidden in the woods, and rarely visited by tourists. The entrance to the tomb is protected by robust grates though you can take a look inside between the bars.

It is a stone tomb hidden under an artificial mound. The tomb consists of a corridor, a vestibule, and a burial chamber. The uncovered corridor (so-called dromos) was built of stone blocks. The passage is separated from the vestibule (foyer) by the entrance in the shape of a trapezoid. Between the vestibule and the burial chamber, there is another door opening, this time – a rectangular one. The tomb is oriented along the north-west to south-east axis, and it measures 12.40 meters in length. The height of the burial chamber is 3.45 meters, and the vestibule is slightly lower.

In the burial chamber, there are three stone benches, called klinai in Greek, arranged in a U-shape along the rear wall and side walls of the chamber. 42 human skulls were found during the excavations, leading the researchers to the conclusion that the deceased people were laid on these stone benches. Other finds from the tomb include urns with human remains and ashes from the cremation.

The essential contents of the tomb were funeral gifts. Around 470 items have been discovered there, including terracotta figurines, oil lamps, perfume bottles, pieces of woolen clothes, baskets, wooden musical instruments, and pieces of furniture. Metal products make an impressive set of 85 items; it consists of jewelry and tools made of gold, silver, bronze, iron, and lead. The most spectacular discovery of Dardanos Tumulus was a collection of gold jewelry, including crowns, wreaths, medallions, earrings, necklaces, and rings, mainly from the Hellenistic period.

VISITOR TIPS

Dardanos Tumulus is located on the premises of one of the campuses of Onsekiz Mart University from Çanakkale. To get to the tumulus it is necessary to obtain a pass from the guard at the entrance gate. The car must be left in the parking lot next to the university buildings, so you need to walk the remaining distance to the tomb. The path leads to the north-east through a forest. After walking 250 meters, you arrive at the tumulus. It is marked with rusty information boards.

GETTING THERE

BY CAR: from the center of Çanakkale, take route E87 in the southern direction, following the signposts to the famous site of Troy. About 10 km from the center of Çanakkale, turn right into Dardanos Caddesi, drive 1 km, and turn left into Eski İzmir

Caddesi. Two kilometers further turn right and enter the campus of Onsekiz Mart University.

Kumkale

Coordinates: 40.0081° N, 26.1996° E

The word Kumkale (Sand Fortress) refers to the ruins of the old Ottoman fortress, but also to the modern Turkish village. Naturally, the remains of the historical fortifications would be much more attractive to tourists than another typical and dusty village, but the fortress is inaccessible to civilians as it currently houses a Turkish military base.

BRIEF HISTORY

Kumkale Fortress was built in the 17th century as a part of the defense system of the Dardanelles, along other Ottoman fortresses in the region: Çimenlik, Kilitbahir, and Seddülbahir. Near Kumkale, you can enjoy an excellent view of the entrance to the strait from the Aegean Sea.

During the First World War, the cannons placed on Kumkale Fortress bombarded the Allied positions on the Gallipoli Peninsula, over the waters of the Strait. The British decided to start an offensive to reduce this threat. After two series of bombings from the sea, on the 19th and the 25th of February 1915, British commandos landed in Kumkale on the 26th of February. The commander of the troops, Lieutenant Eric Robinson, took a solo trip in the vicinity of the nearby tumulus of Achilles. Despite the heavy firing, he was able to detonate the Turkish cannons.

Two months later, French troops landed near Kumkale, with the task to divert the attention of the Ottoman troops from the landing on the Gallipoli Peninsula. Their heroism enabled them to storm the fortress, but the later fate of this unit was dire. They

Kumkale Fortress

were transported to the European shore, where they supported the British soldiers during the Battle of Cape Helles (tr. *Seddülbahir*). During this campaign, the French detachment was virtually wiped out.

Kumkale village, located next to the fortress, was destroyed during the war. It was rebuilt in a different location, to the southeast of the fortress, in the hinterland. It is often referred to as Yeni Kumkale – New Sand Fortress. It is a typical farming village, with a small square, and one mosque. You can see that the days go by quietly, and men spend them drinking tea near the office of the ruling AKP party.

SIGHTSEEING

Currently, Kumkale Fortress, or what is left of it, can be seen only from a distance. The area is fenced off and guarded by heavily armed Turkish soldiers. The entrance to the fortress is strictly prohibited for civilians and foreigners. Taking pictures, even from the distance, is also forbidden.

Near the fortress, surrounded by fields, lies the historical military cemetery (tr. *Kumkale Tarihi Türk Mezarlığı*). On this cemetery, there are graves of the soldiers of the Ottoman army who died during the First World War.

At the entrance to Kumkale village, there is an exhibition of artillery. Their appearance suggests that they are the same cannons that had been damaged by Lieutenant Robinson, but there is no information provided on-site to confirm this impression. On the main square of the village, there are several large pieces of pottery. Also in this case, it remains unclear whether they are ancient originals or their modern copies.

VISITOR TIPS

In Kumkale village, there are several grocery stores and a post office. However, if you are looking for accommodation options, go elsewhere – as there are none to be found there. The most convenient accommodation in the area can be found in Çanakkale or in the village of Tevfikiye, next to the ruins of Troy. A visit to Kumkale is only recommended for the travellers with plenty of spare time as the access is cumbersome, and the place does not offer much to look at.

GETTING THERE

BY CAR: the distance from Çanakkale to Kumkale village is 34 km. If you are travelling from Çanakkale, take the E87 route to the south, following the signposts to the famous site of Troy. Drive carefully to find the turning to Kumkale as it is not the same one that takes you directly to Troy. From the main road turn right, (to the west) about 27 km away from Çanakkale.

To reach the area of Kumkale Fortress, you must drive through the village, heading in a westerly direction and go further 5 km on a very poor road. In some places it is so narrow that you have to drive off it to let tractors pass. About 1 km before the fortress the road turns to the north. Here it connects with the route leading to Kumkale along the Aegean coast. In the vicinity of the intersection, there is a historical military cemetery.

In the center of Kumkale village, there is the intersection of the road leading to the ruins of ancient Troy. It is marked with the appropriate signpost.

Troy

Coordinates: 39.9571° N, 26.2405° E

> Sing, O Goddess, the anger of Achilles son of
> Peleus, that brought countless ills upon the Achaeans.
> Many a brave soul did it send hurrying down to Hades,
> and many a hero did it yield a prey to dogs and vul-
> tures, for so were the counsels of Jove fulfilled from
> the day on which the son of Atreus, king of men, and
> great Achilles, first fell out with one another.

> Homer, The Iliad, Book I, translated by Samuel Butler

For thousands of years, the tale of Troy sung by Homer stimu-
lated the imagination of adventurers and lovers of Greek myths.
Even today, many travellers, bearing in mind the first lines of the
Iliad, direct their steps to Troy, located in the north-western part
of Turkey. However, many of them will be utterly disappointed.
Unfortunately, the remains of the once magnificent fortress of
King Priam do not have much to offer to the tourists, compared
with the impressive streets of ancient Ephesus, a great theater of
Aspendos, or a spectacular stadium of Aphrodisias. Therefore,
when visiting Troy, it is best to keep in mind the magic of the
mythical place, praised by Homer, and not the current state of its
ruins.

To commemorate the events described in the Iliad as well as to
make the visit in Troy more interesting, a replica of the wooden
horse used by the wily Odysseus to outwit the Trojan warriors
has been erected at the entrance to Troy archaeological site. The

wooden construction, currently welcoming the visitors to Troy, arouses mixed feelings. Some people feel outraged at this superficial treatment of the ancient site. Others happily take photos of the horse or climb inside.

BRIEF HISTORY

Trojan War – a myth or a historical fact?

The history of the Trojan War, or actually its last phase, was presented in the Iliad created by the ancient bard Homer. It is not known exactly when this epic poem was composed. Some people believe that it happened shortly after the war, which was supposedly fought in the 12th century BCE, while others, including Herodotus, suggest the 9th century BCE.

The cause of the outbreak of the Trojan War is probably known to almost everyone. As a reminder, of course, it all started because of a woman, the most beautiful one – Helen, wife of Menelaus. The prince of Trojans – Paris – won her thanks to the favourable judgement for Aphrodite, the Greek goddess of love, in the first-ever beauty contest. Paris abducted Helen from Mycenae and brought her to Troy, to the castle ruled by his father – King Priam.

The abduction of beautiful Helen obviously upset the Greeks, even more so as her husband was a legitimate brother of Agamemnon, the king of Mycenae. Greek troops crossed the Aegean Sea and besieged Troy for ten years. In the end, the city fell, mainly due to the cunning of Odysseus, who came up with the idea of constructing a wooden horse. The bravest Greek warriors hid in this bizarre structure, and the remaining troops pretended to withdraw. Jubilant residents of Troy took the horse inside the city and began to celebrate the end of a devastating war. Then, under the cover of night, Odysseus and his companions opened the gates of the city, letting the Greek army in. The slaughter began, followed by complete collapse and burning of Troy.

However, the identification of the ruins located on Hisarlık Hill with the legendary Troy has long been questioned. The events described in the Iliad are not considered by the researchers as a description of the actual history of the city. It is thought that the epic is a compilation of traditions, myths, and stories handed down from generation to generation, concerning different historical events, distorted by time and the ephemeral human memory.

Descriptions left by Homer leave no doubt as to the fact that the Trojan War had been fought in the Troad region, near the Dardanelles. Researchers have long tried to reconcile the poetic vision presented in the Iliad with the historical events that occurred in the late Bronze Age in the Troad. Clay tablets, discovered in the capital of the Hittites – Hattusa – provide two names that may be the missing link in this history. The first name is Wilusa, the land in the north-western Anatolia, whose capital could be Troy. The second name is Ahhiyawa, meaning most likely Mycenae – if we remember that the Greeks called themselves Achaeans. The memory of the ongoing conflicts between Wilusa and Mycenae during the restless period of the late second millennium BCE could survive as the story of the Trojan War.

On the other hand, the archaeological work carried out on the territory of Troy has not provided any convincing evidence that the city was destroyed by the invaders from Greece. It is known, however, that a settlement on Hisarlık Hill was an important regional center, well-fortified and consistently rebuilt after subsequent devastations caused by fires, earthquakes, and wars.

In the course of the archaeological work in the area of the settlement, the researchers tried to link individual layers to the Homeric Troy. Heinrich Schliemann was convinced that the burned citadel belonging to Troy II and its so-called Treasure of Priam constituted a sufficient proof of the truth of the story presented in the Iliad. However, subsequent studies have shown that Troy II was more than a millennium older than the Mycenaean civilization. Dörpfeld, who was responsible for excavations of the Late Bronze Age settlement, argued that the proper identification of Homeric Troy points to Troy VI, but his argument was undermined by Blegen. This researcher argued that small buildings and food storages from Troy VIIa indicate precisely that this layer was a city besieged by the army from Greece. We now know, however, that at the same time, there was an extensive settlement outside the city walls, and the interpretation of traces of fire and several human bones as a proof of the waged war is highly controversial.

Whether or not the famous Trojan War was actually fought in the area, Hisarlık Hill has an invaluable significance for studying the history of this region of Asia Minor. It provides plentiful sources of information about the development of urban centers in the Bronze Age. However, Homer's work has played an important role in culture and art for many centuries. The visitors of the ruins of Troy on Hisarlık Hill should be aware that they follow in the footsteps of great historical figures. This location was visited both by the Persian ruler Xerxes and Alexander the Great of Macedonia, as well as many Roman emperors and Ottoman Sultan Mehmed II the Conqueror. Even the landing of the Allied troops on the Gallipoli Peninsula in 1915 was presented as a 'new Trojan War.'

Location and the chronology of the layers of ruins

Troy is located on a 15-meter-high hill that hides the traces of successive waves of colonization. Although once it lay near the coast, now, as a result of the alluvial activity of river Scamander (now Karamenderes), it is 5 km away from the sea. The location of the ancient settlement – on the coast, on the border of two continents, and at the intersection of trade routes from Asia Minor to the Balkans, the Aegean Sea, and the Black Sea – was crucial to the development and prosperity of its people. In order to systematize the history of Troy, archaeologists divided it into nine historical periods, corresponding to the successive layers of settlements, which in turn are often divided into subperiods.

The history of the city dates back to the early Bronze Age, i.e. around the year 3000 BCE, when the first settlement, marked now as Troy I (3000 BCE – 2550 BCE), was most probably established here. It was a small village, built on terraces on the coast, consisting of interconnected stone and brick houses. The settlement was surrounded by stone walls, repeatedly strengthened. The items found in the earliest layers are mostly dark, hand-produced ceramics, and copper objects. Today, you can admire the restored gate to the village, and one of the houses.

Troy II (2550 BCE – 2300 BCE) actually consists of 7 layers lying one on the other. Each of them was surrounded by city walls, and a monumental ceremonial gate led into the interior of the settlement. The settlement from this period was twice destroyed by fire. In addition, at this time, the first buildings were erected outside the ramparts, gradually creating a vast settlement surrounded by a palisade. It was discovered relatively recently. Archaeological finds from this period include ceramics produced using the potter's wheel, and silver, gold, and amber jewelry. Priam's Treasure found by Schliemann has been dated to this period of Troy history.

Troy III, IV, and V (2300 BCE – 1750 BCE) were the periods of gradual development of the city. We have relatively little information about these stages of the city existence. The scarcity of information results from the progress of the archaeological work, and the severe damage done by Schliemann, who dug through these layers in search of Homeric Troy, irretrievably damaging the chronology of the layers. The findings from these layers indicate the existence of trade relations between Troy and the early Greek city-states, including Mycenae. Ceramics from Troy III is virtually indistinguishable from the vessels of Troy II. More decorative vessels made on the potter's wheel appeared during Troy IV and V.

Troy VI (1700 BCE – 1300 BCE) and Troy VIIa (1300 BCE – 1180 BCE) represent the peak phase of the prosperity of the city in the late Bronze Age. This is evidenced by the remains of fortifications, far exceeding the previous city walls both in the terms of size and quality. However, also in the case of these layers, the possibility of a thorough examination is severely limited, because the center of the settlement was destroyed during the levelling of land for the construction of the Temple of Athena in the Hellenistic period. Moreover, a part of this layer was dug by Schliemann without conducting proper documentation.

It is now known that during this period the city was surrounded by massive walls, encompassing the inner area of 2 hectares. These walls were 5 meters wide and 10 meters high. Inside, there were large detached two-storey buildings, 35 meters long, situated along cobbled streets. The method of their construction – with stone blocks and no windows on the ground floor – can attest to their defensive character. Researchers wonder whether the threat to their residents came from outside, or was the result of conflicts between different clans living in the city.

The buildings belonging to Troy VIIa had a different appearance than the palaces of Troy VI as they were smaller and had well-stocked pantries in the form of massive vessels buried in the floor. Their different nature is the evidence of social change. Both layers – VI and VIIa – were rapidly destroyed, for unknown reasons. This is evidenced by the fallen stone blocks and the traces of fire. The hypothesis put forward by Blegen says that these are the traces of an earthquake, but not all researchers agree with this theory.

Apart from the buildings inside the citadel, outside the city walls developed the so-called Lower City. It was surrounded by two moats, of which the inner one demarcated an area of 30 hectares, and the outer one – an even more extensive area. It is the evidence of the demographic development of the city in the period of Troy VIIa. In the period of Troy VI, its residents began to use horses for the first time.

The finds from Troy VI and VIIa, mostly gray ceramics, testify to the strong ties with Greek civilization. Several vessels imported from Crete, Mycenae, Cyprus, and the Levant have also been found. There is the absence of any signs testifying to relations with Hittite civilization, which at that time was developing in Central Asia Minor.

Troy VIIb (1180 BCE – 950 BCE) was established on the ruins of Troy VIIa. The houses inside and outside the citadel were rebuilt and fortified, and the wall was repaired. The finds from this period, including Protogeometric ceramics, testify to the transition to the Iron Age settlement. The end of this settlement came with another fire, traces of which are visible on some buildings.

In the period between Troy VIIb and Troy VIII (950 BCE –

700 BCE) no traces of settlements have been identified, which means that at that time the hill was uninhabited, or it was only a very insignificant village. Troy VIII (700 BCE – 85 BCE) represents the time of restoration of the city, which occurred after the colonization of the area by Greek settlers. The temples and altars were erected in the Archaic style. After the visit of Alexander the Great in 334 BCE, Troy, then known as Ilion, became a central hub for a confederation of the cities of the Troad. In this time, many splendid public buildings were erected, including a theater and a magnificent temple of the goddess Athena.

In the 80s of the first century BCE, Rome waged war in Asia Minor against the ruler of Pontus, king Mithridates VI. Many Greek cities, including Ilion, granted their support to Mithridates, and were severely punished after his defeat. Ilion was ravaged by a Roman leader called Gaius Flavius Fimbria, who was famous for his exceptional ruthlessness.

Troy IX (85 BCE – 500 CE), which was soon rebuilt on the ruins of Troy VIII, was called Ilium. It was a Hellenistic-Roman city, and the most interesting findings of this layer are an odeon and a bouleuterion. The development and prosperity of the city resulted, among other things, from the cherished belief about the relation of Ilium with the mythical Troy. After all, Roman emperors, especially from the Julio-Claudian dynasty, willingly traced their descent from the Trojan royal family.

After the fall of the Western Roman Empire, Troy fell into disrepair, and was gradually forgotten. With time people ceased to believe in its existence, and the story of the Trojan War has been preserved only in the form of Homer's epic poem.

The search for Troy and archaeological excavations

Although the discovery of Troy is usually attributed to a German amateur archaeologist and adventurer – Heinrich Schliemann – the matter is actually somewhat more complicated. The existence of the mound called Hisarlık was first recorded by Franz Kauffer in 1703. In 1801, Edward Daniel Clarke associated this location with the legendary Troy. In 1822, Charles MacLaren also stated

Roman odeon in Troy

that Hisarlık had been the place where the Trojan War described in the Iliad had been fought.

At the same time, however, the search for the proper Homeric Troy was carried out in the region of the Troad, as many researchers supposed that it had been hidden in a different location. The person responsible for the confusion was ancient geographer Strabo. He claimed that the mythical Troy and Ilion that existed in his days were two entirely different cities. In the 19th century, many scholars pointed to Pınarbaşı village, located about 10 km south of Hisarlık, as the most likely location of Troy.

The first archaeological excavations at Hisarlık were conducted in 1856 by an officer of the British Navy – John Burton. His work was continued in the years 1863-1865 by Frank Calvert, an amateur researcher, who lived in the region. However, the excavations conducted by Calvert did not reach the layers from the Bronze Age.

When Heinrich Schliemann arrived at the Troad in 1870, he began archaeological excavations in Pınarbaşı, but the modest finds were very disappointing. When he was about to abandon the further search for Troy, Calvert pointed out the location of Hisarlık. Schliemann acquired necessary permits to conduct research, and from 1871 until his death he repeatedly returned to Hisarlık, where he excavated the mysterious mound. The notion that Hisarlık is the place where the Trojan War had been fought is the result of an intensive promotional campaign conducted by Schliemann.

Schliemann, eager to find the dreamed-of Troy described by Homer, led the excavations in a manner that caused more harm than good. His work destroyed some of the upper layers of the city, including – as it later turned out – the fragments of the settlement that had belonged to Troy of Homer's epic. In 1873, one of the most sensational discoveries was made by Schliemann. He found a rich collection of objects, consisting of copper pots, bronze weapons and, what was most important to him, silver and gold jewelry. Schliemann announced to the world that he had found the King Priam's treasure, and magnificent gold necklaces and earrings that once belonged to beautiful Helen. In fact, as demonstrated by the dating of the layers of Troy settlements, carried out later by Carl Blegen, these items were much older. Finally, they were assigned to Troy II (i.e. to the middle of the third millennium BCE), which existed some 1,200 years before the destruction of 'Homeric' Troy.

Schliemann secretly took away the rich collection of finds from Asia Minor. The scientific world and the Ottoman authorities learned about this fact when his wife – Sophia – began to show up in antique jewelry in public. Schliemann lost the permission to conduct excavations in Troy. He recovered it later in exchange for the return of the treasure. Some items of the treasure are now in the collections of the Troy Museum. However, the most outstanding exhibits were taken to Germany, where they remained in the Royal Museum in Berlin until 1945. In this year, the collection disappeared in the mysterious circumstances. It was only in 1993 when it reappeared in the Pushkin Museum in Moscow. Since then, multiple efforts have been made for their return, undertaken both by the German and the Turkish authorities, so far – to no avail.

The readers interested in the fascinating biography of Heinrich

Schliemann, an amateur archaeologist, a polyglot and, unfortunately, from the point of view of modern archeology, a vandal, should refer to the extremely interesting book 'Gods, Graves, and Scholars' by German writer C. W. Ceram.

The excavations at Hisarlık were continued by Wilhelm Dörpfeld – a German archaeologist and architect, in the years 1893-1894. He had begun the adventure with Troy earlier, in 1882, as an assistant of Schliemann. After Schliemann's death, Dörpfeld, as the manager of excavations, corrected many erroneous conclusions of his former supervisor.

After a break of almost 40 years, archaeological work at Hisarlık was resumed in 1932, under the leadership of an American archaeologist Carl Blegen and his team from the University of Cincinnati. During the excavations that continued until 1938, it was established that Troy could be divided into nine main layers corresponding to the cities that existed in this location for many millennia. Blegen even proposed the further subdivision into 46 levels.

Another break in the archaeological work lasted until 1988, when Professor Manfred Korfmann, also of the University of Cincinnati, became the director of Troy excavations. At the same time, Professor Charles Brian Rose was responsible for the study of the youngest layers of the city – Greek, Roman, and Byzantine. Manfred Korfmann devoted 17 years of his life to studying Troy. The greatest discovery made while Korfman was responsible for the Trojan excavations, was the determination that Troy had been much bigger than it had been initially thought. In addition to the location on Hisarlık mound, the ancient city covered a wide area around it. Another sensational discovery was associated with the signs of a fight in the city, in the form of bronze arrowheads and human remains, dating to the beginning of the 12th century BCE. These items ignited the imagination of many people and restarted a heated debate on the authenticity of the events known as the Trojan War.

Because of Korfmann's activities, the interest in Troy on international arena increased significantly. In 1996, he assisted Turkish authorities to establish a National Park covering the areas adjacent to Troy. Two years later, Troy became a UNESCO World Heritage Site. A year before his death in 2005, Professor Korfman received Turkish citizenship as a token of gratitude for his achievements. He also adopted a middle name – Osman – officially, as for many years he had been known as Osman Bey. After his death, a library bearing his name, containing his collection of books, publications, and documents was opened in nearby Çanakkale.

A team led by Ernst Pernicka of the University of Tübingen continued Korfmann's work from 2006. However, in recent years, the excavations at Troy became the subject of a dispute. In 2013, an interdisciplinary team of researchers, led by William Aylward of the University of Wisconsin, with the patronage of the University of Çanakkale, was supposed to start working in Troy. However, a few days before the beginning of the expedition, the Turkish authorities withdrew the permissions to conduct the excavations for a hundred participants, including the director. In March 2014, it was announced that new research was planned at Troy, sponsored by a private company and directed by the University of Çanakkale. This was the first Turkish team working in Troy, and Professor Rüstem Aslan was appointed as its director.

Sightseeing

During the tour of Troy do not miss:

- Schliemann's Trench,
- Water Cave of Wilusa,
- Troy Museum.

Visiting Troy is a challenging task, even for hardy travellers who have already visited many ancient sites. The visitors are often confused by a multitude of layers of the settlement on the hill, and the effects of intensive archaeological work. Fortunately, the area open to the public has an excellent infrastructure, which consists of marked paths, platforms, viewpoints, and information boards, which should be studied carefully to get the best of the tour.

Paved ramp of Troy II.

Below, the key points on the route are presented. This route is well marked by signposts, and leads the visitors along a loop, returning to the starting point – the Trojan Horse model (No. 1 on the Plan of Troy on the next page).

2. Excavation House

The building, located near the entrance to Troy ruins, formerly served the teams of archaeologists and currently hosts an exhibition of models and photographs of Troy.

3. Pithos Garden

Behind this mysterious name hides a collection of enormous ceramics, known in classical Greek as pithos. These vessels were up to 2 meters in height and were used to store and transport food. In addition to this exposition, there are ancient terracotta water pipes and stone mortars for grinding grain.

4. Eternal Stone of Troia

It is not a relic from the excavations of Troy, but a symbolic block of granite weighing 20 tons, obtained in the area of the Troad.

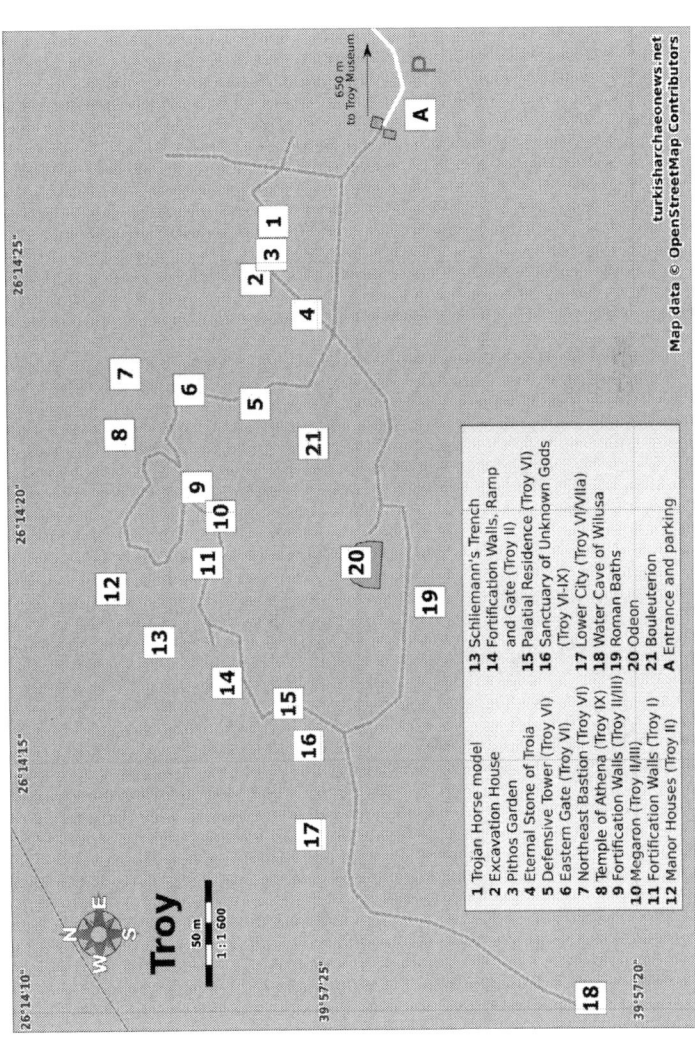

Troy

50 m
1 : 1 600

1 Trojan Horse model
2 Excavation House
3 Pithos Garden
4 Eternal Stone of Troia
5 Defensive Tower (Troia VI)
6 Eastern Gate (Troy VI)
7 Northeast Bastion (Troy VI)
8 Temple of Athena (Troy IX)
9 Fortification Walls (Troy II/III)
10 Megaron (Troy II/III)
11 Fortification Walls (Troy I)
12 Manor Houses (Troy II)

13 Schliemann's Trench
14 Fortification Walls, Ramp
   and Gate (Troy II)
15 Palatial Residence (Troy VI)
16 Sanctuary of Unknown Gods
   (Troy VI-IX)
17 Lower City (Troy VI/VIIa)
18 Water Cave of Wilusa
19 Roman Baths
20 Odeon
21 Bouleuterion
A Entrance and parking

650 m
to Troy Museum

A P

turkisharchaeonews.net
Map data © OpenStreetMap Contributors

Plan of Troy

It was donated to the Foundation of Troy in 2002, as a symbol commemorating the fact that Troy was one of the first places on the border between Asia and Europe, where hewn stone masonry was used. The first examples of the use of this technology in Troy date back to 2,500 BCE, i.e. to the Bronze Age. This technology was applied to build Megaron II A, as well as many other structures belonging to the layers of Troy VI-VIIa.

5. Defensive Tower of Troy VI

After the Eternal Stone of Troia, the sightseeing route of Troy turns right and leads to the fortifications from the times of Troy VI. In the beginning, it is worth paying attention to the remains of the defensive tower. Before you approach closer, stop on the viewing platform, which offers a panoramic view of this part of Troy. The outer walls (on the right side, looking from the platform) are very different from internal walls, slanting to the center of the settlement. This is due to the fact that this part of the external walls was erected later – it was a fence of the outer courtyard of the Temple of Athena.

6. Eastern Gate of Troy VI

The gate leading to Troy VI was placed between two lines of defensive walls – external and internal – overlapping as a spiral. At this point, there was a gate, invisible from the outside and impossible to force using a battering ram as there was no place for its use. In this place, you can also see the connection of the temple walls from Troy VIII and the walls of Troy VI.

7. Northeast Bastion of Troy VI

This is the most massive tower belonging to the citadel of Troy VI. It once rose to a height of 9 meters, and now its ruins are 7 meters high. In the period of Troy VIII-IX this area was built up with the walls surrounding the Temple of Athena.

8. Temple of Athena

Almost nothing has been preserved from the Temple of Athena, that belongs chronologically to Troy VIII and IX. You can see the foundations of the altar and fragments of roofing scattered around the area. Unfortunately, even before the 'discovery' of Troy by Schliemann, local people had known where to obtain excellent building materials. The temple was built as an initiative of Lysimachus, one of the generals of Alexander the Great. The temple, originally erected around 300 BCE, was later renovated at the time of the Roman Emperor Augustus. It is known that its plan had the dimensions of 36 to 16 meters and that the temple was surrounded by a colonnade of Doric order. The temple was the center of the annual celebration in honour of the goddess Athena. One of the best-preserved parts of the building – the relief depicting Apollo/Helios – is currently exhibited in Berlin.

9. Fortification Walls of Troy II/III

It is a very distinctive place in Troy – easily recognizable by modern roofing resembling the sails of a ship, erected in 2003. Most of the visible fragments of red brick walls are a modern reconstruction. The original bricks are inside the wall and go up to a height of 4 meters.

10. Megaron of Troy II/III

The megaron of Troy II/III is located just off the red walls. The term 'megaron' describes a building typical to the ancient culture of the Aegean area, consisting of one covered room and an open atrium. This plan became a prototype of the Greek temples. The Megaron of Troy had stone foundations. A part of the wall, reaching up to 1.5 meters, has been preserved to our times.

11. Fortification Walls of Troy I

Fortification Walls of Troy I constitute the most ancient layer of Trojan buildings. These walls were erected on bedrock, which means that underneath there are no traces of human activity. In this stretch of the walls there was a southern gate, 2 meters wide.

The walls are tilted slightly to the inside of the settlement. The settlement was a roughly circular area, with a diameter of 90 meters. At the defense tower, that forms a part of these fortifications, a fascinating stele has been found. It is adorned with a relief showing the upper half of a human body.

12. Manor Houses of Troy II

The residences of the wealthiest residents of Troy consisted of three parallel buildings (megarons). The largest of them had a size of 30 to 14 meters.

13. Schliemann's Trench

Schliemann's Trench is a reminder of the actions of the famous 'discoverer of Troy' – Schliemann. In search of the castle of King Priam described by Homer in the Iliad, Schliemann made a huge trench in Hisarlık mound. Today it is an illustration of how not to proceed in archaeology. The trench, oriented in the north-south direction, is 40 meters wide and up to 17 meters deep. Schliemann conducted his excavations reaching down to bedrock and destroying the newer layers of the settlement. At the bottom of the trench, there are visible remains of the walls of Troy I. The rows of stone walls are the foundations of houses from this period.

14. Fortification Walls, Ramp and Gate of Troy II

A perfectly preserved paved ramp led into the interior of Troy II. Researchers have discovered that this ramp was situated below a huge tower, under which ran the corridor. Near this place, Schliemann found the so-called Treasure of Priam.

15. Palatial Residence of Troy VI

Not much has been preserved from the Palatial Residence of Troy VI. It reportedly had two floors. Schliemann called this building 'the Palace of Priam'. However, large vessels for storing food, discovered here, testify to the fact that, at least for some time, it was actually a warehouse.

16. Sanctuary of Unknown Gods of Troy VI-IX

The visible remains of buildings date back to the period of Troy VIII and IX. They were erected on the ruins of earlier buildings of Troy VI and VII, perhaps also serving some religious purposes. The best-preserved structure is an altar of so-called Lower Sanctuary. There are also two wells, one of which was used for the collection of blood of sacrificial animals, and the second one – for drawing water. The temple complex was built during the Archaic period of ancient Greece, but the sanctuary was also used later, during the Hellenistic and Roman times, with some modifications. It is not known which gods were worshipped here.

17. Lower City of Troy VI/VIIa

The Lower City of Troy VI/VIIa is located outside the citadel, to the west. Stone foundations of numerous houses have been identified here. The most spectacular finds from the Lower City include a bronze statuette and a terracotta bull figurine. Excavations are still being conducted in this area of Troy, bringing new, exciting discoveries.

18. Water Cave of Wilusa

Water Cave of Wilusa is a place rarely visited by tourists. The distance from the Lower City of Troy VI/VIIa to the cave is about 150 meters. The path leads you along the fields and meadows. The signposts leading from the hill to the cave are quite inconspicuous and easy to miss. The cave is a relatively new archaeological discovery, as it was found and studied in 1997-2001.

Surprisingly, it is an artificial cave, not a work of nature. A 160-meter-long corridor cut in the rock heads to the east. It is connected to the surface by four vertical shafts with a height of up to 17 meters. The corridor was made in the third millennium BCE. It means that in the heyday of Troy VI the cave had already been in use for a thousand years.

The cave was called 'an underground corridor' and associated with a water deity KASKAL.KUR. It is mentioned in the treaty concluded between the Hittite king Muwatalli II and King Alaksandu of Wilusa (as Troy was then called). The King Alaksandu took an oath, invoking the water deity.

19. Roman Baths

On the right side of the path, you can see the ruins of Roman baths. Little has survived of this building, and its floor was once adorned with beautiful mosaics of colourful stones.

20. Odeon

An odeon was a small theater used to enjoy musical performances. It dates back to the Roman times, probably to the end of the first century CE. Marble blocks, lying in front of the odeon, were once a part of its scene.

21. Bouleuterion

A bouleuterion was a place of political gatherings. The bouleuterion in Troy, originating from the time of Augustus, still has a podium and the first row of marble seats.

Troy Museum

In 2012, plans were announced to open a new museum facility – the Troy Museum, which was to operate next to the ruins of Troy. The selection of the project of the building was an important event, and many Turkish and foreign companies took part in the competition.

The Year of Troy was celebrated in 2018 and one of the main events of that year was the opening of the new Troy Museum, situated next to the archaeological site. The collections of the museum include the exhibits previously displayed in Çanakkale Archaeological Museum but also other artefacts, transferred from Istanbul Archaeological Museums and Museum of Anatolian Civilizations in Ankara. Additionally, there are 24 pieces of gold jewellery returned by the US Penn Museum in 2012.

The visit starts at the entrance ramp and follows a story divided into seven chapters on the ground floor. These chapters are devoted to the archaeology of the Troad, Troy Bronze Age, Iliad Epic and Trojan War, Troad and Ilion in the Ancient Period, Eastern Roman and Ottoman Periods, and the history of archaeological excavations. This floor offers information about ancient cities of the Troad region, including Assos, Bozcaada (Tenedos), Parion, Alexandria Troas, Apollo Smintheion, Lampsakos, Thymbria, Tavolia, and Gökçeada (Imbros).

Many finds exhibited in the museum come from two Turkish islands in the Aegean Sea. The biggest attraction from the island of Bozcaada (ancient Tenedos) are the exhibits found in the local necropolis. These finds include the vessels from the 9th century BCE, local wine and olive oil jars (so-called askoi) made from gray clay, dated to the 7th century BCE, Corinthian pottery, also from the 7th century BCE, red-figure pottery from the 5th and 4th centuries BCE, and figurines of the goddess Cybele from the 5th century BCE.

The most valuable finds from the second Aegean island – Gökçeada (Imbros) – have been found in the area of Yenibademli Höyük archaeological site. Archaeological research has been conducted there since 1996, and so far seven architectural layers have been identified. The oldest of them contains the examples of so-called Cyclopean walls and Mycenaean ceramics. The depth of each cultural layer varies from 3 to 5 meters. In addition, a statue of a seated woman from the 2nd century BCE has been brought to Troy Museum.

Fascinating finds have been collected from Dardanos Tumulus, and the visitors to the museum are greatly impressed by golden diadems and wreaths, dated to the 4th and the 3rd centuries BCE, and the treasures from the necropolis (dated to the 4th century BCE), including gold jewelry, statues, and pottery. In addition, the excavations in the area of the tumulus and its surroundings have resulted in the discovery of Hellenistic terracotta figurines, a collection of statues of Aphrodite and Eros, and ceramics from the period between the 4th and the 2nd century CE.

Tavolia and Thymbria are two other sites represented in the museum. Both of them are situated near Troy, and archaeological excavations are still conducted there. The museum displays the vessels found in these sites, from the period from the 6th to the 5th century BCE.

One of the most impressive collections in the museum is the one from Assos (Behramkale). Among the finds from the local necropolis, such as vessels and terracotta objects from the 5th and the 4th centuries BCE, there are fascinating figurines of musicians. Most likely they were funeral gifts because they have been found in the sarcophagi. Perhaps there is a connection between them and the cult of the god Dionysus. The figurines depict musicians playing various instruments, including the lyre, the cithara, the drum, and the flute, as well as people dancing and singing.

Other exhibits have been brought to the museum from Lapseki (ancient Lampsakos), situated on the Asian shore of the Dardanelles. These finds are represented by a stone table leg, a statue of a young man called (so-called kouros) from the 6th century BCE, and the statue of the goddess Aphrodite from the Hellenistic period.

Other archaeological sites represented in the museum are: Cyzicus (a tombstone from the 2nd century BCE), Biga, i.e. ancient Pega (a marble tombstone from the 2nd century CE), Kumtepe (ceramics from the VI-IV millennium BCE), Parion (a bronze amphora and the statue of Orpheus from the end of the first century BCE), and Apollon Smintheion temple (ceramics).

The museum also has among its collections the items found in archaeological sites located on the Gallipoli Peninsula. The sculpture of a horse from the 4th century CE has come from Lysimacheia (near Bolayır), and the gravestone of an athlete from the 5th century BCE has been found in the vicinity of Küçükanafarta (near Eceabat).

The main theme of the second floor exhibition is the Trojan War. The heroes, events, and places of the war as well as coins, pottery, and marble works of this period are presented in drawings, models, and digital programmes. Moreover, the Polyxena Sarcophagus from the 6th century CE, which was brought to light in 1994 in Kızöldün Tumulus near the town of Biga is displayed there. Another sarcophagus is called Altıkulaç and this exhibit in the Greco-Persian style (the 4th century BCE) was found in Çingenetepe Tumulus near Çan.

The museum boasts numerous finds from Troy, including its oldest layers, dated to the years 2950-2550 BCE. From this period, the museum exhibits ceramic dishes such as a fruit platter and a casserole with a lid, as well as marble figurines, which probably served for religious worship.

The objects excavated from the layer of Troy II include the collections of plates, dishes decorated with spatial figures, and many drinking vessels, including the specimens of the so-called depas amphikypellon (a term used by Homer to describe high and narrow vessels with two handles), and the vessels similar in shape to modern mugs. The museum has exhibits from later chronological layers of Troy, including Troy V – dishes and pots, and Troy VIIa-VI – Mycenaean vessels. Also, the museum has several Trojan thematic collections, including bone tools, jewelry, and bronze objects.

Other exhibits are the sculptures of the Roman emperors, including the famous statue of Emperor Hadrian (117-138 CE). The statue of Triton, unearthed in Parion in 2012, is also presented to the visitors on this floor.

The third floor displays historical artefacts from Troy and surrounding settlements from the Ottoman period. There are texts, engravings and photographs describing the Ottoman settlements and the importance of the Dardanelles in the early days of the Ottoman Empire. Other exhibits include the section devoted to the pottery tradition, stonemasonry, and stoneworks as well as coin treasures and ceramics from the Ottoman period. The garden of the Troy Museum is another exhibition place where numerous sarcophagi, columns, steles, and capitals are on display.

Statue of Hadrian found during Troy excavations

Eastern Gate of Troy VI

Opening times and tickets

Troy is a historical site inscribed on UNESCO's World Heritage List (in 1998). Visiting the ruins of Troy is possible every day during the opening hours: in the summer season (April to October) from 8:30 am to 7:30 pm, and in the winter season (November to March) from 8:30 am to 5:30 pm. A ticket costs 35 TL. Small children enter for free. The ticket office closes one hour earlier.

The car park next to the entrance is free of charge. Unfortunately, it is almost entirely unprotected from the sun. Take advantage of the few shady spots under some trees in the corner of the parking lot.

Troy can be visited individually, and you are assisted with the information boards (in English, German, and Turkish). You can also hire a guide for the tour. A guided tour takes about 1.5 hours.

To visit the Troy Museum, it is necessary to buy another ticket, for 35 TL. The museum is open daily, from 8:30 am to 7:30 pm (5:00 pm in winter season). The ticket office closes half an hour earlier.

Accommodation and restaurants

Most of the tourists visit Troy in just a few hours, and then return to Çanakkale or continue the journey further to the south. If you intend to stay near the archaeological site, you can find several restaurants and accommodation options. They are situated in Tevfikiye village, just half a kilometer to the east of Troy. If you get to Troy in the afternoon and find out that the last minibus to Çanakkale had already left, it is worth considering accommodation in the following facilities:

– Hisarlık Hotel – closest to the entrance to Troy. It is a facility run by the family of the renowned Trojan guide Mustafa Askin. The hotel features simply furnished rooms at affordable prices. On the ground floor of the hotel, there is a restaurant serving freshly prepared traditional Turkish dishes. Despite the proximity to Troy and the lack of competition, the dishes are truly delicious, and the prices – reasonable. Dinner dishes include moussaka and güveç (casserole with meat). At the restaurant, there is also a gift shop selling postcards, brochures, and books about Troy, as well as miniature Trojan horses. It is worth comparing the prices offered here to the prices of goods in the official museum shop in Troy. An unusual sight is a wooden hut, adjacent to the hotel. It was commissioned by German television during the filming of a documentary film about Heinrich Schliemann. It reproduces the actual residence of famous treasure hunter, where he lived while working in the area of Troy.

– Troia Pension – located just 100 meters to the west of Hisarlık Hotel. This is a relatively new guest house, run by another experienced guide - Urvan Savas. The facility has only four rooms. The pension has a restaurant and a gift shop. The big advantage of this facility is the possibility of camping in the garden for a small fee.

GETTING THERE

BY PUBLIC TRANSPORT: there are regular minibuses connecting Troy with Çanakkale. Minibuses depart from Çanakkale every hour between 9:30 am and 4:30 pm (in summer till 7:00 pm). The ride takes about 40 minutes. Please note the last return minibus from Troy to Çanakkale departs at 3:00 pm (5:00 pm in summer), which means that you might need to stay in Troy if you decide to visit this site in the afternoon as there are no other public transport options in the evenings.

BY TAXI: it is possible to organize a taxi tour from Çanakkale to Troy and back, and the price depends on the result of negotiations with a driver.

BY CAR: take D550 route from Çanakkale, and turn to the west after 26 km. The turnoff is clearly signposted, and the total distance from Çanakkale is 30 km.

WITH AN ORGANISED TOUR: many travel agencies from Çanakkale and Eceabat organise the tours of Troy.

Lapseki

Lapseki is a small port town located on the Asian shore of the Dardanelles. Its current, inconspicuous appearance can be misleading: as it is a settlement with a rich history. Unfortunately, no significant traces of its old power have been preserved to our times.

Brief history

The city was founded as Lampsakos in 654 BCE by the Greek settlers who came from Miletus and Phocaea, located in the south, on the Asian coast of the Aegean Sea. They were attracted to the north of Asia Minor by extremely fertile lands in the area. In antiquity, the city also was famous for its excellent wine.

In ancient times, under the Roman rule, Lampsakos played an important role. Together with Abydos, located further to the south, at Cape Nara, it exercised total control over the movement of trade through the Hellespont (the Dardanelles) in the direction of the Black Sea. These two settlements were located in one of the narrowest points of this strait.

The most famous historical figure associated with Lampsakos was a natural philosopher Anaxagoras (about 500 BCE – 428 BCE). He was born in Klazomenai – one of the cities of the Ionian League, but for most of his life he was a resident of Athens. His major work about nature has been preserved only in fragments, but it is known that Anaxagoras was the precursor of the scientific explanation of natural phenomena. Because of his views, belittling the role of the gods in the eyes of his contemporaries, he was prosecuted for impiety, and banished from Athens. He spent the last years of his life in Lampsakos, where he was treated with great respect. After his death, an altar dedicated to the Spirit and the Truth was built in his honor in Lampsakos.

Other famous people associated with the city include: Anaximenes of Lampsacus – a historian, an orator, a pupil of Diogenes, and the teacher of Alexander the Great; Metrodoros of Lampsakos – a philosopher and a student of Epicurus; and another Metrodoros of Lampsakos – a philosopher, a student of Anaxagoras, and a commentator on Homer.

Sightseeing

Currently, Lapseki is famous mainly for its cherries – a festival dedicated to this fruit is held there every year in the first half of June. Unfortunately, apart from this event, there is not much to see in Lapseki, as even the ancient artifacts found there are now in the Troy Museum.

Lapseki may be a good choice as a starting point for exploring the historic sites in the northern part of the Troad, including Parion (53 km) and Priapos (74 km).

Visitor tips

Orientation

It is very hard to get lost in Lapseki, because this is a tiny town with only 11,000 inhabitants. It is located on the D200 (E90) route, from Çanakkale in the south to the north-east. In Lapseki, this road takes the name of Atatürk Street. Most of the hotels, shops, and services are situated along this street. The ferry terminal is located on the north side of the town, next to the coach station, and the access road to it is clearly signposted.

Accommodation and restaurants

In Lapseki and its immediate surroundings there are several hotels of tourist standard. In the center, on Fatih Street, there is Orçın Apart Otel, and 3 km outside the center to the north, in the village of Cardak Ovası, there is Linda Apart Otel. Both hotels offer self-catering apartments with a kitchen and a bathroom.

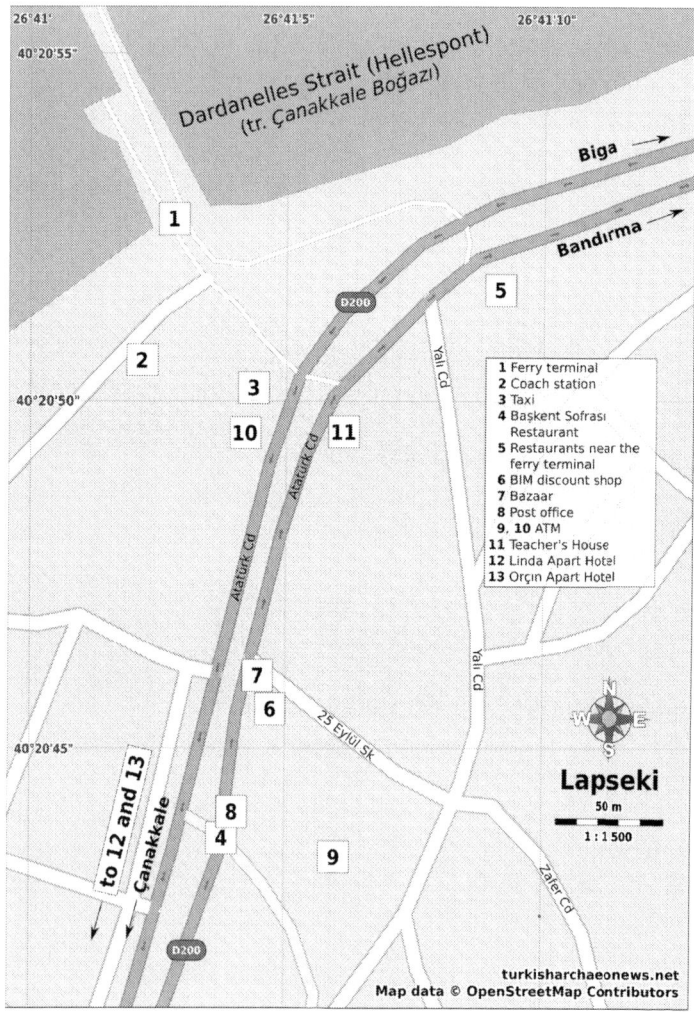

Plan of Lapseki

In the center of Lapseki you can also stay at the Teachers' House, situated opposite the ferry terminal, on Atatürk Street No. 13. The rooms have private bathrooms and are equipped with air conditioning and a refrigerator, but unfortunately, they are not very clean and need a renovation. The price includes a modest breakfast in the Turkish style. A big advantage of the Teachers' House is its tea garden, along with a restaurant where fresh gözleme (traditional Turkish pancakes) and ayran (a yogurt drink) are served.

In the city center, there are several restaurants, clustered close to the ferry terminal. A little further to the south, there is Başkent Sofrası restaurant where tasty green lentil soup with unlimited fresh bread is served. In the menu, there are also several other kinds of soup and dishes with beans and chicken, including döner kebab.

Shopping and services

In the center of Lapseki there is BIM discount store, and on Tuesdays and Saturdays there is a bazaar where fruit, vegetables, clothes, and household goods are sold. In the town, there is also a post office and several banks with ATMs, which can be found right next to the ferry terminal.

GETTING THERE

BY COACH: there are numerous coaches from Lapseki, including local connections to Çanakkale (45 minutes), Bandırma (2.5 hours), Biga (1 hours), and Bursa (4.5 hours). Long-distance coaches go to Ankara (10 hours), Eskişehir (7 hours), Istanbul (6 hours), and many other Turkish cities.

BY CAR: E90 route goes through Lapseki from Çanakkale in the south (34 km). This road takes you further to the east, through Biga and Bandırma to former Ottoman capital city of Bursa (239 km).

BY FERRY: the ferry connects Lapseki with Gelibolu on the European shore of the Dardanelles (30 minutes). If you pay per vehilce, the transport of its all passengers is included in the price.

Parion (Kemer)

COORDINATES: 40.4243° N, 27.0681° E

The ruins of the ancient city of Parion are located on the territory of modern Turkish village of Kemer, in Çanakkale Province, on the coast of the Marmara Sea. The ruins are far from the beaten track, so it is difficult to reach them, and even finding interesting information about this site in a language other than Turkish is a challenge. Thanks to intensive archaeological excavations, conducted in Parion, crucial findings are made every year, shedding light on the history of the settlement.

BRIEF HISTORY

Parion, also called Parium, was a Greek city located on the border of historical lands of Troad and Mysia. In ancient times, Parion functioned as an important harbour for the surrounding settlements. The origin of the town's name has not yet been scientifically explained, but there is a tradition that it comes from Paris, the son of the Trojan king Priam.

The city was founded probably about 3,000 years ago as a colony by settlers from Eretria (a Greek polis from the island of Euboea) and the island of Paros in the Aegean Sea. Parion was a member of the Delian League. In the city, there were defensive towers, and at least four temples.

In the Hellenistic period, it came under the control of Lysimachus – one of diadochi of Alexander the Great. After his death, the city was taken over by the Attalids from Pergamon. As a part of the Pergamon Kingdom, Parion was handed over to the Romans by the will of Attalos III in 133 BCE.

Antique coins from Parion testify to its great importance and advanced minting facilities. The most interesting picture, visible on the coins from the Hellenistic period, is the coat of arms. It depicts the so-called gorgoneion, i.e. the head of the Gorgon – a terrible mythological beast with sharp fangs, and hair in the form of poisonous snakes. In ancient times, gorgoneion served as an apotropaic amulet, reversing evil charms (similar role is now played by nazar boncuğu - a popular Turkish amulet). The relation between the city of Parion and the Gorgon is not fully understood, most likely the monster was chosen as the emblem of the city to reverse bad intentions and repel attacks against its inhabitants. Perhaps it had to do with military power represented by Parion.

In the history of Christianity, Parion appeared as a place where the Christian community already existed before 180 CE. Local martyrs and saints from Parion had some unusual names, such as Onesiphorus, Menignus, or Teogenes. Initially, Parion belonged to the Archbishopric of Cyzicus. From 640, it became an independent Archdiocese, and retained this status until the end of the 13th century. Then, on the orders of the Byzantine Emperor Andronicus II Paleologus, it gained the status of a metropolis, as Pegon kai Pariou.

In the Ottoman times, the ruins of Parion were located in the area of Kamares village, inhabited mainly by the Greeks, and subjected to the sanjak of Biga. Today, the village is called Kemer Köyü and is a small fishing port.

ARCHAEOLOGICAL RESEARCH

Archaeological work has been conducted at the ruins of Parion for many years. The existence of ancient Parion was no secret to the father of the Turkish archeology – Osman Hamdi Bey. He found a sarcophagus there, later transported to the Archaeological Museum in Istanbul. Since 2005, a team of archaeologists in Parion has been directed by Professor Cevat Başaran from Atatürk University in Erzurum.

The most important discoveries made by his team are tombs and sarcophagi from the area of Parion necropolis. Among them,

Parion excavations

it is worth mentioning a 2200-year-old sarcophagus, which was unearthed in 2009. Golden earrings found in it bear the symbol of Eros, and they were accompanied by numerous rings and some fragments of the crown decorated with precious stones. These finds allow the presumption that a rich person was buried there, and she was called the princess of Parion by the discoverers of the tomb. Unfortunately, the bones of the people buried in the necropolis have not been well preserved because of soil moisture due to the proximity of the sea. A royal crown and gold coins with the figure of the sun god were discovered in another tomb.

In addition to these special sarcophagi, around 200 graves have been discovered in the necropolis so far, often with gifts for the dead, including bottles for tears, oil lamps, and toys. Sometimes the funeral gifts enable the identification of the occupation of the person buried there, as in the case of the tomb with bronze fragments of a fishing rod from the 1st century CE. Unfortunately, many of the tumuli surrounding Parion have been plundered by treasure hunters.

Archaeological excavations in Parion are also carried out in a theater, an odeon, and baths, as well as in six areas on a hillside overlooking the ancient city. Important discovery was made in 2011 when a marble block was found, with an inscription in the Phrygian language. Because of this discovery, Parion is now considered as the north-western boundary of ancient Phrygian civilization.

SIGHTSEEING

Based on the excavation findings, Professor Başaran says that Parion was a great city, ruled by the wealthy elite of the Hellenistic era. The professor hopes that the ruins of Parion will become a tourist attraction comparable to Ephesus. Honestly, we need to warn the travellers interested in exploring Parion that these plans relate to the very distant future, as currently the excavations are in no way prepared for visitors.

At the entrance to the village of Kemer, there is a faded information board about Parion (in Turkish). On a hill, in the vicinity of this board, you can see the remains of fortifications. In the center of the village, a signpost leads to the necropolis, where the excavation work is carried out. The official information panel at the necropolis states that the entrance is dangerous and prohibited. However, you can ask for the permission to take some photos. Do not overuse the patience of the archaeologists and do not enter the area of the necropolis.

The most important ancient buildings of Parion are located to the north of the center of Kemer, about 600 meters from the necropolis area. There are the remains of a theater, an odeon, and Roman baths.

The finds from excavations conducted in Parion, dating back to the Archaic, Hellenistic, and Roman periods, are presented in the Troy Museum. One of the most interesting exhibits is a 2400-year-old amphora made of bronze, found in 2005. The vessel is 34 cm high, and it is decorated with the theme depicting the ecstatic procession of dancing figures: the god Dionysus, a satyr, and maenads.

VISITOR TIPS

The village of Kemer is not a place to stop overnight as there are no accommodation options there. We recommend finding a room in a hotel in Lapseki, located to the west. Alternatively, you can book a room in Biga or Karabiga, further to the east. In Kemer, there are no restaurants or shops, so it is worth to stock up on supplies of food and beverages before the trip.

GETTING THERE

BY CAR: take E90 route from Çanakkale to the north-east, through Lapseki. Turn left (to the north) after 74 km, and follow Kemer (Parion) signposts. The local, but good quality road takes you to Kemer village, 12 km from the crossroads.

Biga

Coordinates: 40.2275° N, 27.2413° E

Biga is the largest city in the central part of the Troad, and at the same time, the capital of one of the twelve districts of Çanakkale Province. The city, located on the major transportation route of the region, does not stand out with anything special, but in the past it witnessed an extremely significant event. The first of victorious battles that the troops of the Macedonian leader Alexander the Great fought with the Persians in Asia Minor took place nearby, on the banks of the Granicus River (modern-day Biga Çayı). Because of its location, Biga is a convenient stopover during the journey from the Dardanelles to the east, into the heart of Asia Minor.

Brief history

From the ancient times until the conquest of the Troad by the Ottoman Empire in the 14th century, the city was known as Pegaea (meaning 'river spring' in Greek). The settlement was located on the plain of Adrastea, which is the borderland between the historical lands of Troad and Mysia. As no systematic archaeological work has been carried out in Biga, the oldest history of human settlement remains a mystery to researchers.

The main event that is linked with the history of Biga, happened on the banks of a small river flowing through the city. It is now known as Biga Çayı, although there are also two other names – Çan Çayı and Kocabaş Çayı. This river, flowing from the northern slopes of the massif of Ida Mountain, meets the Sea of Marmara after negotiating 80 km through the area of the Troad. It is best known by its ancient name – Granicus River. In May of 334 BCE, in the Battle of the Granicus, very near modern Biga, the army of Alexander the Great defeated the Persian forces, opening the way for the Macedonians to the conquest of Asia Minor.

SIGHTSEEING

There are several historical wooden houses still standing in the center of Biga. In one of them, known as Halimbey Konağı, operates a small Municipal Museum (tr. *Kent Müzesi*). It hosts a typical collection of ethnographic exhibits. In addition, the city has a remarkable Bazaar Mosque (tr. *Çarşı Cami*), with a beautiful wooden ablution fountain in front of the building.

Biga may be a good base for the tour of the region, including the visit to the ruins of the ancient city of Parion, situated 30 km to the north-west, and the ramparts of ancient Priapos, located in Karabiga village, 23 km to the north.

VISITOR TIPS

Currently, Biga has 80 thousand inhabitants. It is located on an important communication route, running from west to east along the coast of the Sea of Marmara. Just at the point where the city is situated, D200 route leaves the coast in a gentle curve towards the south. The city lies on the southern side of the route, but even though it is surrounded by a vast plain, its center is a maze of narrow, crowded streets.

Due to its location, Biga is mainly a transit city for the travellers who go to the east of the country. In the city, several hotels may provide convenient accommodation. If you plan to spend the night in Biga, consider the following hotels:

- MRG Hotel – Ihlamur Street No. 3, in a renovated house from the Ottoman era. It is the most stylish lodging option in the city, although according to the opinions of many travellers the quality of service and equipment of the rooms are not up to the standard expected for the price of a room.
- Edahan Hotel – İnönü Street No. 31, located in the heart of the city and very well rated.
- Biga Palas Hotel – İstiklal Street No. 152, is apparently the

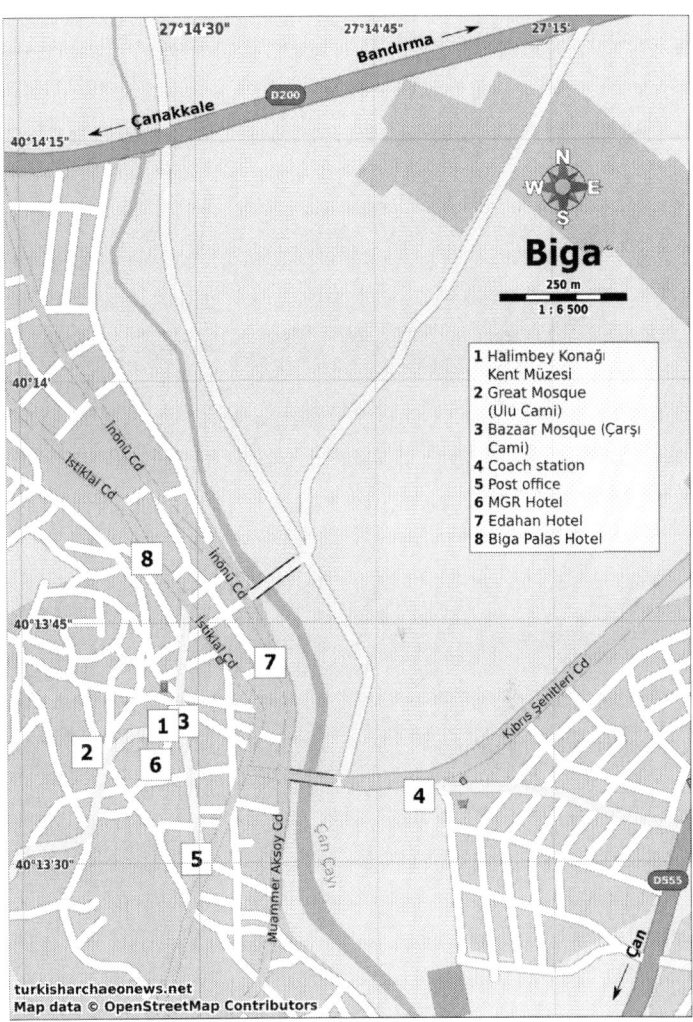

Plan of Biga

best hotel in town. The price of a room includes breakfast in the form of a buffet with local, fresh produce.

Getting there

By public transport: there are regular coaches from Biga to Bandırma, Çan, Çanakkale, Lapseki, and Karabiga.

By car: Biga is situated on D200 route, connecting Çanakkale (94 km) and Lapseki (60 km) in the west, with Bandırma (75 km) in the east. D555 route starts in Biga and takes you to the south – to Çan (33 km). There is also a local road to the north, to Karabiga (23 km).

Karabiga (Priapos)

Coordinates: 40.4036° N, 27.3062° E

Karabiga is a small port town, situated on the shore of the Sea of Marmara in Çanakkale Province. The fascinating history of the town is inextricably linked with the cult of the god Priapus, from which came the ancient name of the settlement. The location of the city, near the mouth of the Biga River, in a small bay, favoured the development of the settlement as a trading port. Even today Karabiga is an important harbour for container ships.

Brief history

Priapus, who gave his name to the ancient city, was a minor deity of the Greco-Roman pantheon. His task was to protect farm animals, fruit trees, vineyards, gardens, and male genitalia. Priapus can be easily identified on paintings, mosaics, and sculptures from the ancient times because of his enormous erect penis.

The cult of Priapus had its roots in Asia Minor, near Lampsakos (now Lapseki), that is situated not far from Karabiga. Gradually, it spread to the whole area of ancient Greece, and later – the Roman Empire. The exact relationship between the name of this deity and the name of the village is not known, but it can be assumed that it was connected with the famous local vineyards.

Karabiga, known in antiquity as Priapos or Priapus, was founded by the Greek settlers who arrived on the coast of the Marmara Sea from Miletus in the 7th century BCE. An alternative version of the history of the settlement is that the city was founded as a colony of Cyzicus. The Greek geographer Strabo mentioned that the area had produced exceptionally tasty wine, and the historian Thucy-

Fortifications of Priapos

dides wrote that it had housed the base of warships.

In 334 BCE, the city surrendered without a fight to Alexander the Great before the Battle of the Granicus. This battle with the Persian army was the first victory of the Macedonian leader in Asia Minor. The famous Granicus River is, in fact, a rather large stream, flowing into the Sea of Marmara in the vicinity of Karabiga. In Byzantine times, the city was a fortified stronghold. The Ottomans conquered this region of Asia Minor in 1364.

The relatively small amount of information available about the history of Karabiga results from the lack of archaeological excavations conducted in this location. Preliminary studies were carried out in 1997 by Professor Cevat Başaran from Atatürk University in Erzurum. However, this scholar finally decided to undertake the excavations in nearby Parion instead.

Sightseeing

The biggest tourist attraction of Karabiga are the remains of city walls, beautifully situated in the hills about 2 km from the town center. Once there stood a huge castle with 24 towers, guarding the dual harbor of Priapos. The ruins of these fortifications are not signposted, but fortunately they can be seen from afar. Admission to the ruins is free of charge.

During the tour, be careful because the area of the ruins is not fenced off, and lies next to a high cliff. Beautiful views pose an additional threat, as a moment of inattention may cause an unpleasant accident. In addition, the area is overgrown with thorny bushes, so it is advisable to wear sturdy shoes and long trousers.

In addition to visiting the ruins, it is worth climbing the hill to admire the cliffs towering above the sea waters and hidden bays between them. You can use these coves to take a swim in the sea. Seagulls and cormorants often occupy the rocks protruding from the waters of Marmara Sea.

Maritime Festival (tr. *Karabiga Priapos Deniz Festivali*) takes place every year in late June and early July. During this festival, you can enjoy performances of local artists and take part in sports competitions.

Coast in Karabiga

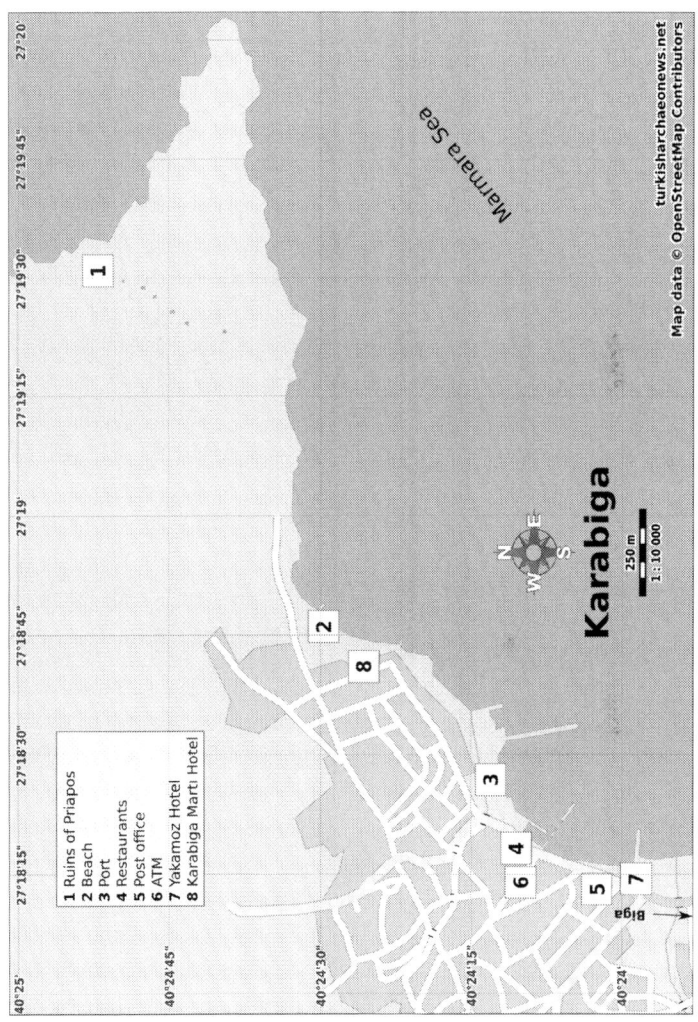

1 Ruins of Priapos
2 Beach
3 Port
4 Restaurants
5 Post office
6 ATM
7 Yakamoz Hotel
8 Karabiga Marti Hotel

Marmara Sea

Karabiga

250 m
1:10 000

turkisharchaeonews.net
Map data © OpenStreetMap Contributors

Biga

Plan of Karabiga

Orientation and services

Between the center of Karabiga and the ruins of Priapos in the north, there is a summer cottages district, popular among Turkish families. There is a beach with sun beds, bars, and cafes. In the city center, there are several grocery stores, a post office, and ATMs. Friday is a market day in Karabiga.

Accommodation

In the center of Karabiga, next to the harbour, there is Yakamoz Hotel, offering 18 rooms with private bathrooms. Moreover, in the beach district of the town operates Karabiga Martı Hotel, boasting its own outdoor swimming pool and a private beach.

Restaurants

Several small restaurants are situated along the main street of Karabiga – Cumhuriyet Caddesi – that runs along the waterfront and next to the harbour. We recommend Angaralı Halil Usta restaurant, specializing in fish dishes, but also serving good köfte with pilav (i.e. meatballs with rice). Among other venues, New Vitamin stands out as the most fashionable restaurant in town, offering pizza and breakfast menu, and Karabiga Cennet Cafe & Restaurant is seen as the family-friendly option.

GETTING THERE

BY CAR: the easiest way to get to Karabiga is by car. If you come from the direction of Çanakkale, follow E90 route to the northeast, through Lapseki. 86 km away from Çanakkale turn off this road to the north (to the left) and follow Karabiga (Priapos) signposts. After 20 km you will reach Karabiga.

An alternative route takes you through the secondary roads but allows the exploration of Parion ruins on the way. Turn off E90 route 74 km away from Çanakkale, following the signposts to Kemer (Parion). After 12 km the road reaches the village of Kemer, where the ruins of the ancient city of Parion are situated.

Up to this point the road is excellent, but further on it becomes very poor, with potholes made by trucks servicing a nearby factory. Moreover, you have to drive just next to this factory, listening to the megaphones that may scare unsuspecting travellers by announcing suddenly *Dikkat, fabrika çıkışı!* (i.e. Warning, this is the exit from the factory!). Then a gravel road leads through a countryside dotted with low hills, with the coast of the Marmara Sea in the distance, to the beach holiday village Aksaz. The total distance from Parion to Karabiga is 27 km, and it is not easy and enjoyable ride, despite some fabulous views.

By COACH: there are hourly coaches from Biga to Karabiga (23 km).

By FERRY: there are irregular ferry connections between Karabiga and Barbaros – a harbour on the opposite shore of the Marmara Sea, 9 km to the south-west from Tekirdağ.

Çan

COORDINATES: 40.0296° N, 27.0528° E

Çan is one of those towns located in the Troad, where the travellers will not find any fascinating sights. It is located somewhat off the beaten track from the main transportation routes, and is usually bypassed by tourists travelling through this region of Turkey. Meanwhile, there are at least two reasons why it is worthwhile to visit Çan: its local ceramics, and a small restaurant, serving the tastiest meatballs (tr. *köfte*) and bean salad (tr. *piyaz*) throughout the country.

BRIEF HISTORY

Little is known about the history of Çan, although the traces of numerous ancient settlements have been identified in the vicinity of the town. Unfortunately, they are very weakly preserved. Some researchers identify Çan with Gergis settlement, where Gergithes tribe mentioned by Homer used to dwell, but these assumptions have not been confirmed yet.

During the Greco-Turkish War, which was fought after the First World War, Çan was destroyed by the retreating Greek army. Turkish troops retook the city in September 1922.

Today Çan has about 30,000 inhabitants and is the capital of the district of the same name, belonging administratively to Çanakkale Province. The primary source of income for the town is the ceramic industry. In the area of Çan, there are significant deposits of kaolinite and feldspar – essential raw materials used in the production of ceramics. For this reason, the largest ceramics factory in Turkey currently operates in Çan, giving employment to many people from the surrounding areas.

Orientation

The town is divided into two parts by D555 route. The centre of Çan, with shops, restaurants, and services, is located on the north-west side of the road. The second part of the city is the industrial and residential district, known as Seramik Mahallesi.

Accommodation

Because there are many thermal springs in the vicinity of Çan, the town authorities are planning to transform it into a holiday resort. They want to attract tourists looking for relaxation in a quiet environment of forests and hills. Currently, there is only one spa hotel in the town – Ataol Çan Termal Otel & Spa (on Çannakale-Balıkesir Yolu), and the construction of other spa centres is dependent on the success of this first outpost of tourism in the district.

If you do not plan to relax in the spa, and only seek accommodation before the onward journey through the Troad, the best option is to stay at Sergis Hotel. It is conveniently located just off the access road to Çan from Biga (tr. *Çan-Biga Yolu*).

Restaurants

One of the main reasons why it is worth to stay in Çan is a small restaurant called Gülen Piliç on Oran Street. As its name suggests, it specializes in chicken dishes. There you can enjoy delicious grilled chicken breast fillets, with exceptional flavor and juiciness, and ideal köfte (meatballs) which in Çan take the form of small meat rolls. Order piyaz (bean salad) as an appetizer – in contrast to the bean soup with the same name from the area of Antalya, in the Troad it is the salad made of many vegetables with cooked white beans. The chefs from Çan achieved the national championship in their execution of this dish, and in addition to the excellent flavor, it is very aesthetically served. To wash it down, you can order only non-alcoholic drinks, and the best addition to the food is a yoghurt

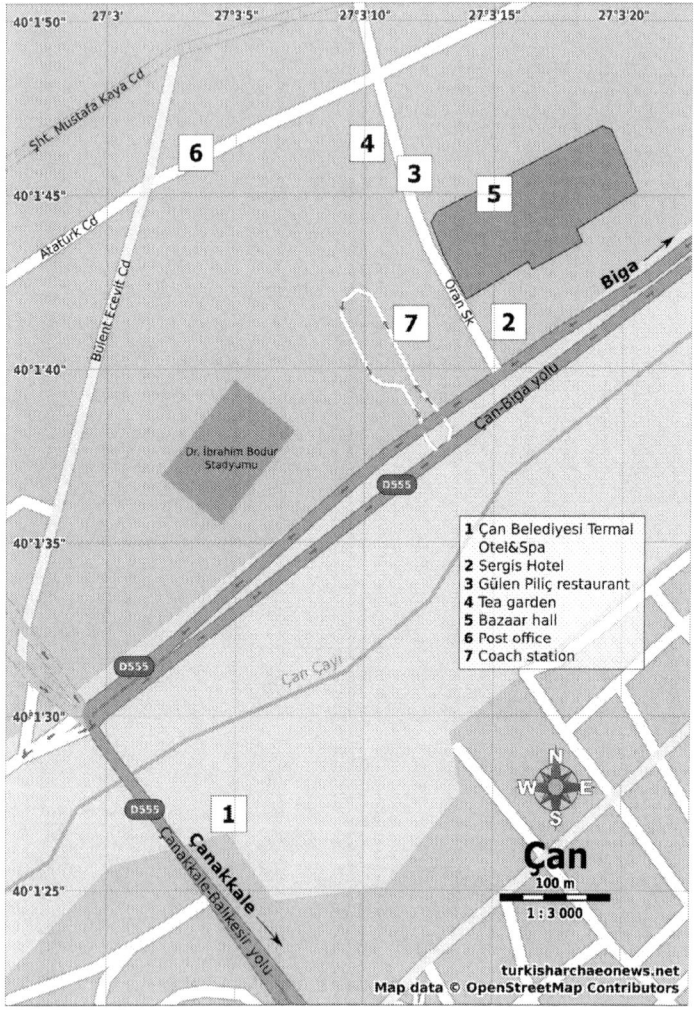

Plan of Çan

Bean salad (piyaz) from Çan

drink called ayran.

Of course, in Çan there are many more restaurants, all serving typical Turkish cuisine. The easiest way to find a place that suits your needs is to stroll along Şht. Mustafa Kaya Street, running through the center of the town.

An excellent place to rest is the spacious square, delimited by the streets of Millet, Oran, Atatürk, and Belediye. You can recognise it by the monument of Mustafa Kemal Atatürk. There are ponds where ducks swim and a lovely tea garden to relax.

Shopping and services

The biggest bazaar in Çan is held every Sunday in a specially con-structed hall (tr. *Çan Belediyesi Kapalı Pazar Yeri*). There are also numerous grocery stores, as well as clothing and industrial shops plus several supermarkets and discount stores of BİM network (on Atatürk and Çanakkale streets), Şok network (on Çanakkale Street), and A101 network (on Banka Street).

Banks and ATMs are mainly located along Şht. Mustafa Kaya Street. The post office is located at Atatürk Street.

Getting there

By coach: Çan coach station is situated on D555 road, next to the bazaar hall and Sergis Hotel. The coaches departing from it go to many cities and towns in the Troad (Altınoluk, Biga, Çanakkale, Yenice) and other destinations, including Ankara (11 hours), Bursa (4 hours), and Istanbul (8 hours)

By car: it has already been mentioned that Çan is located far away from the main communication routes of the Troad. The town is hidden in central Troad, far away from the sea. The easiest way to get there is by taking D200 route from Bandırma to Çanakkale. Turn off this road to the south in Biga and drive 35 km along D555 route.

Yenice

COORDINATES: 41.2001° N, 32.3281° E

Of all the twelve districts of Çanakkale Province, Yenice is probably the least likely to be visited by travellers. This is not surprising – as this district, located deep inland in the Troad region, has almost nothing to offer to visitors. There are no interesting sights or coastal beaches, only dense forests, among which a few villages and settlements of the district are hidden. The capital of the district – Yenice – is a tiny town, with only eight thousand inhabitants, and a provincial ambience where the sight of a foreigner still causes a surprise.

BRIEF HISTORY

The history of human settlement in the area of Yenice district is very long, as evidenced by the ruins of buildings from the Roman and Byzantine times, scattered on its territory. However, they have not been excavated so far and are extremely difficult to find among fields and dense forests. The exception is the nearby Yenice Tumulus, where researchers have found the remains of buildings from the Hellenistic period. Several exhibits found there are now in the collections of the Troy Museum.

However, the area around Yenice has always remained somewhat on the margin of the main events in the region. When the first president of the Turkish Republic – Mustafa Kemal Atatürk – travelled through Yenice on the way to Çanakkale, this event made a great impression on the locals. They even erected a suitable commemorative fountain in the place where he stopped for a brief chat with the villagers to remember about this extraordinary event.

The history of Yenice is marked with frequent earthquakes. Seismographic studies have shown that the town lies on the Yenice-Gönen Fault, which is an extension of the North-Anatolian Fault. It is a geological boundary between the Anatolian plate and the Eurasian plate. The earliest earthquake recorded by historians leveled Yenice to the ground in 1440. However, it is known that it was not the first earthquake in this area, and seismologists say that the frequency of these events is about 660 years. The most recent earthquake with the epicenter in Yenice, of magnitude 7.4, occurred in 1953, and its consequences were tragic. 998 people were killed in the district, and thousands of buildings collapsed. The tremors were felt even in Greece and Bulgaria, and the size of the disaster prompted the authorities of Turkey and Greece to introduce new building regulations.

Yenice was completely rebuilt after the earthquake, according to the new urban plan. The modern layout of the town is now visible in the form of wide streets, that distinguish Yenice from the villages that have preserved the traditional form of settlement – concentrated along narrow and winding lanes. The residents of the town are engaged mainly in agriculture – planting cereals, beans, tomatoes, and tobacco. There is a factory of tomato puree – famous domates salçası – an indispensable ingredient of many Turkish dishes.

SIGHTSEEING

Although Yenice does not have a lot of tourist attractions, the town authorities are making efforts to lure tourists to this part of the Troad. The main attraction of the district are beautiful pine forests with the endemic species Abies equi-Trojani, i.e. the Trojan fir. The most popular type of entertainment in Yenice area is wild boar hunting.

There is also small Ethnographic Museum (tr. *Belediye Türkevi Müzesi*), with exhibited costumes, ceramics, carpets, and jewelry. The venue is open every day except Sunday. In addition, there is a centuries-old plane tree, treated as a local curiosity by Yenice inhabitants.

The most important historic building in the area is a 600-year-old wooden mosque, located to the north-east of Yenice, on the road connecting Çakıroba and Seyvan villages. This building, standing among old Ottoman-period tombs, underwent a complete renovation in 2014.

VISITOR TIPS

Yenice is situated on the route D555, almost entirely on its southern side. Just before entering the town, this road forks off, and two parallel streets – Biga Caddesi and Mareşal Fevzi Çakmak Caddesi – run through the center of Yenice. Along these streets, the most important institutions of the town are located, including a town hall, a post office, and several banks (with ATMs). Also in this area, operate grocery stores, including – discount stores of BIM network, as well as bakeries and pastry shops. The bazaar area is situated along Çarşı Caddesi. Nearby, you can also find several simple eateries, restaurants, and a tea salon, oriented mainly to male clientele.

The only hotel in the center of the city – Aksu Otel – is located on the corner of Maresal Fevzi Çakmak and PTT streets, but its decor does not encourage staying there for a night. If you want to spend the night in Yenice, Kazdağ Göknar Hotel is a much better choice. It is located at the southern end of the town, on the Çukur Sokak Street No. 54. This hotel has an outdoor swimming pool in the garden, rents bicycles for its guests, and offers barbecue facilities and wireless Internet connection. Breakfast is included in the price and the hotel also has a restaurant and a bar. A hiking trail leading up to the mountains starts near the hotel.

The most luxurious accommodation option nearby is İliada-Kazdağı Hotel, located in the town of Kalkım, about 23 km to the south of Yenice. This hotel offers the possibility of hiking in Ida Mountain massif and many types of outdoor activities.

GETTING THERE

BY PUBLIC TRANSPORT: coaches and minibuses heading to Ayvacık, Bayramiç, Biga, Çanakkale, Ezine, Kalkım, and Küçükkuyu pass through Yenice.

BY CAR: Although Yenice is located in the heart of the Troad, all major transport routes in the region lead along the coast of the Aegean Sea, the Dardanelles and the Sea of Marmara. As a result of such an organization of roads in the region, despite the apparent time saving resulting from taking a shortcut through the center of the Troad, this inland route will take much more time than a longer way around. If you decide to drive through Yenice, then you have to take D555 route, from the western or the eastern direction. Alternatively, there are winding local roads linking Yenice with Biga in the north (45 km), and Edremit in the south (60 km). The distance to Çanakkale in the west is 90 km, and to reach Balıkesir, located in the south-east, you need to travel 100 km.

Southern Troad

From a historical and geographical point of view, two parts of the Troad – the Northern and the Southern – are an indivisible entity. The suggested division is applied to facilitate the planning of itineraries and selecting a convenient accommodation base. Therefore, by the Southern Troad, we will understand this part of the Biga Peninsula, which lies to the south of an imaginary line drawn at a latitude of Troy. The south-eastern part of the peninsula, near Edremit, belongs administratively to the Balıkesir Province. However, historically and geographically, this division is not well founded, so this region of the Troad is covered by this guidebook.

The Southern Troad is relatively unknown among tourists. While the northern part of the Biga Peninsula is famous because of the ruins of Troy and the bustling capital of the province – Çanakkale – its southern part is often omitted in travel plans. This state of affairs is due to the location of the biggest tourist attractions of the region: at a considerable distance from the main transport route leading to the south, in the direction of well-known holiday resorts on the Aegean Sea.

Do not miss

During your stay in the region of Southern Troad necessarily visit:

- Mount Ida – an excellent hiking and nature-watching destination;
- Babakale – the westernmost tip of Asia Minor;
- one of the ancient cities of the region, with Assos being the most picturesque one.

Gallipoli Peninsula and the Troad

Geography and transportation

The main road leading through the Southern Troad is the E87 route. It goes from the north, from the direction of Çanakkale, through Ezine and Ayvacık, to Edremit. Between Ezine and Küçük-kuyu this road takes an inland route, far away from the coast, so it is not really scenic. Also, to see the most famous monuments of the Southern Troad, it is necessary to take other, local roads, in the direction of the Aegean Sea.

The Southern Troad is dominated by the massive of Ida Mountain, known from the mythology as the place from where the Greek gods observed the actions of the Trojan War. The southern slopes of the mountain descend to the Aegean coast, where numerous holiday resorts are located. This stretch of the coast reaches the town of Edremit in the eastern direction.

Suggested sightseeing route

It is possible to travel very quickly from Ezine to Edremit, by taking the international route E87. However, in order to see the most impressive archaeological sites of the region, exit this road near Ezine, and head to the south-western part of the Troad along narrower and less frequented roads. In this way, you can reach the ruins of Alexandria Troas and Neandria, the Temple of Apollon Smintheion in Gülpınar, Babakale fortress, and the extensive remains of ancient Assos. Then you can get back to the E87 route near the town of Ayvacık. Next, by following the E87 route along the southern coast of the Troad, you get to the massif of Ida Mountain and can visit ancient Antandros and modern Edremit, before embarking on the journey to the south or the east of Turkey.

If you select the shorter variant of the itinerary, bypassing the south-western Troad, you will have about 85 km to drive from Ezine to Edremit. This way only one day is enough to visit the nearby tourist attractions, unless you stop for the night on the coast, or decide to explore the peaks of Ida Mountain. However, in the case of a more thorough exploration of the Southern Troad, along the longer route through Gülpınar, Babakale, and Assos,

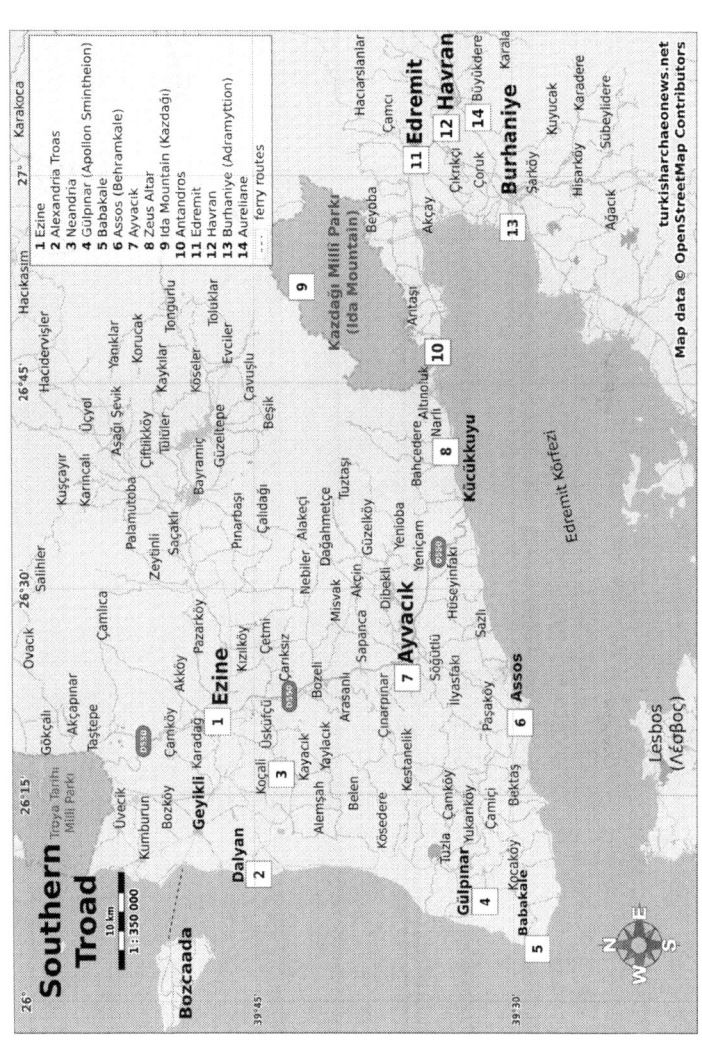

Map of Southern Troad

the minimal time required to appreciate the region is two days, and the route is about 165 km long. Keep in mind that public transport between the villages of the Troad is virtually nonexistent. Without a car, be prepared for long waiting hours for minibusses, and take into account the possible need to postpone sightseeing until the next day.

ACCOMMODATION

The majority of towns and villages described in this guidebook offers at least one hotel, a guest house, or a teachers' house. The widest choice of accommodation options can be found in Assos (Behramkale), and in the holiday villages located on the coast below the southern slopes of Mount Ida. You can also find accommodation in the villages located in the massif of Ida Mountain. Detailed advice on accommodation options available in particular towns is presented in the relevant chapters of this book.

VIEWPOINTS AND BEACHES

The most beautiful viewpoints in the Southern Troad are located on the peaks of local hills and mountains. The region looks especially attractive from the ruins of Neandria, and from the peak of Mount Ida. Scenic views of the Aegean Sea can be observed from the so-called Altar of Zeus, located in Mount Ida massif. Remember also about the castle of Babakale, standing on the westernmost point of Asia Minor. Unforgettable views of the Aegean Sea and its coast stretch from this fortress.

The E87 route is not a particularly picturesque road in this region of the Troad, because it is far away from the coast, winding through forests and vast fields. It gets back to the coast near the village of Küçükkuyu, but this part of the Aegean coast is densely built-up by the summer cottages. Here you can find the best options for sunbathing and relaxing at the seaside.

An additional attraction of the Southern Troad is a cruise to a Turkish island in the Aegean Sea, known as Bozcaada. Ferries to the island leave from the harbor of Geyikli İskelesi, located 4 km to the west of Geyikli town.

Ezine

COORDINATES: 39.7844° N, 26.3375° E

Ezine is a small town located in the southern part of Çanakkale Province. Its location makes this sleepy little town an excellent base for the tourists visiting the sights in the Biga Peninsula, i.e. the ancient Troad region. The most famous product from Ezine is the local cheese, called, of course, Ezine peyniri. It is made from cow, sheep, and goat milk, and the secret of its flavour lies apparently in the process of maturation in tin containers. This cheese can be purchased at many stores throughout the town. It's hard to miss the opportunity to buy this speciality, even if you are only passing through Ezine via the main road, as signs and ads are visible everywhere.

BRIEF HISTORY

The earliest traces of human settlement in the area of Ezine were found on nearby Çaltıkıran Tepe mound. However, the history of the town started only with the arrival of Turkish tribes to the area of Asia Minor. The local Danishmend tribe contributed significantly to its development, establishing the Great Mosque (tr. *Ulu Cami*). It is known that at that time, i.e. in the 14th century, the settlement was known as İğne – 'Needle.'

SIGHTSEEING

The most famous mosque in Ezine is Seferşah Camii, also called Abdurrahman Camii. It was built in the 14th century, during the reign of Sultan Bayezid I. It is one of the earliest examples of the mosques in typical Ottoman style. The walls were built of stone, and the vaulted ceilings – of bricks. The wall with the mihrab has four windows on two levels. Apparently the building material was obtained from the ruins of the ancient city of Neandria. Next to the mosque, there is the tomb of the fourteenth-century hermit called Ahi Yunus. In the neighborhood, on Tea Street (tr. *Çay Sokak*), there is Seferşah Hamamı bathhouse, built at the same time as Seferşah Mosque. The bathhouse has been restored and still welcomes customers, separately men and women as the tradition dictates.

Another notable mosque in Ezine is the Great Mosque (tr. *Ulu Cami*), also known as Yazicizade Cami, built in 1382, during the reign of a local Danishmend dynasty, but completely rebuilt in 1828. It is near the bridge over the Akçin River, on Ulucami Kısığı Street. You should also look into the Olive Mosque (tr. *Zeytinli Cami*), standing at the intersection of Nahit Şenoğul and Uzun streets, on the western side of the town. Both these buildings were erected with the fragments of Roman buildings, and it is worth paying attention to their porches with clearly visible ancient columns.

To the east, just a few hundred meters away from Ezine, flows Karamenderes River, in ancient times known as Scamander. One of its tributaries – Akçin River – flows through the center of the town, although the view of this brook is not attractive in the middle of summer. A city park is an excellent place to spend an afternoon, with an inherent tea garden and a playground for children. The tea served there is tasty, strong, and cheap.

Ezine is a convenient base for exploring the sights in Southern Troad. The ruins of the ancient city of Neandria are located only 14 km from Ezine and the ruins of Alexandria Troas are 22 km away. The Temple of Apollon Smintheion, i.e. the Lord of Mice, is situated 50 km from the town.

Orientation

Ezine is located near D550 transit route, and the historic district is situated on the western side of this road, on Akçin River. To get to this part of Ezine, turn into Atatürk Street from D550 road, and drive in the direction of Seferşah Mosque. If you head westward from this point, you will reach Long Street (tr. *Uzun Sokak*), with the buildings dating back to the early 20th century. If you go to the south, down Seferşah or Çay streets, you arrive at the bridge over the river, leading into the city park. The modern part of the town extends to the south of D550 road.

Accommodation

Baransel Hotel is located in the centre of Ezine, on Çay Sokak no. 6/C. The hotel has an official category of two stars, and the rates are quite high. The rooms are not very big but equipped with a private bathroom and a refrigerator. Not all rooms have balconies, there is no elevator, and the floors are high. Service is friendly and willing to help, but only Turkish is spoken by the staff.

The big advantage of the hotel is breakfast, served in the restaurant on the top floor. You can dine in the spacious hall or the terrace overlooking the town. Breakfasts are generous, and the choice of ingredients is much wider than in many other hotels. Another attraction is the chance to taste the famous local cheese.

The second option of accommodation in the town center is the local Teachers' House, on Zubeyde Hanım Meydanı Square. It has 12 guest rooms, but often they are all occupied by teachers.

Restaurants

Steer clear of Pino Restaurant, located next door to Baransel Hotel. Maybe we were unlucky, but the dumplings (tr. *mantı*) that were served to us were extremely distasteful and dry. Fortunately, a delicious beef and vegetable stew compensated this unfortunate experience. Stuffed peppers (tr. *biber dolma*) were prepared correctly. The prices for non-alcoholic drinks were at a medium level.

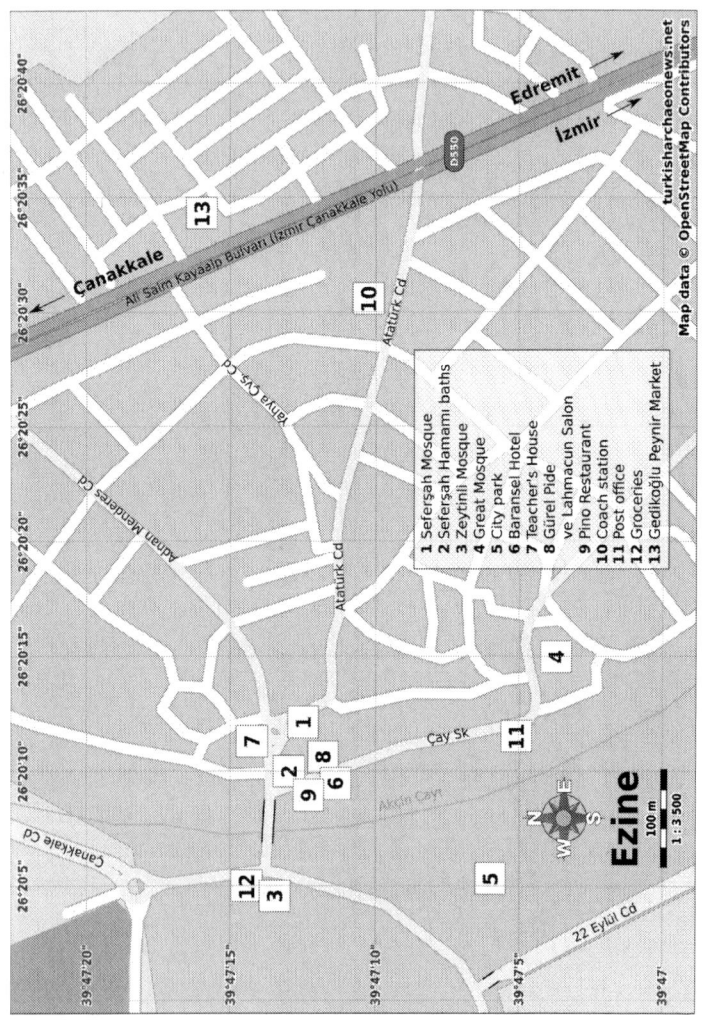

1 Seferşah Mosque
2 Seferşah Hamamı baths
3 Zeytinli Mosque
4 Great Mosque
5 City park
6 Baransel Hotel
7 Teacher's House
8 Gürel Pide
  ve Lahmacun Salon
9 Pino Restaurant
10 Coach station
11 Post office
12 Groceries
13 Gedikoğlu Peynir Market

Ezine
100 m
1:3 500

Plan of Ezine

Opposite Baransel Hotel, there are several small eateries, specializing in various Turkish dishes. The bar called Gürel Pide ve Lahmacun Salonu offers different varieties of Turkish pizza (tr. *pide*), and several kinds of soups and kebabs. While pide was delightful, ezogelin soup and Adana kebab were too heavily salted, which unfortunately happens very often in restaurants operating in the Troad region.

Shopping and services

The biggest cheese shop in Ezine – Gedikoğlu Peynir Market – is located right on the transit route D550. In the center of the town, there are many groceries, bank branches with ATMs, and a post office. The local bazaar is held every Monday.

Getting there

By car: the distance from Çanakkale to Ezine is 47 km via E87 (D550) route. This road has been rebuilt for many years now, and the journey may be painfully slow.

By coach: local coach connections from Ezine include: Ayvacık, Çanakkale, Dalyan (near Alexandria Troas), Edremit, Gülpınar (with the Temple of Apollon Smintheion), and Babakale. Long-distance coaches go from Ezine to Ankara (12 hours), Antalya (12 hours), Aydın (7 hours), Denizli (9 hours), İzmir (5 hours), Istanbul (9 hours), and many other locations.

By ferry: the ferry terminal to Bozcaada Island is situated 17 km to the west from Ezine. The terminal is known as Yükyeri İskelesi, near Geyikli village. The ferries usually depart three times per day, and the cruise takes 30 minutes. The road to the ferry terminal is clearly signposted. The terminal is also served by minibuses from Çanakkale and Ezine.

Alexandria Troas

COORDINATES: 39.7527° N, 26.1553° E

Alexandria Troas was the ancient port city in the Troad, founded by Antigonus I Monophthalmus – one of the generals of Alexander the Great – as Antigoneia. After the death of Antigonus, another Macedonian commander – Lysimachus – controlled the Troad. The city was then renamed to Alexandria, in honour of the great Macedonian leader. Because there were many cities called Alexandria in those days, this particular Alexandria was given the term 'Troas' or 'from the Troad.'

BRIEF HISTORY

According to ancient sources, the settlement in the area of Alexandria Troas had already existed before the Hellenistic period, and it was called Sigeia (Sigia). Antigonus I Monophthalmus only contributed to its development, through the resettlement of the residents of the surrounding towns of Gargara, Hamaxitos, Neandria, Kolonai, Larisa, Kebren, and Skepsis. It happened about 310 BCE.

With time, Alexandria Troas became the most important port city in the north-western part of Asia Minor, as well as the richest city of the Troad. It owed its spectacular development to its strategic position, on the Aegean coast near the entrance to the Dardanelles. It meant that Alexandria was a convenient harbour for the transit of goods transported on the route from the east to the port of Neapolis in Macedonia, and further – to Rome. Additional sources of income for the city were salty springs in Larisa, mines, farmland, and the income from the temple of Apollon Smintheion.

ALEXANDRIA TROAS

In the Roman times, Alexandria Troas acquired the status of a free and autonomous city. It is estimated that the city had a population of 100,000 people in the days of its greatest prosperity. Successive Roman emperors, including Augustus and Hadrian, contributed to the development of the city. A famous Roman statesman, philosopher, and man of substance – Herodes Atticus – was appointed by Emperor Hadrian to the position of the prefect of the free cities of Asia, in 125 CE. While holding this title, he funded the aqueduct of Alexandria Troas, fragments of which have been preserved to our times. Herodes Atticus was also a sponsor of a local theater and baths.

A small Christian community already existed in Alexandria in the middle of the first century CE, as we know from the New Testament, namely the Letters of St. Paul, and the Acts of the Apostles. Because Alexandria Troas was an important port, it was the starting point for St. Paul when he set sail to Europe during his second missionary journey (50-52 CE). The Apostle visited the city again, during his third missionary journey (53-58 CE). According to the New Testament, during his stay, he restored to life a young man named Eutychus. This man came to Alexandria Troas to hear the speech of St. Paul, but he fell asleep from exhaustion and fell from the third floor.

In the Byzantine era, Alexandria Troas held the rank of a bishopric, and the names of some of its bishops are known. Even in the 10th century CE, it appears in historical records as a diocese governed from Cyzicus. Currently, the city is still the seat of the titular bishop of the Roman Catholic Church as Troadensis, but its last titular bishop – Joseph-Alphonse Baud – resigned from this function in 1971. Alexandria Troas is also the titular diocese of the Orthodox Church.

Apparently, Emperor Constantine the Great had an intention of making Alexandria Troas the new capital of the empire, but in the end, his choice fell to Byzantium, later known as Constantinople. It is not known exactly when the city was abandoned, but with the growing importance of Constantinople, Alexandria Troas lost

Ruins of Alexandria Troas

its leading position in the region. In 267 CE, the Goths sacked the city, which had a substantial negative impact on its economic situation. It is known that over time the port was silted up, and the town fell into disrepair. In medieval times, travellers who saw the remains of Alexandria from the sea suspected that these had been the ruins of the legendary Troy.

In the first half of the 14th century, the Troad fell under the control of the Karasid dynasty, one of the nomadic Turkish tribes. They formed the so-called Karası Beylik, i.e. a small Turkish principality governed by a bey, covering the area of the current provinces of Balıkesir, Çanakkale, and Bergama. In 1336, Karası Beylik was conquered by Orhan Gazi from the Ottoman dynasty. This way, the Ottomans gained a convenient starting point for the campaign of conquest of European territories, located on the other shore of the Dardanelles.

In the Ottoman times, the ruins of Alexandria Troas were known as Eski Istanbul, i.e. Old Istanbul. The reason for the prosperity of the city in ancient times - its location at the crossroads of land and sea routes – became the reason for the current, deplorable condition of the ruins of Alexandria Troas. Since the city was easy

178

to reach, it was not difficult to demolish it, to obtain excellent construction materials. For example, the columns adorning the Yeni Valide Mosque in Istanbul were transported from Alexandria Troas.

In the 18th century, European travellers reported that Alexandria Troas was abandoned and completely ruined. They also complained that it was a good hiding place for local robbers, lurking for travelers. It was also reported that the ruins were used by the Ottoman government that exported architectural elements to Istanbul. Local farmers used the sarcophagi as cisterns of street fountains, and granite blocks were transformed into cannonballs for the Ottoman army.

Archaeological research has been conducted in Alexandria Troas since 1993, under the management of scientists from the Westphalian Wilhelm University of Münster.

SIGHTSEEING

The ruins of Alexandria Troas occupy the area of about 400 hectares, but most of it is heavily overgrown with bushes. The outline of the old city walls is still visible, in some places quite well preserved. The total length of the walls was once 10 km, with defensive towers placed at regular intervals. One of the main roads to the city led through the Eastern Gate, also known as the Neandria Gate, built in the 3rd century BCE.

The preserved ancient buildings of Alexandria Troas include five odeons, a bath, a theater, a gymnasium, a necropolis, a nymphaeum, and a recently discovered stadium, dating back to 100 BCE. The aqueduct of Emperor Trajan is located in the eastern part of the city.

At the highest point in the area of Alexandria, there are the remains of the theater from the Hellenistic times. The people in the audience, in addition to the performances taking place there, could admire stunning views of the entire city, distant buildings of Neandria, the islands of Bozcaada and Lesbos, and the Aegean Sea.

The best preserved Roman building in Alexandria Troas is a complex consisting of a gymnasium and baths, built with the funds provided by Herodes Atticus. The ruins of this building are now

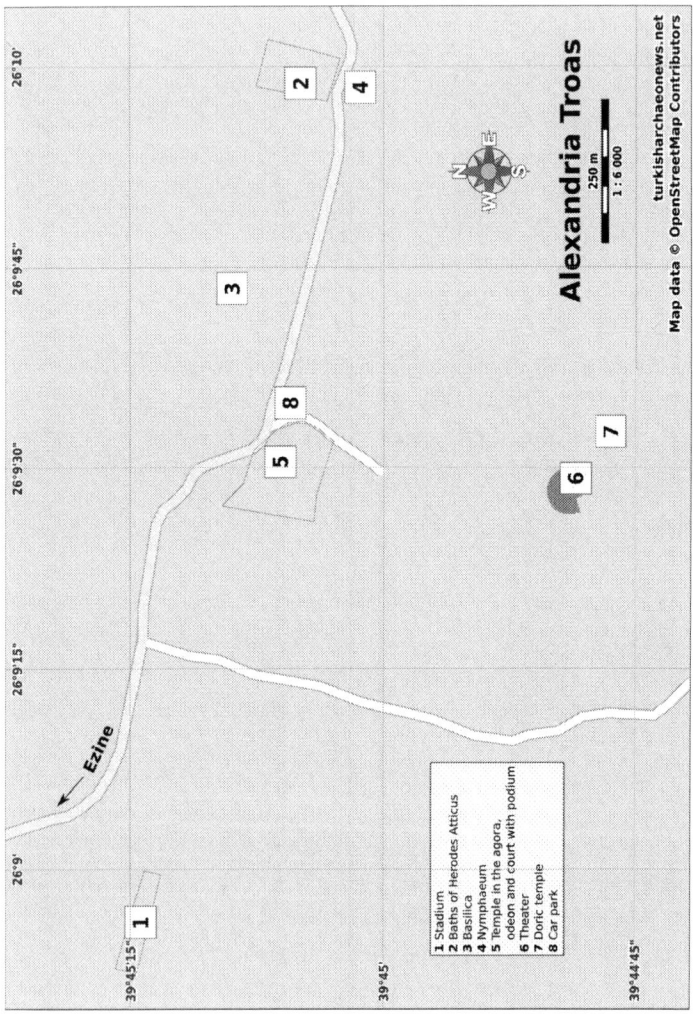

Alexandria Troas

1 Stadium
2 Baths of Herodes Atticus
3 Basilica
4 Nymphaeum
5 Temple in the agora,
  odeon and court with podium
6 Theater
7 Doric temple
8 Car park

turkisharchaeonews.net

250 m

1 : 6 000

Map data © OpenStreetMap Contributors

Ezine

Plan of Alexandria Troas

Baths of Herodes Atticus in Alexandria Troas

known among the local population as Bal Saray or Honey Palace. The dimensions of the baths are 123 to 84 meters.

The former harbour, consisting of two bays, is now completely silted up. Archaeological work has recently been conducted on its territory.

VISITOR TIPS

The ruins of Alexandria Troas are located near the village of Dalyan in Çanakkale Province, about 10 km to the south of the town of Geyikli. The area to visit is quite large, located on both sides of a road. A part of the area is heavily overgrown, so take care to protect your legs and feet from thorny bushes. Admission to the ruins is free of charge. The site is open to visitors every day, from 8:30 am to 7:00 pm (5:00 pm in winter months).The parking place is situated on the right side of the road, if you are coming from the north, next to the temple in the agora.

Accommodation

Just 1 km north of Alexandria Troas, on the Aegean coast, lies the tiny holiday resort of Dalyan. If you plan to stay overnight in this area, it is worth checking if there are places available in local hotels: Odunluk Taş Konak, Sunset Troia, and Geyikli Aqua Otel.

Getting there

By public transport: in summer season there are hourly minibuses from Ezine and Geyikli to Dalyan. In winter, the frequency of minibuses is much lower. You have to walk or hitch-hike the last leg of the trip – from Dalyan to Alexandria Troas.

By car: drive to the west from Ezine, through Geyikli to Dalyan. In Geyikli take the road heading to the south (to the left), as the road going straight ahead leads to the ferry harbour. The total distance from Ezine to Alexandria Troas is 22 km.

Neandria

COORDINATES: 39.7233° N, 26.2737° E

Neandria ruins are the remains of an ancient city in the area of the Troad, on the slopes of Çığrı Mountain. The ruins of Neandria are not very impressive, but getting there is the challenging part of the travel experience. Additionally, the views from the mountain top may reward the hiking efforts.

BRIEF HISTORY

Neandria was founded as a Greek colony by Aeolian settlers, most probably around 700 BCE. From 454 to 431 BCE, the city was a member of the Delian League as Neandreies. In 399 BCE, it was incorporated into the Persian Empire. The city history is relatively short because around 310 BCE Neandria was entirely abandoned by its inhabitants who were resettled in the newly founded harbour city. The person responsible for this decision was Antigonus I Monophthalmus – one of the generals of Alexander the Great. After the death of the Macedonian king, Antigonus became the ruler of the western Asia Minor. His goal, however, was to conquer all the lands once controlled by Alexander. His ambitions enraged the other Macedonian leaders who joined their forces and defeated him at the Battle of Ipsus in 301 BCE.

Before his death, Antigonus founded the harbour city Antigoneia, later known as Alexandria Troas. The inhabitants of Neandria were resettled there. However, the issue of the city walls that encircle Neandria remains one of the archaeological puzzles. There is some evidence that suggests that the city was not fortified during the Persian rule. The archaic walls surrounded the acropolis

Ruins of Neandria

area only. The style of the walls encircling the whole settlement indicates that their construction took place in the early Hellenistic period, just before the abandonment of the city or even afterwards.

An interesting hypothesis has been put forward by F. E. Winter from the University of Toronto. According to his suggestions, after the inhabitants of Neandria had been resettled to Alexandria Troas, the ruler of this region, Antigonus I Monophthalmus or the victorious general of the Battle of Ipsus – Lysimachus, decided to transform Neandria into a fortress. The strategic location of Neandria in the south-western Troad seems to confirm their motivation for this move. The mountain where Neandria once stood offers a magnificent view over the valley of river Scamander (now Karamenderes) and the vast plain from the Dardanelles to the mouth of the river Satnioeis (now Tuzla Çay). In the turbulent times after the death of Alexander the Great, the great tactical importance of such a well-situated fortress was difficult to neglect.

The Winter's hypothesis is further confirmed by the reinforcement of the defensive walls and the erection in the central area of Neandria of evenly planned buildings (barracks) as well as the complete lack of any traces that could testify to the existence of the city (e.g. coins or graves) in this location after 310 BCE. The civil buildings (a temple, an agora, and a theatre) were neglected after this date.

However, even if a fortress existed in Neandria in the late 4th century or the early 3rd century BCE, it was also abandoned, in 280 BCE at the latest. There are also some premises to believe that in Roman times a small settlement existed there. It would have had a connection with the nearby quarries where the marble has been acquired until today. No traces have been found so far from this Roman village.

ARCHAEOLOGICAL RESEARCH

The first archaeological excavations in Neandria were conducted in 1865 by Frank Calvert – a British diplomat and amateur archaeologist who is more widely recognised as the discoverer of Troy, several years before Heinrich Schliemann. The second scholar who demonstrated some interest in Neandria was J. T. Clarke, who visited it in 1880.

Most of the work in Neandria ruins was conducted in 1899 by the German architect and amateur archaeologist Robert Johann Koldewey. He is mostly known from his excavations in Babylon. His interest in Neandria lasted for one season only and, although he expressed the opinion that further work would have been fascinating, no one has taken up this challenge until now.

SIGHTSEEING

Although Neandria has been abandoned for almost 2.5 thousand years, its remains are in quite a good state of preservation. This fact results from the location of this ancient city – far away from modern human settlements. Therefore, the ruins were not used as a convenient source of construction materials.

The defense walls that surround Neandria are of a polygonal shape. They encompass the area 1400 meters long and 450 meters wide. The walls are 3 meters thick, and their total length is more than 3 km. The older parts of the internal city walls surrounded the acropolis in the north-eastern part of the city.

Ruins of Neandria

The most important discovery in Neandria were the ruins of the Apollo Temple, built the 7th or 6th century BCE. This is the oldest known example of a Greek temple in the area of Asia Minor. This building consisted of one room 9 meters wide and 20 meters long. The columns of this temple, decorated with the capitals of Aeolian order, can be seen in the Archaeological Museum in Istanbul.

Moreover, in the Neandria area, a necropolis was found with sarcophagi, monumental tombs and pithoi i.e. large clay vessels used for the storage purposes.

VISITOR TIPS

The entrance to Neandria is free of charge. Wear sturdy hiking boots and remember about protection against strong sun. Bring your own supplies of food and water.

Accommodation

The nearest accommodation options are available in Ezine and Çanakkale.

GETTING THERE

Getting to Neandria is not an easy task. It is practically impossible to get there without a car. If you have one, drive to a small village called Kayacık Köyü. The distance from Çanakkale is 58 km and from Ezine – 14 km. If you are heading to Neandria from Çanakkale, keep to E87 route until you reach Ezine. There turn in the south-western direction and drive to Kayacık Köyü.

The car is useless in the further part of this journey, so leave it in the village, in its main (and only) square. From there you must continue on foot. The trail leads up, and the path is rocky and uneven. The total distance to walk is 1.8 km – take your own water and cover your head from the sun. If in doubt, ask the villagers for directions to the ruins.

Gülpınar (Apollon Smintheion)

COORDINATES: 39.5362° N, 26.1175° E

The ruins of a temple dedicated to Apollo 'Lord of Mice' Smintheus are located in a quiet village of Gülpınar on the Biga Peninsula. Why did one of the gods of the Greek pantheon earn the nickname associated with rodents, and why was his temple built in the Troad? There are no clear answers to these questions, but when searching for them it is necessary to start from the source, that is, from Homer.

BRIEF HISTORY

Apollo – Lord of Mice?

The history of Apollo as the Lord of Mice started with the following fragment of the Iliad:

> 'Not a word' he spoke, but went by the shore of the sounding sea and prayed apart to King Apollo whom lovely Leto had borne. 'Hear me,' he cried, 'O god of the silver bow, that protectest Chryse and holy Cilla and rulest Tenedos with thy might, hear me oh thou of Sminthe. If I have ever decked your temple with garlands, or burned your thigh-bones in fat of bulls or goats, grant my prayer, and let your arrows avenge these my tears upon the Danaans.'
>
> Homer, the Iliad, Book I, translated by Samuel Butler

With these words, the priest of Apollo, Chryses, begs the god to bring the revenge on the Greeks. Their main commander,

188

Agamemnon, abducted his daughter, Chryseis. Apollo listened to this request, sent the plague onto the Greek army, and Chryseis was returned to her father. This situation became a source of conflict between Agamemnon and Achilles, the main theme of the Iliad.

The most enigmatic word in the quoted passage is the nickname 'Sminthe', given by Chryses to Apollo. The ancient Greeks had already found this word incomprehensible and attributed its origins to one of the Anatolian languages. Modern linguists agree with this opinion and derive the word from the Luvian language. Unfortunately, the epic poem of Homer does not provide any hints at the meaning of this word. Therefore, subsequent myths of Apollo tried to explain this nickname on the basis of the context in which it had been used in the Iliad. Since Apollo sent the plague on the Greeks, he was associated with rodents as major disease carriers. Therefore, Apollo as the god that could send or finish an epidemic, became the 'Lord of Mice'.

SETTLEMENT MYTHS AND ERECTION OF THE TEMPLE

All mythical stories about the foundation of the Greek city of Chrysa in the Troad are associated with the erection of the Temple of Apollon Smintheion. According to the earliest tradition, derived from Callinus of Ephesus from the 7th century BCE, a settlement was founded by the Cretans of Trojan origins. The oracle ordered them to set up the city in the place where they had been attacked by 'the sons of the earth.' It was very unclear, typical style of the oracle, but the prophecy was clarified when the settlers were attacked by mice that ate all the leather parts of their inventory. In a place where this unusual attack occurred, the town was founded and the temple of 'the Lord of Mice' was built.

Please note that the name of Chrysa is sometimes used alternately with the name Hamaxitus, while other sources claim that the settlement Chrysa was far away from the Temple of Apollo, which was in Hamaxitus. This would mean that they were two different places.

It is now known that the Temple of Apollon Smintheion was located in a place rich in sources of clean water. They were cru-

Temple of Apollon Smintheion

cial for the business of the Apollonian oracle. The sanctuary in Hamaxitus was known in ancient times, not only among the inhabitants of the Troad, but also among the pilgrims from all over the Aegean Sea region.

ARCHITECTURE OF THE TEMPLE

The Temple of Apollon Smintheion was built in the mid-second century BCE, in the so-called pseudodipteral style. It was a typical plan in the Hellenistic period, and its creation was attributed to Hermogenes of Priene. The name of the architect of the Temple of Apollo is unknown, but it can be assumed that he was a disciple of Hermogenes.

The temple represents the Ionic order. The dimensions of the foundations are 22.40 to 40.27 meters. Originally, it was surrounded by the colonnade, with eight columns on the front and back of the building, and 14 columns at each side. All columns stood on a marble platform. The body of each column comprised of seven drums. The highest drum was decorated with scenes from the Iliad or a bucranium, i.e. bas-relief decorative motif in the shape of the head of an ox. The capitals of the columns were in the Ionic order.

In the central part of the temple, i.e. in its naos, a statue of the god Apollo once stood. The fragments of this statue, found by archaeologists, allowed to estimate that it was about 5 meters high. Its creator was, most probably, a well-known sculptor Skopas of Paros. The exact appearance of the statue in all its glory is not known. However, the coins found in nearby Alexandria Troas show a figure standing in front of the Temple of Apollo and trampling a mouse. An alternative version is that mice presented on the statue were not being trampled, but they were surrounding the deity.

The entablature of the temple was richly decorated. The architrave was separated from the frieze by the so-called cymatium, i.e. a continuous sculptural element. Two motifs present on the cymatium from the Temple of Apollon Smintheion are 'egg-and-dart' (or egg-and-tongue) – consisting of an egg-shaped object alternating with an element shaped like an arrow, and the 'string of pearls' (bead-and-reel) – alternating spherical and cylindrical elements.

The most interesting preserved architectural element of the temple is its frieze, where the scenes from Homer's Iliad are presented in bas-relief. Decorative elements of the entablature are complemented by the teeth (denticuli) – rectangular cubes on the bottom of the cornice, and the sima – the upturned edge of a roof which acts as a gutter.

The marble, from which the temple was built, came from the island of Proconnesus, located on the Marmara Sea, now known as the Marmara Island. The island has been known from excellent deposits of white marble since the ancient times. Both the modern name of the island, and the whole sea are derived from this material.

ARCHAEOLOGICAL RESEARCH

In modern times, the Temple of Apollon Smintheion was mentioned in 1785. It was then discovered by Jean-Baptiste Lechevalier who saw it while travelling from Babakale to Alexandria Troas. This French astronomer, explorer, and writer, was at the moment a secretary at the French embassy in Istanbul. This position allowed him to travel around Asia Minor. His memoirs of the journeys were published in 1799 under the title 'Voyage dans la Troade, ou tableau de la plaine de Troie dans son état actuel'.

In 1853, British Admiral Thomas Abel Brimage Spratt visited the temple during his work on the creation of maps of this region of Asia Minor. He identified the visible remains of buildings as the sanctuary of Apollo Smintheion, on the basis of some inscriptions. The map prepared by Spratt was later used by Heinrich Schliemann, known as the discoverer of Troy. The so-called Spratt map was made in collaboration with the German professor of classical history. Troy was already marked on this map, although with a question mark over its name.

The first archaeological excavations at the Temple of Apollo were carried out by the English architect Richard Popplewell Pullan. He received funding for the work at Teos, Priene, and the Temple of Apollon Smintheion, in the years 1863-1869. Systematic excavations were later conducted in the temple in the period

1971-1973, under the auspices of the Archaeological Museum of Çanakkale. Since 1980, ongoing excavations have been conducted by a team from the University of Ankara, under the leadership of Professor Coşkun Özgünel.

In 2004, the archaeologists working on the temple grounds found the traces of a much older settlement, from prehistoric times. So far one cultural layer has been identified, and initial dating places it in the first half of the fifth millennium BCE. According to the chronology adopted for western Anatolia, it belongs to the Middle Copper Age. Culturally, this layer of settlement from Gülpınar was included in the so-called Kumtepe A/Beşik-Siviritepe/Gulpinar horizon.

Since the resumption of archaeological excavations, the site has gained a number of sponsors, including numerous public institutions and banks, as well as Efes Pilsen brewery. This company has been financing the restoration of the temple since 1998.

Sightseeing

The main attraction of the site is the Temple of Apollo, the Lord of Mice, or rather what is left of it. Its southwestern corner has been restored, with the stairs and re-erected fragments of columns.

In addition to the temple, you can see long stretches of a road from the Roman era, along with the plumbing. There are also remains of several buildings from the Roman period. The bath building is the largest and best preserved of them. Between the Roman baths and the temple, there are the remains of Roman cisterns.

A local museum is located in a small building at the excavation site. The most important objects displayed here are the friezes from the temple, decorated with bas-reliefs depicting the scenes from the Iliad. Admission to the museum is included in the ticket to the excavation site.

Visitor tips

Visiting the ruins of the Temple of Apollo is possible every day, during the opening hours, from 8:00 am to 5:00 pm. A ticket costs 6 TL.

At the excavation site there is a small parking lot, restrooms, and a restaurant specializing in Turkish pancakes (gözleme) – especially tasty with cheese filling.

In the nearby village of Gülpınar, there are several shops and restaurants, but not a single hotel. However, you can find a post office and an ATM there.

GETTING THERE

BY COACH: several coaches per day connect Gülpınar with Ayvacık, Behramkale, Çanakkale, and Ezine.

BY MINIBUS: from Babakale, Behramkale, and Ezine.

BY CAR: drive in the south-western direction from Ezine, passing the villages of Koçali, Uluköy, and Tavaklı. The route is clearly marked with brown 'Apollon Smintheion' signposts. To reach the temple turn right in Gülpınar, into a secondary road, following the singposts. The total distance is 49 km.

From the direction of Ayvacık (from the east), there is a road to Gülpınar through Behramkale (Assos) and Bademli. The distance is 42 km.

Babakale

COORDINATES: 39.4794° N, 26.0644° E

Babakale is a small village, which lies on the south-western tip of the Troad, at the foot of an Ottoman fortress. You can get to the village only via a winding road that takes you through picturesque rock formations and forested areas. The difficulties of the travel are soon rewarded with the views of the Aegean Sea, extending from the eighteenth-century fortifications. Babakale village has an extraordinary location at Cape Baba (tr. *Bababurnu*). This cape is the westernmost point of Asia Minor, and consequently – the whole of Asia. Its location is marked by a lighthouse, standing on the cliff above the sea.

BRIEF HISTORY

In antiquity, Cape Baba was known as Lekton. According to Strabo, there was the altar of the Twelve Olympian Gods, built by Agamemnon. No traces of this ancient structure have been preserved to our times.

The present name of the village and the cape is derived from the Turkish holy hermit, called Baba, i.e. Father, who once lived in this place. Sailors from the ships passing that way threw him packets of food. When he died, a tomb was erected at the cape, and the generations of hermits took care of this shrine. They also received food from the sailors. The Ottoman name of the cape – Emek Yemez Burnu, i.e. the Cape of Doing Nothing – probably comes from those hermits and their way of spending time.

According to local stories, the village was founded by the prisoners, who got their freedom back as a reward for the work on the

Babakale Fortress

construction of the fortress. Later, their community was joined by fishermen and their families, and thus the settlement grew steadily. Currently, it has about 500 residents.

SIGHTSEEING

The main attraction of the village is a fortress towering over the area. Babakale Fortress stands out in two ways among other fortress built during the reign of the Ottoman dynasty. First of all, it is located exactly at the westernmost point of the Asian continent. Secondly, it is the last stronghold erected on the territory of modern Turkish Republic during the reign of the Ottomans.

The fortress was build in order to assist the local garrison in the fight against the pirates ravaging this part of the Aegean Sea. According to the information board located inside the fortress, the building was erected by Admiral Mustafa Pasha. He is also credited as the builder of the village mosque, baths, and a fountain.

A more extended version of the history of the fort says that it was commissioned by Sultan Ahmed III. Apparently, when he sailed nearby a storm hit the sea, and his ship sought a refuge in the local harbor. During a short stay in Babakale, the sultan learned of the enormous injustices, which his subjects experienced at the hands of pirates. For this reason, he ordered the castle to be erected. It was built by prisoners in 1720.

A stone inscription in Arabic alphabet is carved above the main gate leading into the fortress. The area inside the walls is partially overgrown with shrubs, and partially cleared out for a small football pitch. Apparently, local celebrations and weddings are also held in the fortress.

Looking from the top of the battlements, the outlines and foundations of several buildings that stood on the castle grounds are visible. One of the towers houses a modern lighthouse. The appearance of the walls indicates their recent renovation, with visible modern infill. It is possible to walk around the fortress on its ramparts as there is a narrow sidewalk. However, please note that there are no security barriers to protect you against a fall from a considerable height. Therefore, we recommend great caution while walking and taking photos.

Within the fortress, there are no additional attractions for visitors, such as a museum or an exhibition. On the other hand, the views that extend from the walls are most impressive. You can see the Aegean Sea and two islands – a Turkish one – Bozcaada, and a Greek one – Lesbos. Looking in the opposite direction you can observe Babakale village and steep hills surrounding it.

At the foot of the fortress, from the sea, there is a small cemetery with the tomb of the famous Muslim hermit Baba. In Babakale village, there is a mosque, which was built at the same time as the fortress. It is also possible to spot many well-preserved stone houses from the Ottoman era, built in a style typical for this region of Turkey.

VISITOR TIPS

Admission to Babakale fortress is free of charge. A parking lot is directly in front of the fortress.

In Babakale, you can enjoy a delicious meal at one of several restaurants that specialize in fish and squid dishes. They are located next to the castle and the harbour.

Babakale may prove to be the ideal choice for a few days of relaxation in a place far away from the hustle and bustle of civilization. There are at least three hotels, each of them has a restaurant, and offers rooms with the views of the sea and the fortress: Narcissus Motel, Balıkçı Motel, and Denizhan Hotel.

Most of the travelers decide not to stay overnight in Babakale, but go further to the east, to Assos (20 km), where the selection of accommodation options is much wider.

Getting there

By coach: there are coaches to Babakale from Ezine (2 hours) and Gülpınar (15 minutes).

By car: there is only one road to Babakale. It starts in Gülpınar (the town that boasts the Apollon Smintheion temple). If you travel along the main road of this region of the Troad, turn right in Gülpınar, and follow the signposts to Babakale. It is only 9 km away from Gülpınar.

Assos (Behramkale)

COORDINATES: 39.4920° N, 26.3368° E

The ruins of the ancient city of Assos are situated on a rocky hill that stands above the Aegean Sea. Tuzla stream, in ancient times known as Satnoieis, flows to the north of Assos. The relics from the ancient settlement are located on the territory of the modern Turkish village and holiday resort of Behramkale.

BRIEF HISTORY

In search of the earliest mentions of Assos, some historians go back to the Hittite texts. Around 1400 BCE, Hittite king Tudhaliya I defeated a confederation of city-states of western Anatolia, which operated under the name Assuwa. The hypothesis was put forward that the name is connected with Assos. It would mean that the city has a much longer history than is testified by the currently available archaeological evidence. Other historians say that the name of the entire continent of Asia derives from Assos.

In the Iliad, there is information that a certain Elastos, killed by Agamemnon, had come from Pedasos, located on a steep mountain, near Satnoieis river. From this geographical description, it can be concluded that Pedasos was the same city that later was known as Assos. However, the ancient geographer Strabo, who lived at the turn of the first century BCE and the first century CE, wrote that Pedasos, one of Lelege cities, was abandoned in his times. This statement belies the theory that Pedasos can be equated with Assos, which was inhabited continuously from the moment of its founding in the 7th century BCE.

Archaeological findings help to reconstruct the history of Assos from the days when it was founded in the 7th century BCE by Aeolian settlers. They came to Asia Minor, probably from the city called Methymna located on the Aegean island of Lesbos. In the 6th century BCE, Assos came under the rule of the kingdom of Lydia, and then shared the fate of this country, becoming a part of the Persian Empire. The satrap of this Persian province, called Ariobarzanes, joined the so-called Great Satraps' Revolt. Persian governors of the provinces, despite the support obtained from the Egyptian Pharaoh, the king of Sparta, and several Greek cities, suffered defeat at the Battle of Assos in 365 BCE.

In the period after the Battle of Assos, Persia began to lose control over the area of the Troad. This reflected the general weakness of the central government of the Persian kings. As a result of this crisis, the control over an area stretching from Assos to Atarneus (now Dikili near Bergama) was seized by a banker named Eubulus. Eubulus ruled as a despotic tyrant, but with time he started sharing the power with his former slave Hermias.

At a young age, Hermias was sent to Athens, where, for several years, he studied philosophy under the guidance of Plato and Aristotle. At that time, he became a friend of Aristotle. Shortly after returning to Asia Minor, in 351 BCE, Eubulus died, and Hermias inherited the power over Assos and Atarneus. The Macedonian king Philip II soon became interested in Hermias as a potential ally during the planned military campaign in Asia Minor.

At the command of Philip II, Aristotle went to Assos to join his friend Hermias for 'political reasons'. During his stay in Asia Minor (348-345 BCE), Aristotle had a huge influence on Hermias, who softened the form of government and saw the potential resulting from an alliance with Macedonia.

However, Philip II unexpectedly completely cut off his relation with Hermias. This radical political change occurred under the influence of a blackmail on the part of Athens. This city-state threatened an attack on Macedonia with Persian support, if Philip II had not abandoned the plans of the conquest of Asia Minor. Left alone, Hermias was arrested by a Greek mercenary on the orders of the Persian king Artaxerxes III. Hermias was sent in chains to Susa – the winter capital of Persia. There he was subjected to torture, to reveal the information on the plans of the Macedonian invasion of Persia. Hermias died without revealing anything, and the last words he asked to convey to his friends were that 'he did nothing shameful or unworthy of a philosopher.'

The Persian control over the Troad ended definitively with the arrival of Alexander the Great, son of Philip II, to Asia Minor in 334 BCE. In the years 241-133 BCE, Assos belonged to the Kingdom of Pergamon, ruled by the Attalid dynasty. The last king of this dynasty – Attalos III – bequeathed the whole kingdom to Rome.

Saint Paul visited Assos during his third missionary journey (53-58 CE). He walked to Assos from Alexandria Troas (it's only 55 km away), to meet with St. Luke and sail to the island of Lesbos.

From the times of Alexander the Great, Assos began its decline, losing importance in the Troad to Alexandria Troas. In the days of the late Byzantine Empire, Assos shrunk to the size of a small village. After the capture of Assos by the Turks in 1306, Turkish settlers gave the town a new name – Behramkale. The development of this settlement occurred only with the increase in popularity of tourism in the second half of the 20th century. Even now, only 1,100 people live in Behramkale permanently.

ARCHAEOLOGICAL RESEARCH

The existence of ancient ruins of Assos in the area of Behramkale has never been a secret. In 1838, the Ottoman Sultan Mahmud II gave the French archaeologist Raoul Rochette few blocks with sculptures from the Temple of Athena. They are now in the Louvre Museum.

The first archaeological excavations in Assos were conducted by the expedition of the American Archaeological Institute under the direction of J.T. Clarke and F.H. Bacon in the years 1881-1883. During the works, the scholars examined and documented the Temple of Athena, a gymnasium, an agora, a theater, a bouleuterion, and the tombs in the necropolis. Under the mutual agreement, 2/3 of the exhibits were given to the Sultan, and 1/3 – were taken to America. They are on display in the Museum of Fine Arts in Boston.

After a break of nearly one hundred years, in 1981, new research in Assos was started by Professor Ümit Serdaroğlu. For him, the research of Assos became the life's work. When the scientist died in 2005, he was buried in Assos. Since 2006, the work has been headed by Dr. Nusret Arslan from the University of Çanakkale.

SIGHTSEEING

The Acropolis, where the ruins of the city of Assos are located, is surrounded by mighty fortifications. These city walls are considered as one of the best preserved ancient Greek ramparts. Most sections of the fortifications date back to the 4th century BCE. Several gates, each of different and original concept, lead to the area of the ancient city. The main gate is located on the western side. The eastern tower of this gate, reaching up to 14 meters in height, has been preserved to our times.

The ruins of the Temple of Athena stand on the highest point of the Acropolis hill of Assos. This temple was built around 530 BCE in the Doric order. However, its later elements, including the architrave, are characterized by the Ionic order. Originally, the temple was surrounded by the colonnade, with 13 columns on the longer sides, and six columns on shorter sides.

The stylobate, i.e. a stone base of the building, which was carrying the entire structure, has been preserved. Its dimensions are approximately 14 to 30 meters. Six of original 38 columns are still standing. Great reliefs, once adorning the temple, are scattered in the museums in Istanbul, Paris, and Boston, and the Doric capitals of the columns and other parts of the building lie around the area. From the top of the hill, of a height of 238 meters, there are magnificent views of the valley of Satnioeis River and the Bay of Edremit.

The remains of the agora, the gymnasium, and the theater are located on the terraces of the southern slope of the Acropolis. The agora, which was the main square of the city, was delimited

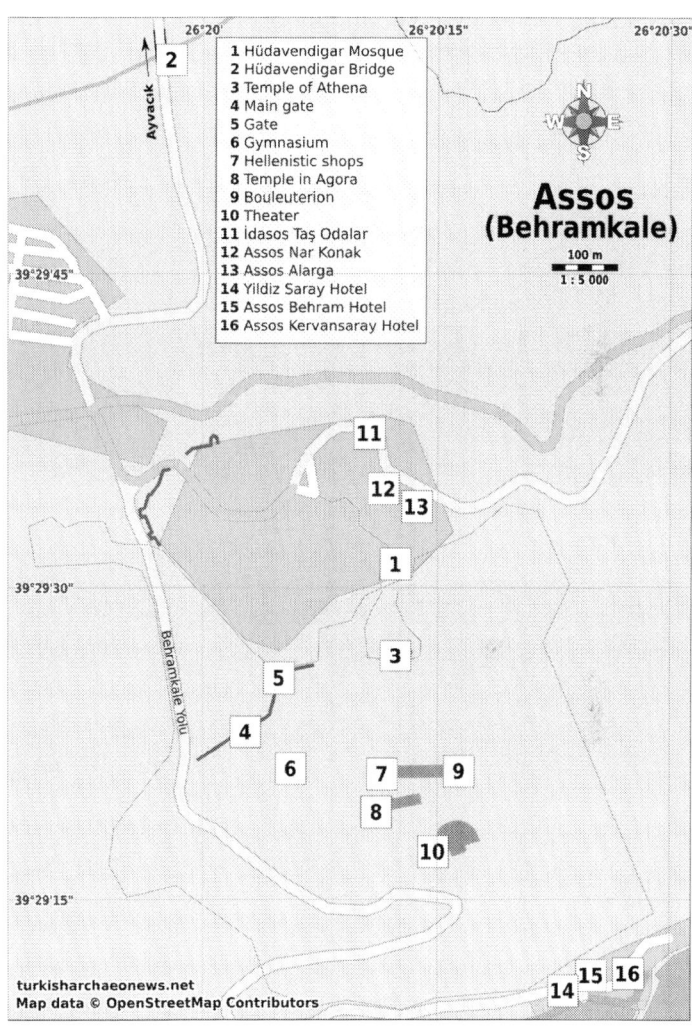

1 Hüdavendigar Mosque
2 Hüdavendigar Bridge
3 Temple of Athena
4 Main gate
5 Gate
6 Gymnasium
7 Hellenistic shops
8 Temple in Agora
9 Bouleuterion
10 Theater
11 Idasos Taş Odalar
12 Assos Nar Konak
13 Assos Alarga
14 Yildiz Saray Hotel
15 Assos Behram Hotel
16 Assos Kervansaray Hotel

Assos
(Behramkale)

100 m
1 : 5 000

turkisharchaeonews.net
Map data © OpenStreetMap Contributors

Plan of Assos

from the northern and southern sides by elongated columnar halls known as the stoas. The northern stoa was built in the Doric order and had two floors, and its length was 111 meters. On the southwest of the agora and the west of the northern stoa, there were stores that probably specialized in the sale of luxury goods. Only their foundations have been preserved to our times.

The southern stoa had three floors, the lower two of them opened in the southern direction, and the highest one – both to the north and to the south. The inhabitants of ancient Assos could stroll along shaded walkways, which had great views of the area of the agora and the Aegean Sea. The middle storey of the southern stoa housed 13 shops in a form of a covered bazaar. In the basement there were two water cisterns, there were also 13 public toilets available to Assos residents.

The entrance to the agora, in the form of a wide gate topped with an arch, was situated on the western side. Just outside the entrance, on the right, there was a small temple, later converted into a Christian church. Only the foundations have remained from this structure.

On the narrower, eastern side of the agora, there were the most important public buildings of the city, including the bouleuterion, i.e. the place of meetings of the municipal council. The buildings within the agora date back to the 3rd and the 2nd century BCE.

Between the main gate of the city and the agora, there was a gymnasium – a school where boys trained sports and studied music, literature, and philosophy. Its cobblestone courtyard measuring 40 to 32 meters has been preserved. Once, it was surrounded by colonnades. In the north-eastern part of the courtyard, a church was erected in the Byzantine era, and in the south-west corner, there is a water cistern.

Just below the agora, in the southern direction, stands the theater. It was built in the 3rd century BCE, and it underwent a renovation in Roman times. The design of the theater is a typical example of Greek architecture. It uses the natural slope of the hill and is oriented towards a beautiful, panoramic view. The theater

Greek Theatre in Assos

could accommodate 5,000 spectators. Apparently, even a hundred years ago the state of its preservation was much better. Now there are visible attempts to rebuild it and restore to its former glory.

The road leading to the main gate of Assos runs through the necropolis. A lot of sarcophagi and statues can be seen in this area. The oldest tombs discovered in Assos are the burials in large clay pots (pithos), from the 7th century BCE. In the 6th century BCE, the first cist graves, enclosed within stone walls, appeared. The first sarcophagi date back to the 5th century BCE. The burials in sarcophagi continued until the Byzantine era.

Greek sarcophagi were simple in appearance, with flat covers and no inscriptions. Roman sarcophagi stand out with their elaborate carvings, inscriptions, and the monumental size. The sarcophagus of Publius Varius, from the first century BCE, is one of the best-preserved examples of Roman sarcophagi from Assos. The sarcophagi of Assos, made of local stone, were famous in the ancient world and widely exported.

Most of the buildings in Assos were constructed with local materials, including andesite, which is a rock with the structure of porphyry. The famous sarcophagi were also produced of andesite, since this material accelerated the decomposition of the bodies and cleaning the bones of the dead, which in ancient times was seen as the great advantage.

In addition to the remains of the ancient city of Assos, there are several interesting buildings in Behramkale. The most important of them is the Hüdavendigar Mosque, built in the 14th century, during the reign of Sultan Murad I. The dome of the mosque is about 10 meters in diameter. Above the entrance door of the mosque, there is a carved cross and a Greek inscription, which indicate that the building was erected with the stones from the church of the Byzantine era.

The appearance of other parts of this building suggests that the builders acquired the supplies from the Temple of Athena. The construction of the mosque is typical of the early Ottoman-style architecture. It is one of two surviving mosques of this kind in Turkey (the other one is the famous Green Mosque in Bursa).

If you arrive at Assos from the northern direction, just before reaching the destination, pay attention to the historical bridge, located on the left side of the road. Hüdavendigar Bridge was built in the 14th century over Tuzla stream that is mentioned in the Iliad as Satnoieis River. Four arches, on which the bridge is supported, are original, but the other elements of the bridge are from later periods and are the result of renovation works.

The name of the bridge comes from the nickname that was given to the Ottoman Sultan Murad I, who reigned from 1361 to 1389. Hüdavendigar is the word with Persian origins, and means 'Similar to God.' This nickname demonstrates the huge power of the ruler. What did Murad I do to deserve such a nickname? Firstly, he moved the capital of the Ottoman Empire to Edirne, and from there he led an army to conquer the Balkans and forced the Byzantine Emperor to pay him tribute. Secondly, he was the first ruler of the House of Osman who took the title of the Sultan. Thirdly, Murad I organized the famous Janissary corps and implemented a method of recruitment into its ranks – the devşirme – taking young Christian boys from the Balkans and turning them

Hüdavendigar Bridge over Tuzla stream

into Muslim warriors. He also created a system of government in which a significant role was played by the divan headed by a grand vizier. Moreover, during the reign of Murad I, the system of land distribution was implemented, in the form of so-called timars for the people serving in the army. Finally, Murad I introduced the division of the empire into two provinces: Anatolia and Rumelia.

Currently, Hüdavendigar Bridge is closed to car traffic, that is directed to a modern bridge, located slightly to the west. This new bridge offers a perfect view of the historical structure. The travellers can take a walk across Hüdavendigar Bridge as it is open to pedestrians.

VISITOR TIPS

The admission to Assos costs 15 TL. There are three gates: to the temple of Athena, to the necropolis, and to the theatre. The ruins are open from 8:30 am to 7:30 pm (April–October) or to 5:30 pm (November–March). The ticket office closes half an hour earlier.

Orientation

Behramkale is divided into two districts, which the locals call Liman (a harbor) and Köyü (a village). If you arrive in Behramkale from any direction, you first get to Köyü district. From there, you can reach the Acropolis by walking or driving uphill. The ruins of the Temple of Athena stand in the highest point of the hill.

If you go down from the Acropolis, on the way to the harbour area (Liman), you will pass the necropolis and the ancient theater, clearly visible from the road. Then, driving along a steep and narrow road, you will reach the harbour. The road sharply descends towards the sea and leads to the quarter of Behramkale known as İskele. In this area, there are preserved old stone houses, converted into restaurants and guesthouses. Nearby there is a small pebble beach. Ship cruises are organized along the coast.

Accommodation

In Behramkale, both in the village area, as well as in the harbour, there are plenty of guesthouses and hotels. Many of them are housed in stone, traditional buildings. Spending the night in the village district is recommended for people who value peace and quiet, and in the harbour area – for people looking for entertainment and the views of the sea. In the summer, most of the owners of B&Bs insist on selecting the half board option (tr. *yarım pansiyon*).

Among the accommodation options in the village district, located close to the ruins of Assos, you may consider the following options:

- Assos Nar Konak – opened in 2013, in a stone mansion. It offers stylish rooms, a tree-lined courtyard, and breakfasts prepared from local ingredients.
- Assos Alarga – has only three luxury rooms, and offers a sauna, a swimming pool, a private parking lot, and a library.
- İdasos Taş Odalar – in a stone building. Its guests can enjoy a private garden and a restaurant.

While seeking accommodation at the harbor, in İskele district, we recommend the following hotels:

- Yildiz Saray Hotel – an animal-friendly establishment with a fish restaurant, right by the sea, with a private parking lot.
- Assos Kervansaray Hotel – a traditional stone building, with tastefully furnished rooms. The hotel has an indoor pool and a sauna.
- Assos Behram Hotel – with a panoramic terrace, a private parking lot, and a restaurant.

Many accommodation options are also located on the stretch of the coast located about 3.5 km to the east of Assos. There are, among others:

- Gidisim Camping – camping grounds with a private beach and a restaurant. You can rent a 2-person tent with breakfast included in the price.
- Assos Park Hotel – a hotel with a private beach and a swimming pool.

Restaurants

The restaurants situated on the coast have higher prices than the restaurants located on a hill, in the heart of the village district. Most of the premises at the harbuor specialize in seafood dishes. The restaurants in the rural district offer a variety of lamb and goat dishes as well as rural specialties such as Turkish pancakes (tr. gözleme).

Services

Despite the significant popularity among tourists, Behramkale does not offer many facilities. ATMs are only available in the upper part of the town. There is also a pharmacy.

GETTING THERE

By COACH: there is a coach from Çanakkale (1.5 hours) to Ayvacık, situated 25 km away from Assos.

By MINIBUS: there are minibuses to Assos from Ayvacık (20 minutes), Gülpınar (1 hour), and Babakale. In summer, there are also connections from Küçükkuyu (1 hour) and Ezine. Regular minibuses finish their route in the village district. In the summer season, some of them go as far as the harbour district. Village and harbor districts are also connected with shuttle buses.

BY CAR: from Ayvacık take a road to the south – the distance to Assos is only 18 km. If you drive from Babakale, go in the western direction for 30 km. The roads are very good, despite their local category.

Ayvacık

COORDINATES: 39.6009° N, 26.4008° E

Ayvacık is a town in Çanakkale Province, located at some distance from the sea. Because of its location at the foot of the mountains – at a height of 251 meters above sea level – the town may surprise travellers with rapid changes in the weather, and even torrential rains in the middle of summer.

BRIEF HISTORY

The history of the town is linked to the story of Ümmühan Hanım, a woman who came from Tbilisi (the present capital city of Georgia). She owned an inn there. During the war waged by the Ottomans against the Iranian Safavid dynasty in 1514, Ümmühan Hanım married one of the Ottoman soldiers, who often stopped at the inn and moved with him to Ayvacık. She started visiting local villages, urging their inhabitants to move to Ayvacık, and thus helping the development of the town.

SIGHTSEEING

Currently, Ayvacık with its 7.5 thousand inhabitants is a small town, with a strong rural character. Back in the 80s of the twentieth century, John Freely described Ayvacık in his book 'The Western Shores of Turkey' as the largest village in the southern part of the Troad. This area is a meeting place for the nomads of western Anatolia, known as the Yürüks, who come to Ayvacık to celebrate panayir – a spring festival that lasts a whole week. They lead a nomadic life, moving on horses and camels, together with the herds of goats and sheep.

The nomads spend the winters in the lowlands, located on the shores of the Aegean and Mediterranean seas, and in the spring they move their herds to the alpine meadows (tr. *yayla*) in the Taurus Mountains and other mountain ranges. On the way to the pastures, they stop to celebrate the annual migration in the old Anatolian towns. The name of the spring festival comes from the Greek word panegyria, that was adapted by the ancestors of the Yürüks. They came to Asia Minor after the Seljuk victory over the Byzantine army at Manzikert in 1071.

In Ayvacık, there is a historical mosque – Ümmühan Hatun Camii – which was built by the famous founder of the city. Her statue stands in the center of the town.

Ayvacık and its surroundings are famous for making traditional, small-sized carpets, produced by the local community, including the descendants of the nomads. On the main road to Çanakkale, two kilometers outside Ayvacık, there are the headquarters of the Dobag Project (i.e. Research and Development of Natural Dyes – Dogal Arıstırma Boya ve Geliştirme Projesi). It was established in 1981 to encourage the villagers to keep up the tradition of weaving carpets from naturally dyed wool. In the building, you can visit the exhibition and buy carpets made of such materials. The prices, though high, are favourable compared with those that you have to pay for similar carpets displayed on bazaars of large cities. The quality of local products is supervised and guaranteed by the Marmara University in Istanbul. Each rug has a label of quality and is marked with the symbol of the village and the person who produced it.

Every Friday, a large rural market is held in Ayvacık. Local farmers flock to the town to sell vegetables, fruit, and hand-made baskets. The descendants of the nomads can be seen among the vendors, distinguished by satin coats and brightly coloured scarves on the heads of women.

Ayvacık can be a base to explore Assos, Babakale, and the Temple of Apollon Smintheion in Gülpınar.

The Teachers' House is situated in the center of town, on Gemedere Street No. 2. It offers 25 beds in 12 guest rooms. The rooms are spacious, with a bathroom, but no air conditioning. The rooms are equipped with wireless internet connection. Breakfast is extra paid. A nice restaurant in the Teachers' House garden serves a few dishes, but baked mushrooms (tr. *kiremitte mantar*) and roasted chicken (tr. *kiremitte tavuk*) turned out to be nice in appearance, but oversalted.

Car rental agency Göktuğ is located opposite the Teachers' House. It offers a choice of several models of Fiat and some motorcycles.

In addition to the weekly bazaar, you can go shopping to a grocery store, located in the center of the town. It belongs to Uysal chain of stores, operating in Çanakkale Province. In the center of the town, there is also a post office and an ATM.

GETTING THERE

BY COACH: there are coaches to Ayvacık from Çanakkale (1.5h).

BY MINIBUS: minibuses connect Ayvacık with Behramkale, Ezine, and Küçükkuyu.

BY CAR: from Çanakkale take route E87 to the south, through Ezine. The distance is 70 km, but this road goes away from the coast of the Aegean Sea, thus bypassing the most impressive monuments of the southern part of the Troad (Assos, Babakale, the temple of Apollon Smintheion, Neandria, and Alexandria Troas). To visit them, you should take the longer route along the Aegean coast.

From Ayvacık, you can go further to the east, to Edremit, following E87 route. The first section of the road runs through the mountains and is somewhat troublesome because of the large volume of heavy traffic. After 25 km, in the vicinity of Küçükkuyu, the road descends to the coast and runs along the Gulf of Edremit on an entirely flat terrain, through holiday villages. The total distance from Ayvacık to Edremit is 63 km.

Mount Ida

Coordinates: 39.7024° N, 26.8642° E

The massif of Goose Mountain (tr. *Kazdağı*), located along the northern coast of the Gulf of Edremit, is known for many mythical events that took place on its slopes. Today, travellers can benefit from the possibility of trekking while wondering whether the view that they have in front of their eyes is similar to that observed by the gods of Greek mythology who watched the events of the Trojan War from the peak of this mountain.

Mount Ida massif covers an area of about 700 square kilometers and its highest point – Karataş peak (in ancient times called Gargarus) – rises to 1,774 meters above sea level. Several villages, connected by paths, are located within the massif. Most of the streams with the sources on Mount Ida find the outlets in the waters of the Gulf of Edremit, but the most important river in the region – Karamenderes (ancient Scamander) – which begins its course here, flows in the opposite direction, into the Dardanelles.

The peak of the mountain is not covered with trees, but the mountain slopes are overgrown with forests, with numerous endemic species, being a remnant of the last ice age. You come across deer, wild boars, and jackals, and less often – wolfs, lynx, or even bears. Despite the unique ecosystem, only the area of 2.4 square kilometers of Ida Mount is now protected as the Kaz Dağı National Park, created in 1993.

Legends and mythology

The most important story related to Mount Ida is the history of Paris, the son of the Trojan king Priam. When the prince was born, his mother dreamed that instead of the child she gave birth to a burning torch. Additionally, on the day when Paris was born, a soothsayer predicted that a child born on this day in the royal family would contribute to the fall of Troy.

The parents of Paris – King Priam and Queen Hecuba – were not able to kill their own child, despite the pressure from a priestess of the god Apollo. In the end, Priam delegated this task to his chief shepherd, Agelaus. However, Agelaus also decided that the task was too difficult. Therefore, instead of murdering the baby, he abandoned Paris on the slopes of Mount Ida. When he returned after nine days, he discovered that the baby survived, nourished by a she-bear. The shepherd took Paris to his home, where he raised him as his own son.

The famous and fateful event, known as the judgment of Paris, also took place on Mount Ida, near a holy spring. He decided to give a golden apple from the Garden of the Hesperides to the most beautiful of the goddesses – Aphrodite. In exchange, she offered him the love of a beautiful woman called Helen. Unfortunately, Helen had already been married, and her spouse – Menelaus, the brother of the Greek king Agamemnon – did not appreciate her abduction by Paris to Troy. In this way, the Trojan War started. It ended with the fall of the mighty city of Troy. The developments of the war were followed attentively by the Olympians, who often interfered in its course. They chose Mount Ida as a convenient vantage point, instead of the distant Mount Olympus.

The Turks know Mount Ida as Goose Mountain, and naturally have their own legends and stories related to the massif. Its name is explained by the story of a beautiful young girl named Sarıkız (the Blonde). She lived on the mountain with her old father. Her only entertainment was a flock of geese that kept her company. When her father went on a pilgrimage to Mecca, the girl was harassed by the suitors, but she rejected all of them. Unfortunately, after returning from Mecca, her old father died, and the mourning girl took refuge in the yard with her geese. A huge cloud covered the mountain, and when the weather cleared, the girl and her geese

Settlement in Mount Ida massif

disappeared without a trace.

SIGHTSEEING

Mount Ida is a popular holiday destination, especially for hikers and for people suffering from asthma as the mountain is famous for its very clean air with high oxygen content. There is a road for motorists, leading into the depths of the mountain range, to several picnic areas. Jeep safaris are also organised so it is possible to spend a night in a tent on a mountain slope.

Tourist Information Office

Tourist Information Office in the Kaz Dağı National Park is located in Zeytinli village, 3.5 km to the north of the route E87. This office operates in a renovated building, and offers lots of maps, plans, and brochures with information on Mount Ida massif.

Hiking trails

Four hiking trails have been prepared in the massif of Mount Ida. The easiest route leads from the mountain meadow (tr. *yayla*) located above Pınarbaşı village to Bear River (tr. *Ayı Çayı*), where you can have a picnic. The length of this route is 7 km, and in the suggested direction, it descends from an altitude of 800 meters above sea level to 574 meters above the sea level. The hike is possible all year round, even for untrained walkers. It leads through the forest of chestnut trees and Calabrian pines.

The second trail, with a length of 10 km, is slightly more difficult and leads to the place known as Tozlu, through the forests of the National Park, to Çeyiz stream. The altitude difference between the start and end points of the route is 350 meters. Because of the location, at an altitude of over 1000 meters above sea level, this trail is not recommended for walking in winter.

The other two hiking trails lead through the canyon of Şahin stream. The first section leads from Avcılar village to a place known as the Manzara Seyir. It has a length of 8 km and an elevation of approximately 500 meters. The second section, with a length of 6.5 kilometers, leads in the direction of the coast, from the vantage point above Altınoluk village. Both sections of the trail are accessible all year round and easy to walk.

Cycling routes

In addition to hiking trails, two cycling routes have been prepared on the slopes of Mount Ida. The first one, of medium difficulty, has a length of 17 km, and requires cycling up from 110 meters above sea level to an altitude of 525 meters. Along the route, you can observe numerous animals, including – wild boars, deer, and falcons.

The second cycling route has been developed for inexperienced cyclists. It has a length of 15 km but leads down from an altitude of 730 meters asl to a point located at an altitude of 445 meters asl. The biggest attraction of this trail are centuries-old plane trees. Because the trail leads mainly along shaded forest paths, it can be enjoyed at any time of the day.

Zeus Altar on Mount Ida

Zeus Altar

COORDINATES: 39.5603° N, 26.6178° E

On Mount Ida, and more specifically – on a small hill of the height of 300 meters above sea level – there is a mysterious structure, carved in the rock. Although there is no archeological evidence of its origins, it has been known as the Altar of Zeus since the days when Heinrich Schliemann visited the area in the late 19th century. Schliemann, a lover of Homer and the discoverer of Troy, identified this hill of the peak of Gargaros, where Zeus sat and observed the Trojan War. How Schliemann came to this conclusion remains a mystery, especially since the views from the hill are to the south, in the direction of the Aegean Sea, and not in the opposite direction where Troy is situated.

To reach this place you should turn off from the E87 route in the coastal town of Küçükkuyu, as indicated by a brown signpost, and then follow a narrow and winding road for about 3.5 km. Leave the car in the place where a signboard of the Altar of Zeus stands (unfortunately, only in Turkish), and walk 700 meters through the woods to get to the structure.

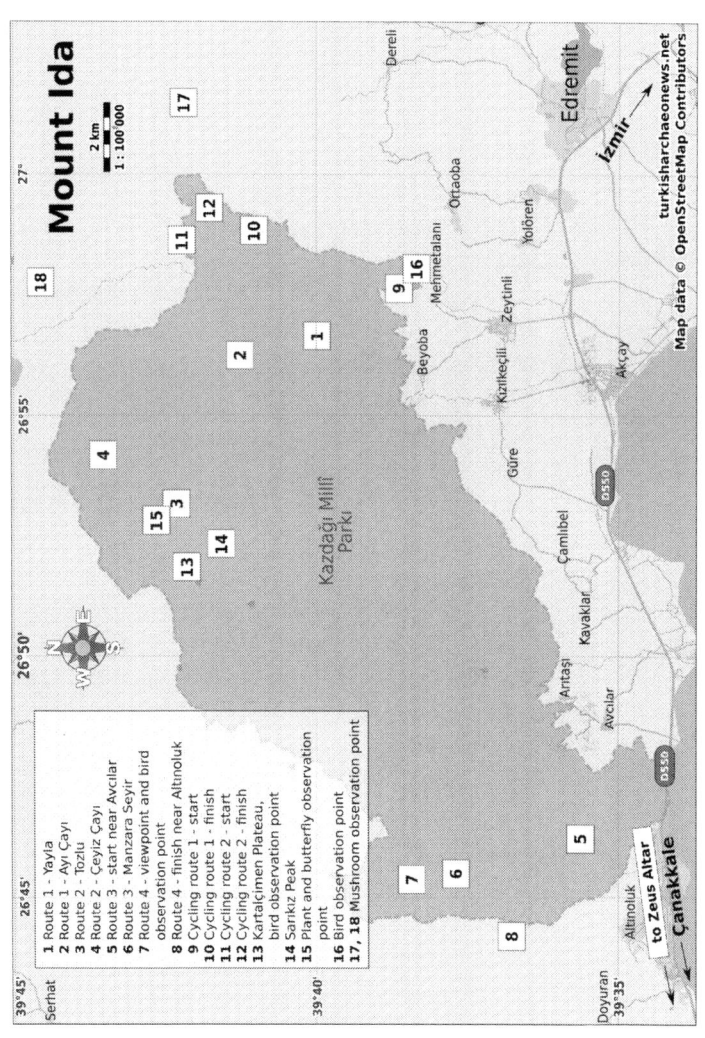

Mount Ida

2 km
1 : 100'000

Kazdağı Millî Parkı

Serhat

1 Route 1 - Yayla
2 Route 1 - Ayı Çayı
3 Route 2 - Tozlu
4 Route 2 - Çeyiz Çayı
5 Route 3 - start near Avcılar
6 Route 3 - Manzara Seyir
7 Route 4 - viewpoint and bird
observation point
8 Route 4 - finish near Altınoluk
9 Cycling route 1 - start
10 Cycling route 1 - finish
11 Cycling route 2 - start
12 Cycling route 2 - finish
13 Kartalçimen Plateau,
bird observation point
14 Sarıkız Peak
15 Plant and butterfly observation
point
16 Bird observation point
17, 18 Mushroom observation point

to Zeus Altar
Altınoluk
Çanakkale

Doyuran

turkisharchaeonews.net

Map data © OpenStreetMap Contributors

Edremit

İzmir

Touristic map of Mount Ida

NATURE OBSERVATION POINTS

Endemic plants

The most important endemic species of plants from Mount Ida may be encountered in three observation points. In Tozlu, at an altitude of 1,475 meters above sea level, a species of fir Abies equi-trojani grows. On Kartalçimen plateau (1,742 meters above sea-level), you can find a species of thyme – Thymus Pulvinatus, a species Silene Compacta, also known as Catchfly, Digitalis Trojana (foxglove), and Asperula Sintenisi. Near the peak of Sarıkız (1,730 meters a.s.l.) grows Sideritis Trojana and Hypericum Kazdaghensis. It is worth remembering that in the massif of Ida Mountian there are as many as 32 endemic species of plants, most of which bloom in July and August.

Butterflies

The most beautiful butterflies in the Ida Mount can be seen in the distant valley, located on the northern side of the massif. The rich vegetation and the proximity to the stream attract such species of butterflies as Satyrium abdominalis (the Gerhard's Black Hairstreak in the family Lycaenidae) – very rare in Europe but common in Turkey, Melitaea didyma (the spotted fritillary), and Vanessa cardui (the painted lady or the cosmopolitan) – in the family Nymphalidae, as well as Pieris rapae (the small white).

Birds

Bird-watching fans will appreciate the fact that Mount Ida is a place where, only in 2009, 120 different species of birds could be observed. In the recommended observation points various species can be seen, including European greenfinches (Carduelis Carduelis), ordinary greenfinches (Carduelis Chloris), robins (Erithacus Rubecula), great tits (Parus Major), grey wagtails (Motacilla Cinerea), Syrian woodpeckers (Dendrocopos Syriacus), ravens (Corvus Corax), long-legged buzzards (Buteo Rufinus), golden eagles (Aquila Chrysaetos), and hoopoes (Upupa Epops). These sites are located at altitudes from 900 to 1750 meters above sea level.

Mushrooms

Mount Ida is an area extremely rich in different species of mushrooms, which are easiest to observe in the autumn season. The most common species include: Lactarius salmonicolor, common morel (Morchella esculenta), wood blewit (Lepista nuda), fly agaric (Amanita muscaria), Hygrophorus chrysodon, and tinder fungus (Fomes fomentarius). The points of observation of these species are situated at altitudes of 650 and 1,100 meters above sea level.

Visitor tips

Mount Ida massif is located in the southern part of the Troad. From the south, the slopes of the mountain descend in the direction of the Aegean Sea. The coastal road E87 goes along this coast, from Çanakkale and Ayvacık to Edremit. The stretch of the coast located between Küçükkuyu (in the west) and Akçay (in the east) is actually one long holiday resort, covered with summer cottages, hotels, and guesthouses. The travellers, looking for some peace and quiet, and wishing to stay in a place situated on the slopes of the mountain, should visit one of two villages hidden in the massif a certain distance from the coast – Adatepe and Yeşilyurt.

In Küçükkuyu, you can stop for a moment to visit the Olive Museum, open from 9:00 am to 7:00 pm. The process of olive oil production has been demonstrated in this venue. Adatepe village is located north of Küçükkuyu village, and is accessible via a winding road, 4 km long.

Adatepe is a charming cluster of restored historical houses, and its surroundings encourage hiking in the mountains, abundant in waterfalls and interesting rock formations. There is a nicely preserved Roman bridge near the Başdeğirmen Waterfall. In Adatepe, you can find several places to stay for the night. The best appreciated by travellers is Hünnap Han – a beautifully decorated hotel in the historical homestead, with a garden and a stone courtyard.

Yeşilyurt, located a little further to the west, is even prettier than Adatepe. In the center of the village, there is a cobbled square surrounded by stone houses, several of which have been converted into boutique hotels. The most frequently recommended ones are Manici Kasrı, Çetmi Han, and Erguvanlı Ev.

GETTING THERE

BY PUBLIC TRANSPORT: the coaches that connect Çanakkale in the north with Izmir in the south go along the coastal E87 route. They stop in several towns, including Küçükkuyu. In the summer, Küçükkuyu and Behramkale (with the ruins of Assos) are connected by minibuses. You need to take a taxi to get to Adatepe and Yeşilyurt.

BY CAR: take the coastal E87 route from Çanakkale and Ayvacık (in the north), and from Edremit (in the east).

Antandros

COORDINATES: 39.5710° N, 26.7858° E

Only 15 years ago, almost none of the travellers knew of the existence of the ruins of the ancient city of Antandros, located on the Gulf of Edremit, in the southern part of the Troad. The only visible traces of the once mighty city were the scattered fragments of buildings, hidden in an olive grove, and not encouraging an in-depth exploration. However, a lot has changed since then, and the team of researchers led by Professor Gürcan Polat has made remarkable discoveries in Antandros. The biggest attraction of this place is a wonderfully preserved Roman villa, adorned with mosaic floors and wall frescoes. So if you are travelling along the coastal road to Edremit, make a stop in the holiday village of Altınoluk, and search for the traces of ancient Antandros.

BRIEF HISTORY

Even in ancient times, there was no consensus as to who founded Antandros. According to Alcaeus, a Greek poet from the island of Lesbos, the city had been founded by the Anatolian tribe of Leleges, in the 7th century BCE. The most famous Greek historian, Herodotus, gave information that the settlement was founded by the Pelasgians, the people also from the territories of Asia Minor. Thucydides, writing several decades later, was the first of the authors who claimed that Antandros was a Greek settlement, colonized by the immigrants from Aeolia. However, the tradition of the local origins of the founders of the city survived in historiography, mentioned again by Aristotle. He explained that the alternative names of Antandros – Edonis and Kimmeris – were derived from the names of the Thracian tribe of the Edonians, and the nomadic Cimmerians from the east.

Two versions of Antandros history that combined the contradictory information were presented by Conon, a Greek grammarian and mythographer, who was active during the reign of Emperor Augustus. According to the first version of events, the city had been ruled by Ascanius the son of Aeneas, until he was kidnapped by the Pelasgians. They received Antandros in exchange for his release. The second version explains that the city was founded by the exiles from the Aegean island of Andros, which was reflected in the name of their new place of residence.

Antandros appears on the pages of history in 512 BCE, when it was conquered by the Persians. Due to its location, at the foot of Mount Ida, the city had access to the rich resources of timber and resin, essential materials for the shipbuilding industry. These considerations meant that Antandros was a tasty morsel for all military powers, seeking to expand their war fleets. The city repeatedly passed from hand to hand, it was controlled by the Greeks and the Persians, and it was even an autonomous settlement for a short time.

ARCHAEOLOGICAL RESEARCH

The first attempts to locate the ruins of Antandros were made in 1842, when Heinrich Kiepert, a German geographer and cartographer, discovered an inscription from Antandros built into the wall of a mosque in the nearby village of Avcılar. Kiepert climbed Kaletaşı Hill, which, as he suspected, concealed the remains of an ancient settlement. He actually found many pieces of marble and ceramics there, thus confirming his theory. However, for more than 150 years after the discovery of Antandros, only superficial studies were conducted there.

Only in 2001, systematic archaeological work began in Antandros, conducted under the auspices of the Museum in Balıkesir by Professor Gürcan Polat. These studies demonstrated that the ceramic fragments found in the area of the Greek necropolis date back to the 8th and the 7th century BCE. It means that the Greeks inhabited the area two centuries earlier than it was previously thought. This also means that the theories of the Greek origins of the city have gained in importance, moving the claims about the local founders of the city into the shadows.

SIGHTSEEING

The villa or so-called Terraced House (tr. *Yamaç Ev*) from the Roman period, i.e. from the 4th century CE, is a must-see while visiting the ruins of Antandros. There are six rooms of the house arranged around an inner courtyard, preserved in excellent condition. The mosaics decorating the floors and wall frescoes are beautiful and reminiscent of the decoration of houses in Pompeii.

In addition to the villa, in Antandros you can see the remains of huge baths, Roman cisterns, and an extensive necropolis.

VISITOR TIPS

Entry to Antandros is currently free of charge. There are continuous efforts aimed at opening an archaeological museum in this place. This venue would display the exhibits from Antandros, currently stored in a warehouse. With the opening of this facility, most probably official ticketing system and opening hours will be introduced.

In the nearby village of Altınoluk, you can easily find a place to stay at one of the seaside hotels or B&Bs. There are also numerous restaurants, grocery stores, a post office, and ATMs.

GETTING THERE

BY PUBLIC TRANSPORT: the buses and minibuses connecting Küçükkuyu (in the east) with Edremit (in the east) pass right in front of the entrance to the area of ancient Antandros. You just need to ask a driver to stop there.

BY CAR: Antandros ruins are situated between Altınoluk and Avcılar, on the E87 route.

Edremit

COORDINATES: 39.5915° N, 27.0175° E

The town of Edremit administratively belongs to the Balıkesir Province. However, because of its location – on the Gulf of Edremit (tr. *Edremit Körfezi*), which marks the border of Biga Peninsula – it can be counted as one of the cities of the Troad. It is situated in the south-easternmost point of this region. The city bears the name derived from the ancient Adramyttion, but in fact, the ruins of this settlement are located further to the south, in Burhaniye. Edremit is a modern town, where it is difficult to find spectacular sights or tourist attractions. The importance of Edremit to the travelers results from its position at the crossroads of many significant roads. If you are travelling around the western part of Turkey, in Edremit you need to decide whether to go further south along the coast of the Aegean Sea, or turn east, deeper into Asia Minor.

BRIEF HISTORY

The earliest history of human settlement in the area is associated with the nearby Adramyttion. This history is presented in the chapter on the town of Burhaniye. The history of Edremit started only in 1093 when Adramyttion was destroyed during the invasion of troops under the command of the Seljuk general Çaka Bey. The city was rebuilt in a new location in 1109 by the Byzantine commander Eumathios Philokales. Emperor Manuel I Comnenus, who reigned in the years 1143-1180, strengthened the city in the face of the growing threat of the Turkish attack. In the 14th century, Edremit was finally conquered by the Turks of the Karasid dynasty

Gulf of Edremit seen from Mount Ida

(tr. *Karesioğullari*). They formed a small independent state in the area of the current provinces of Balıkesir and Çanakkale. Soon afterwards, during the reign of Sultan Orhan, Edremit became a part of the Ottoman Empire.

In the 19th century, the economic importance of Edremit grew because of the intensification of the production of olive oil. After the end of World War I and the Turkish-Greek war (1919-1923), this industry developed significantly, at the expense of Ayvalık, located further to the south. This was due to the fact that the farmers from Edremit area were largely of Turkish origin, and the cultivation of olive trees in Ayvalık had been in the hands of the Greeks before the wars. After the signing of the peace treaty of Lausanne, the Greek inhabitants of the Aegean coast were relocated to the territory of modern Greece, and their place was taken by the Turks who had no experience in the production of olive oil. It gave a huge advantage to the experienced producers from Edremit, and thus, the city is now known as the 'Turkish Capital of Olive Oil.'

SIGHTSEEING

If the value of tourist destinations could be judged by the number of brown signposts indicating their location, then in the case of Edremit, the priority would belong to a sanctuary called Üçler Dede Türbesi or the Tomb of Three Grandfathers. The place is exactly what its name indicates – the burial place consisting of three tombs. The whole complex is very modest and tiny, as if all the financial resources have been allocated to the signposts, and it should be considered only as a local curiosity.

A much more attractive place (on the Edremit scale) may be the Ethnographic Museum (tr. *Ayşe Sıdıka Erke Etnografya Müzesi*). It operates in a restored house from the Ottoman era, on the Boulevard of Azerbaijan (tr. *Azerbeycan Bulvarı*), near the coach station. The facility presents a collection of old photographs of the city, a few traditional costumes, and everyday objects. The museum is open daily, from 8:00 am to 6:00 pm.

The second museum in Edremit is the Museum of Olive Oil Production (tr. *Edremit Evren Ertür Tarihi Zeytinyağı Aletleri Müzesi*). It is located outside the center of Edremit, on route E87, in the direction of Akçay village. The exhibits include a variety of devices used for the production of olive oil, from ancient times to the present day. They have been collected by Ertürk family that has been manufacturing olive oil for over 40 years.

The oldest building in Edremit is the Lead Mosque (tr. *Kurşunlu Camii*), built in 1231. It is located on the Lead Boulevard (tr. *Kurşunlu Bulvarı*), in Kapıcıbaşı district. It is a simple building, covered with a single dome, built of hewn stones. The columns in the Corinthian order that support the arches of the narthex are particularly noteworthy. They were, most likely, collected from the ruins of ancient Adramyttion. Another curiosity comes in the form of two ostrich eggs, hanging inside the mosque, for no apparent reason.

Another historical building in Edremit is Tahta Mosque, standing on the road in the direction of Akçay, in a suburb of Kadıköy. This wooden structure was moved here from Kızılcabayır village,

Lead Mosque (Kurşunlu Camii) in Edremit

located in a remote Çorum Province.

A hill known as Ülkü Tepesi rises on the eastern side of the town. There stands a monument to the first president of Turkey – Atatürk. Apparently this is the highest monument of its kind in the country, but any such claims should be treated with suspicion in the case of Turkey.

VISITOR TIPS

The centre of Edremit is located on the east side of the route E87. Because there are relatively few places of interest in the centre, we discourage driving into the heart of the city. Although it is inhabited by only 55,000 people, there is heavy traffic, and traffic jams occur frequently. The very center of Edremit is situated near Menderes Boulevard, where there are many shops, restaurants, bank branches, ATMs, and a post office. The biggest shopping mall – Kipa AVM – lies on the west side of the city, on the route E87.

If you plan to stay in the area for the night, the most attractive hotels are located outside the city center – in Bostancı district, and in nearby holiday villages – Akçay, Güre, and Burhaniye. In Bostancı, next to the local airport, you should consider two hotels:

- Adramis Thermal Hotel – equipped with a sauna, swimming pools, and a Turkish bath.
- Entur Thermal Hotel – slightly cheaper, also with swimming pools and a spa.

GETTING THERE

BY CAR: Edremit is situated on the crossroad of E87 and D230 roads. E87 road connects Çanakkale (in the north-west, 130 km) with the cities situated to the south, including Burhaniye (17 km), Ayvalık (45 km), and Izmir (190 km). To the east of Edremit city centre, D230 branches of the E87 route, taking the travellers to the east, to Balıkesir (86 km).

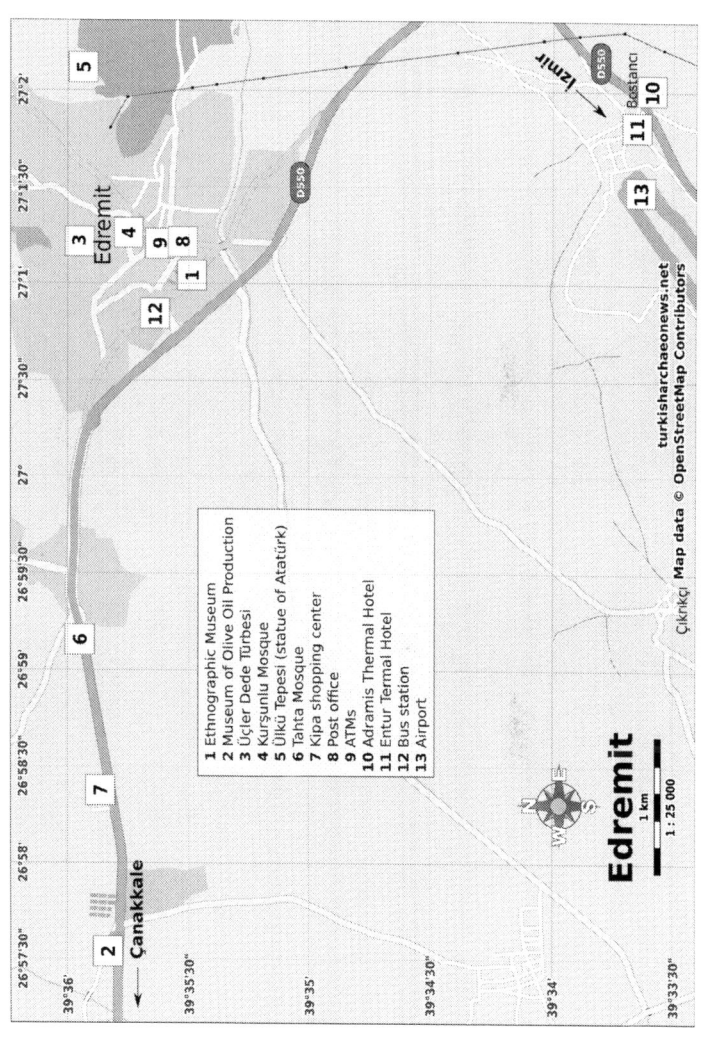

Edremit

1 Ethnographic Museum
2 Museum of Olive Oil Production
3 Üçler Dede Türbesi
4 Kurşunlu Mosque
5 Ülkü Tepesi (statue of Atatürk)
6 Tahta Mosque
7 Kipa shopping center
8 Post office
9 ATMs
10 Adramis Thermal Hotel
11 Entur Termal Hotel
12 Bus station
13 Airport

Edremit

1 km
1 : 25 000

Çıknkçı Map data © OpenStreetMap Contributors

turkisharchaeonews.net

BY PUBLIC TRANSPORT: some long-distance coaches start from Edremit coach terminal. They travel to many cities in Turkey, including Ankara, Bursa, Çanakkale, Istanbul, Izmir, and Manisa. Minibuses also depart from this terminal to many towns and villages situated on the Gulf of Edremit, including Akçay and Altınoluk.

BY PLANE: Edremit Airport (tr. *Edremit Körfez Havalimanı*) is situated in Bostancı district, to the south from the centre. There are daily flights to Ankara and Istanbul.

Havran

COORDINATES: 39.5583° N, 27.0983° E

This small town in Balıkesir Province is famous throughout Turkey for its roasted chickpeas (tr. *leblebi*), a war hero Seyit Ali Çabuk, and cheese halva (tr. *hoşmerim*). If you visit Havran during your journey, you will find that this is a pretty and nice town, where you can buy goods made from olive oil at very reasonable prices.

BRIEF HISTORY

The oldest discovered traces of human activity in and around Havran come from the Neolithic period, as evidenced by the so-called Neolithic stone altars. They are located in the area between Havran and Burhaniye. The term 'Havran' is, most likely, the distortion of the name of the ancient city of Aureliane. Its meager remnants are located approximately 4 km to the south, in the village of Büyükdere. In turn, the name Aureliane comes from the Latin word for gold – aurum – as this metal was once mined in the area.

The best known person born in Havran was Corporal Seyit Ali Çabuk, the hero of the First World War. He became famous during the campaign on the Gallipoli Peninsula. When the crane used to load missiles broke down, Corporal Seyit manually loaded the cannon with three shells, each weighing 275 kg. Apparently one of the missiles hit the British warship Ocean, which later sank after hitting a mine in the Dardanelles. Corporal Seyit had many monuments erected in his memory, including the ones in Eceabat and Kilitbahir.

Old building in Havran

SIGHTSEEING

There is not much to see in Havran. The biggest tourist attraction is the old town center, where several wooden houses from the Ottoman period have been preserved. The prettiest of them is facing the Street of the Republic (tr. *Cumhuriyet Caddesi*), opposite the Ebubekir Mosque.

During a stopover in Havran, you should also look for the local specialty – cheese halva (tr. *hoşmerim*) – which is served in local pastry shops. This delicacy is traditionally produced from unsalted sheep or goat milk, with the addition of semolina, i.e. fine bulgur wheat, and powdered sugar.

VISITOR TIPS

Havran is a very peaceful town with only 11,000 inhabitants. It is located on the route D230, and is a convenient stopover during the journey from the Troad region to the east. The center of the town is marked by Yılmaz Akpınar Boulevard. There you can find a post office and several banks with ATMs. Nearby there are several eateries, where you can taste delicious fried chicken liver.

The most important reason why it is worthwhile to visit Havran, are the shops selling goods manufactured locally from olive oil. The offer of these shops includes a variety of products based on olive oil, including excellent soap, sold at sensationally low prices, unprecedented in major drug stores and places frequented by tourists. Friday is the market day in Havran, and the goods offered are mainly vegetables and fruit.

If you want to spend a night in Havran, there are not many accommodation options to choose from. It is worth checking if there are rooms available in the local Teachers' House (tr. *Havran Öğretmenevi*), located on the west side of the town, at the junction of Sakarya, Menderes, and Yılmaz Akpınar streets. However, much larger selection of hotels can be found in Edremit and Burhaniye.

GETTING THERE

BY CAR: take D230 route from Edremit in the west (10 km) or the capital of the province – Balıkesir in the east (81 km).

BY MINIBUS: there are regular minibuses from Edremit to Havran.

Burhaniye (Adramyttion)

COORDINATES: 39.4985° N, 26.9362° E

Despite the widespread belief that the ancient city of Adramyttion was situated in the area of modern Edremit, whose name is a corruption of the ancient name, in fact, the case is a bit more complicated. The ruins of Adramyttion are located in the beach district of the town of Burhaniye, known simply as Ören, i.e. ruins, located 24 km to the south of Edremit.

BRIEF HISTORY

Recent archaeological research conducted in the area of Burhaniye has provided the evidence that the traces of human activity in the area date back to prehistoric times. It is testified by altars and monuments carved into the rock, dating back to the Neolithic period and associated with the cult of the Mother Goddess. In total, sixteen such places have been identified so far, hidden in the hills between Burhaniye and Havran.

The origins of the settlement, that became an important port city in the region during the Greek and Roman periods, are lost in the mists of history. There are two main theories about the city's foundation. According to the first one, the city was founded in the 6th century BCE, at the behest of Adramys, the son of the King of Lydia – Alyattes – and the brother of the famous king Croesus. Apparently, Croesus, the last king of Lydia, before ascending to the throne, acted as the governor of Adramyttion. The second theory claims that the settlement is much older, and it was founded, under the name Adra-Mudra, by native Anatolian people – the Luvians who lived in Asia Minor in the second millennium BCE.

For many centuries, Adramyttion functioned as a harbour and the center of trade in products originating from forests growing on the slopes of Mount Ida and the plains stretching to the east. The turning point in the history of the city was the year 422 BCE. In this time the inhabitants of the island of Delos settled in the city, expelled by the Athenians from their homeland. The Persian satrap of Daskyleion, who managed the western Asia Minor, agreed to accept their presence. Since then, the city of Adramyttion was Hellenised, and figured in the lists as 'a Greek city.' The laws applied by the rulers of Adramyttion were studied by Aristotle, who presented a typology of political systems of city-states in his work 'Politics'.

In the Hellenistic period, due to the strategic location of Adramyttion, frequent battles were fought between the heirs of Alexander the Great near the city. The city was conquered in 302 BCE by Prepelaus, a general in the service of the king of Macedonia. However, in the same year, he lost it to Demetrius I, known as 'the one who besieges cities.' In 201 BCE, the city was plundered by Philip V of Macedon, and in 190 BCE – by Antiochus III the Great, the ruler from the Seleucid dynasty. Finally, Adramyttion was incorporated into the expanding Kingdom of Pergamon, whose kings contributed to its development and prosperity.

Under the Roman rule, Adramyttion flourished, and new public buildings were erected, including a shipyard and a school of rhetoric. Until the reign of Emperor Gallienus, i.e. the middle of the 3rd century CE, the city was minting its coins. The famous Roman historian, Pliny the Elder, wrote that Adramyttion was famous for the production of valuable medicated ointment. In the first century CE, the city was repeatedly visited by St. Paul, during his missionary journeys. The city had the status of a bishopric from 431, and its representatives participated in a number of councils and synods.

The golden era of Adramyttion ended because the harbour was silted up. The end to the city's existence was put by the Seljuk commander Çaka Bey, who invaded and destroyed the city in 1093.

The memory of its existence has been preserved in the name of the nearby town of Edremit, founded shortly afterwards by the rulers of Byzantium.

The Turks founded a new village in the vicinity of the ancient Adramyttion, under the name Taylıeli. At the beginning of the 14th century, it was managed by the Karasid dynasty (tr. *Karesioğulları*), when it developed and attracted many immigrants. In the days of the Ottoman Empire, the settlement was renamed as Kemer and attached administratively to Edremit. In 1866, the town became the capital of the district under the name of Burhaniye, derived from the name of the Ottoman prince Şehzade Burhanettin. During the Greco-Turkish War, on the 29th of 1920, the Greek army occupied and set fire to Burhaniye, destroying the main mosque of the town.

Currently, Burhaniye is a small town with the population of about 40,000 residents, administratively belonging to Balıkesir Province. It has its harbour and a beach district – Ören – where the ruins of ancient Adramyttion are located. Besides tourism, the main source of income of its residents is the production of olive oil.

SIGHTSEEING

The ruins of ancient Adramyttion, located in the coastal area of Ören, are the most important place that can be seen during a visit to Burhaniye. Unfortunately, they are surrounded by a fence protecting the archaeological site, so the opportunity to visit them depends on your power of persuasion when talking to the researchers working there. Out of excavation season, the possibility of legal entry into the Adramyttion is virtually nonexistent. If you are lucky, during the visit to this place you will see the fragments of marble blocks with inscriptions, lying near a bay, that once served as a harbour. Under the water, you can even see the outline of an ancient pier.

The ruined Byzantine church, dating back to the 10-11th century CE, is the most attractive building unearthed in Adramyttion so far. It was discovered in 2001. The researchers found out that

Mosque in Burhaniye

the building was erected in the area of a necropolis, dated to the late Roman period. The church was built on a rectangular plan, with stone blocks bound with mortar.

Do not be deceived by brown signposts, placed in Ören that indicate the direction to an open-air theater (tr. *açık hava tiyatrosu*). It is a modern structure, built for the organization of concerts and cultural events, and not an ancient Greek or Roman theater.

In Ören district, you should look for the Museum of Turkish National Movement (tr. *Kuvay-ı Milliye Müzesi*). Its name is somewhat misleading, because the exhibits collected there are a standard mix of archaeological finds from the area of Burhaniye, and ethnographic objects. The museum is next door to Koca Mosque (tr. *Koca Camii*), built in 1841.

In addition, around Burhaniye you can find the so-called neolithic stone altars. Sixteen such places have been discovered so far. They are hidden in the hills between Burhaniye and Havran. An altar usually stands on a hill with a water soure. It is a carved rock niche, with stairs, used in prehistoric times for religious purposes. The most famous of these altars are called Dedekaya and Deliktaş.

VISITOR TIPS

Orientation

Burhaniye is divided into two main districts – the central one, bearing the name of Cumhuriyet, and the seaside one, known as Ören. They are situated about four km away from each other, which is troublesome for visitors because intercity buses arrive only to Cumhuriyet. All tourist attractions of the town are located in Ören, so you have to take a taxi, wait for an infrequent city bus, or just walk the distance.

Accommodation

The best idea is to look for accommodation in a seaside district of Ören and in small towns located further to the south. Highly recommended hotels are listed below:

– Idahan Hotel – located in the center of Ören, Sur Street

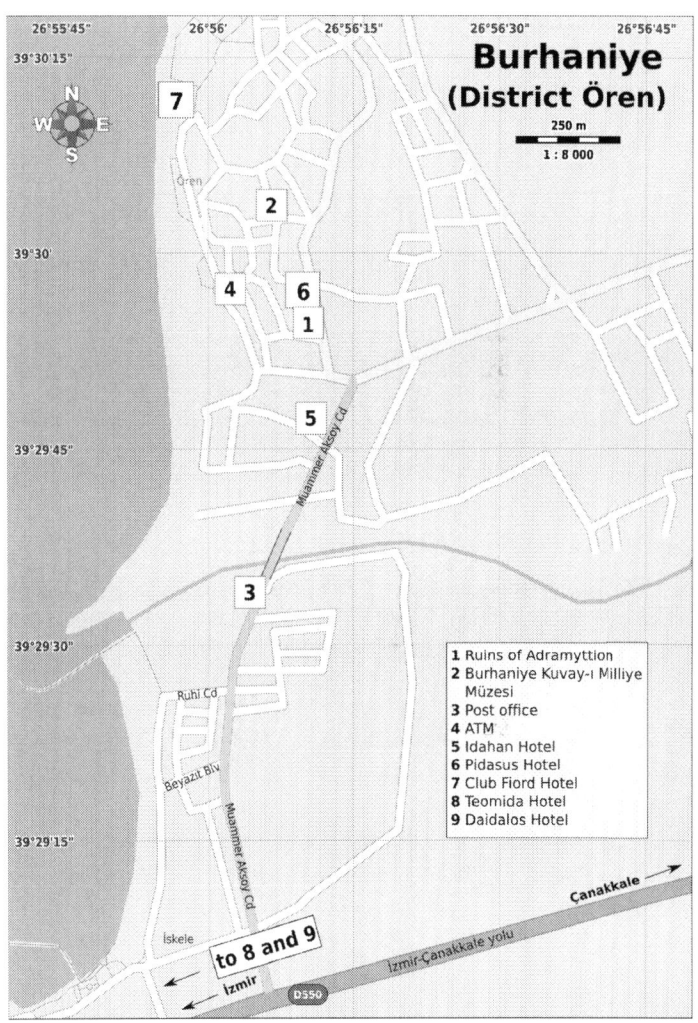

Plan of Burhaniye, district Ören

No.17, 200 meters from a sandy beach.

- Pidasus Hotel – also located in Ören, Avni Meto Street No.2. It has a swimming pool, and a beach is just 150 meters away.
- Hotel Club Fiord – located in Ören, Ayakli Street No.77, right on a private beach. It has a wide range of rooms and suites – from double rooms to five-bed apartments.
- Teomida Hotel – a luxurious hotel, located close to the coast in İskele district, to the south of the center of Burhaniye. The hotel has an outdoor swimming pool, a steam bath, and a restaurant.
- Daidalos Hotel – a boutique hotel, located in Taylıeli village, 7 km to the south from the center of Burhaniye. The main advantage of this hotel is its quiet surroundings, and the guests can use a swimming pool and a beautiful garden.

Shopping and services

In Ören, in addition to many hotels and B&Bs, there are grocery stores, restaurants, ATMs, and even a post office. However, you should not compare this town with well-known holiday resorts such as Bodrum and Alanya. It is just a small district, with numerous summer houses, and out of summer season almost all shops and restaurants are closed.

Getting there

By public transport: there are minibuses from Edremit and Ayvalık (via Gömeç) to the centre of Burhaniye. To get to Ören district, take a taxi, a city bus, or walk 4 km.

By car: the road E87 (D550) goes through Burhaniye from Edremit in the north (17 km), to the cities situated along the Aegean coast further to the south: Ayvalık (30 km), Izmir (181 km), and Aydın (283 km).

Aureliane

Coordinates: 39.5366° N, 27.0779° E

The modest ruins of the ancient city of Aureliane are a serious challenge, both for the travellers and for the lovers of historical puzzles. To reach Aureliane, the travellers must turn off the main route that runs in an arc around the Gulf of Edremit, and find Büyükdere village near the town of Havran, concealed among a tangle of narrow rural paths.

Brief history

In ancient times, Aureliane was situated in the area known as Mysia, on the river Euenos (now known as Havran). Apparently St. Paul passed through Aureliane during his second missionary journey. The name of the city reportedly comes from the name of the Roman emperor Marcus Aurelius, who reigned between 161 and 180 CE. An alternative explanation derives it from the Latin word for gold – aurum – as this resource was once mined in the area. A reminder of the existence of this ancient settlement is the name of the nearby town of Havran, which is a strong distortion of the world Aureliane.

Visitor tips

If you manage to get to Aureliane, there is some bad news for you: there is no possibility of entry to the ruins of the city. They are located behind a solid fence, in the area of a quarry. The only remaining option is to take some photos from behind the fence. For this reason, a visit to Aureliane is the task only for the most avid history buffs and the searchers of archaeological trivia. Other persons are advised to explore some other sites in the Southern Troad that are better preserved and open for visitors, such as Alexandria Troas or Assos.

GETTING THERE

BY CAR: the distance between Aureliane and the nearest significant city, i.e. Edremit, is 14 km. Take the E87 route from Edremit to the south-east. After 4 km turn off this road in the direction of Havran. Drive 6 km more, and turn to the right (to the south). The distance from this point to Büyükdere is 4 km. The ruins of Aureliane are situated near the village, on the left side of the road, in the area of a quarry.

Aegean Islands

If you suddenly start craving for a sea cruise during your stay on the Gallipoli Peninsula or in the region of the Troad, you are in luck. It is an excellent opportunity to make a trip to one of two Aegean islands that belong to Turkey. These islands are located in the north-eastern part of the Aegean Sea. They are currently known as Gökçeada and Bozcaada, and they are the only inhabited islands of the Aegean Sea that are controlled by Turkey. They were granted to this country under the Treaty of Lausanne in 1923.

The provisions of this Treaty have exempted the Greek population living in these islands from the obligation to resettle into the lands belonging to Greece. However, do not believe in the advertised 'Greek' ambiance of these islands, as almost all Greeks who used to inhabit Gökçeada and Bozcaada, left the islands many years ago, because persecutions and unfavorable laws. Therefore, these islands are now inhabited almost exclusively by the Turkish population.

Both islands are served by ferries from the Turkish mainland. The easiest way to get to Gökçeada is from the Gallipoli Peninsula, and more precisely – from Kapatepe ferry terminal – located on its western shore. To get to Bozcaada, take a ferry from Geyikli İskelesi harbour, located on the western coast of the Troad. There are also less frequent ferries and hydrofoils to both islands from the city of Çanakkale.

The smaller of the islands – Bozcaada – is regarded nowadays as a fashionable holiday destination for the wealthy residents of Istanbul, so accommodation there is more expensive than on a larger, but less scenic Gökçeada. Please bear in mind that off-season the ferries are less frequent, and many hotels and B&Bs close down for the winter.

DO NOT MISS

During your stay on the Aegean Islands necessarily visit:

- the fortress on Bozcaada,
- one of Greek villages on Gökçeada,
- beautiful beaches on both islands.

Gökçeada

COORDINATES: 40.1941° N, 25.9048° E

The island, now known officially as Gökçeada, and before that, for many centuries, called Imbros, is in many respects a unique place. Firstly, it is the largest island that belongs to Turkey, and at the same time – one of only two inhabited Turkish islands in the Aegean Sea. It is also the westernmost point of the Turkish territory. What's more, because of the exclusion clause in the Treaty of Lausanne in the 20s of the twentieth century, preventing local Greek population from resettlement, Gökçeada still is inhabited by a small Greek community, whose ancestors settled on it in ancient times.

BRIEF HISTORY

Mythical beginnings

The island, under the name of Imbros, first appeared in Greek mythology. On the waters of the Aegean Sea, between Imbros and Samothrace, there was a palace belonging to the Thetis, the sea nymph who married a mortal – Peleus – and bore him a son, a famous warrior Achilles. Between Imbros and Tenedos (currently Bozcaada) there were stables of winged horses of the god of the oceans, Poseidon.

Ancient times

According to Homer and Hesiod, before the arrival of the settlers from Greece, a mysterious tribe of the Pelasgians lived on the island. Archaeological finds from Yeni Bademli mound indicate that the island was inhabited at least since 3000 BCE.

Landscape of Gökçeada

Greeks thought of Imbros as the island of Hephaestus – the god of metallurgy. This belief was reflected in locally minted coins, depicting this deity. After the reign of the Persians, in times of the greatest development of the power of Athens, Imbros was its cleruchy, i.e. a colony whose inhabitants enjoyed the Athenian citizenship. Not much has been preserved to our times from the period of Roman domination on the island, but we know that in the second century CE, Imbros had a certain degree of autonomy.

Ottoman period

In 1456, just three years after the conquest of Constantinople by the Ottomans, Imbros also came under the control of the Turkish rulers. Due to the strategic location of the island, a fortress was erected on the site where the Greek Acropolis once stood. During the fifth Ottoman-Venetian War (1645-1669), Venetian army temporarily conquered Imbros because of the rich sources of drinking water, required by the crews of warships stationed at the mouth of the Dardanelles.

After these events, the Turks strengthened the fortress on Imbros, but that did not prevent the Venetians from re-occupation of the island – in 1698 and 1717. Another battle took place on Imbros during the Ottoman-Russian war in the years 1768-1774. The Russians managed to control many of the islands in the Aegean Sea, including Imbros. Ultimately, as a result of the peace treaty, it was returned to the Ottoman Empire.

During the Balkan wars, between November 1912 and September 1913, Imbros was under Greek control. After the end of hostilities, as a result of pressure from the British, the island was returned to the Turks due to its strategic location.

First World War and afterwards

In 1915, the Allies were stationed on Imbros, and the island was the headquarters for the troops fighting on the Gallipoli Peninsula. At that time, a field hospital, an airport, and administration buildings were erected on the island. In 1918, on the waters near Imbros, a sea battle was fought between the British and Turkish warships. As a result, the Turks lost their two most valuable units – the cruisers Midilli and Yavuz Sultan Selim. Thus, they could not take any offensive action in the Aegean Sea until the end of the First World War.

The peace treaty signed in Sèvres in 1920, gave the island of Imbros to Greece. This state did not last long – as a result of the victorious war fought by the Turkish army under the leadership of Mustafa Kemal Atatürk against the Greek troops, the provisions of Sèvres treaty were renegotiated. Under the new treaty, signed in Lausanne in 1923, Imbros was included within the boundaries of the Turkish Republic. At the same time, due to the fact that the island was inhabited mostly by the Greeks, it was granted a special autonomous status, and its population was excluded from the population exchange between Greece and Turkey.

The provisions of the treaty were not respected – already in 1927 the special rights granted to the Greeks of Imbros were revoked. The similar situation occurred on the island of Tenedos (now Bozcaada). The Turkish education system was imposed on the Greeks of these islands, and at the same time they were deprived of the right to appoint local tribunals. The further harassment

Traditional building in Gökçeada (Panaghia Balomeni)

occurred after World War II: Turkish settlers from the Black Sea region were gradually moved to Imbros, and the Greeks had to give away their farmlands. Successive waves of resettlement in 1946, 1973, 1984, and 2000, and the harassment of the local population deprived its Greek inhabitants of their means of subsistence. Most of them decided to leave the island and go into exile to Greece and the United States, and even to distant Australia.

Currently, Imbros is an island inhabited almost entirely by the Turks, with only a small Greek community whose ancestors have lived there since the ancient times. It is enough to compare the proportions of Greek and Turkish inhabitants in 1927 (6555 Greeks and 157 Turks) and 2000 (254 Greeks and 8640 Turks) to illustrate the demographic changes on the island.

The most famous Greek, born in Imbros, is the current Patriarch of Constantinople, Bartholomew I. He was born in 1940 in the small village of Zeytinli, formerly known as Aghios Theodoros.

Gökçeada today

The island, officially known as Gökçeada since 1970, administratively belongs to Çanakkale Province. It is located in the Aegean

Landscape of Gökçeada

Sea, at the entrance to the Gulf of Saros (tr. *Saros Körfezi*). Cape İncirburnu, situated on the island, is the westernmost point of Turkey.

Gökçeada, the largest Turkish island, has an area of 279 square kilometers, and its highest point is the summit of İlyas Dağ mountain (673 meters asl). The island is almost devoid of forests but is famous for its vineyards and wine production. The island residents also make living from fishing, sheep and cattle husbandry, and the cultivation of olive trees. As there is a large Turkish military base on the island, a large part of its land is not available for tourists.

Gökçeada is now one of the 15 Turkish members of the Cittaslow or 'Slow Town' movement. It started in the Italian Tuscany in 1999, with the aim to promote sustainable tourism and cultural diversity, environmental protection, promotion of traditional local products, and the desire to improve the quality of life.

SIGHTSEEING

The first contact with Gokceada may sometimes be highly disappointing for the newcomers as there is no town around the ferry terminal at Kuzu Limanı. It is a unique phenomenon in the case of the Aegean islands. After arrival, most of the tourists head directly to Gökçeada town, situated 6 km away from the coast.

Gökçeada (Panaghia Balomeni) - the capital city of the island

The main town on the island is Gökçeada, also known as Çınarlı, and in the old days – as Panaghia Balomeni. In the town there is not much to look at – there is a fish market, a closed Orthodox church, and several stone houses. The whole town makes an impression of being neglected. Most visitors who arrive here straight from the ferry or from the nearby airport quickly move on to other villages of the island.

The people arriving at Gokceada are usually mostly interested in traditional Greek villages of the island. For the reasons mentioned above, they are now called Greek mainly for historical reasons – their names were changed in 1926 to the Turkish ones, their Greek residents emigrated en masse from the island, and many buildings have fallen into disrepair. However, it is possible to observe timid and slow efforts to revitalize these villages and attract more visitors. Most frequently visited are four of them – Kaleköy, Zeytinli, Tepeköy, and Dereköy.

Kaleköy and Yukarı Kaleköy (Kastro)

Kaleköy village lies on the coast, about 4 km north of Çınarlı. A ruined Genoese fortress towers over it, but very little has been preserved of this structure. Just beneath the fortress there is a district known as Yukarı Kaleköy (the Upper Castle Village), consisting mainly of abandoned Greek stone houses. There's also a church, currently under restoration, that was built in 1949. Its portico is supported by marble columns probably obtained from an earlier Byzantine building. On the coast, you can find a recently established yacht marina.

Zeytinli (Aghios Theodoros)

In this inconspicuous village, located 3 km west of Çınarlı, Patriarch Bartholomew was born. Currently, only 50 people live there, mainly engaged in the sale of traditional coffee, known as

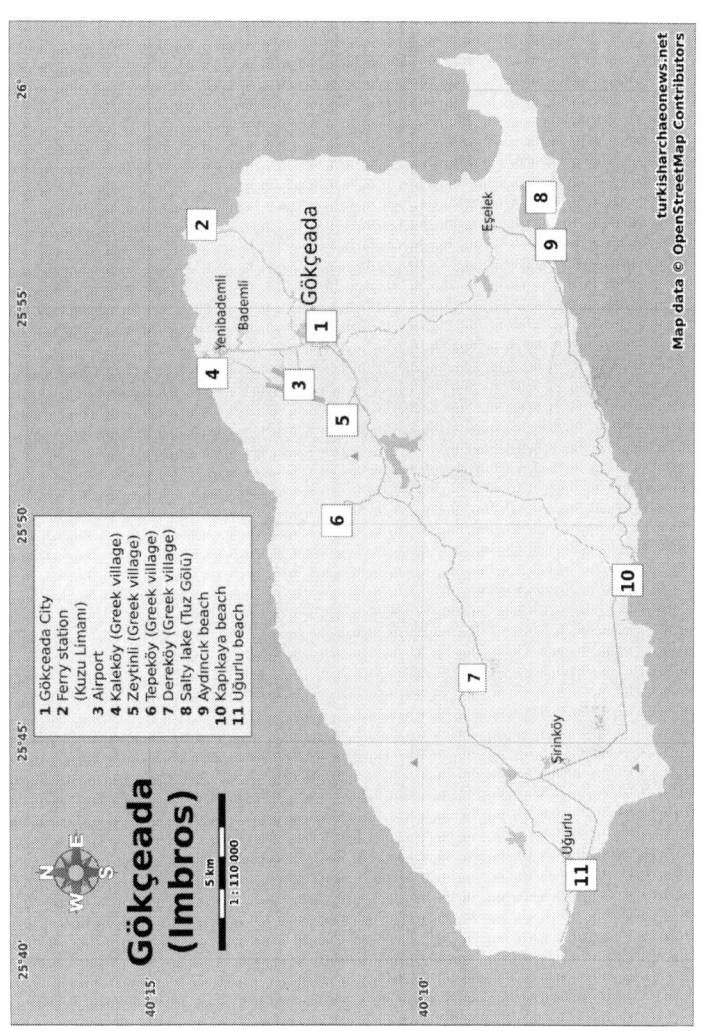

Map of Gökçeada island

Orthodox church in Gökçeada (Panaghia Balomeni)

dibek kahvesi. At the same time, the efforts are made to develop the tourist interest in the village, where one hotel has been opened so far.

Tepeköy (Agridia)

In Tepeköy village, you can almost feel the old, Greek climate of the island as this place is inhabited by the majority of Gökçeada's Greek population. The village is located 9 km west of Çınarlı, at the foot of an extinct volcano İlyas, which is the highest peak on the island. In the area of Tepeköy, there are old Greek houses and a complex of religious buildings, which consists of a church and a school.

Dereköy (Schoinoudi)

It is said about Dereköy that it was once the biggest village on the island, and perhaps in the whole of Turkey. However, currently so few people live there that most of the buildings are uninhabited and are falling into disrepair. The former glory of the settlements is only visible in two churches – closed to visitors, but kept in good condition. The village comes to life once a year, on August the

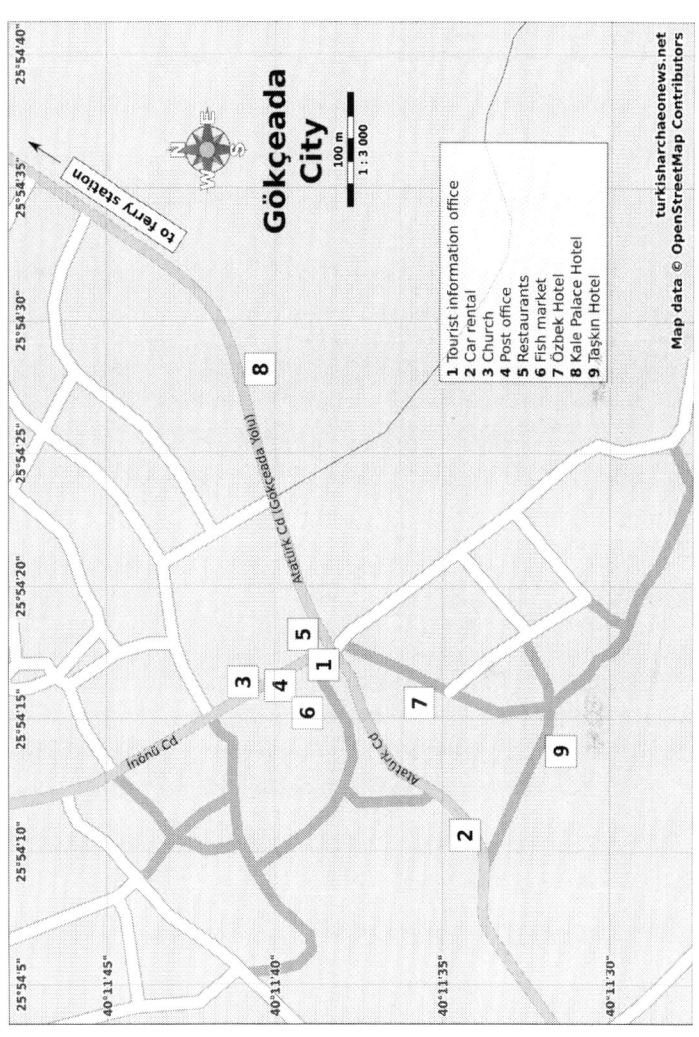

Gökçeada City

100 m
1 : 3 000

to ferry station

Atatürk Cd (Gökçeada Yolu)

İnönü Cd

Atatürk Cd

1 Tourist information office
2 Car rental
3 Church
4 Post office
5 Restaurants
6 Fish market
7 Özbek Hotel
8 Kale Palace Hotel
9 Taşkın Hotel

Plan of Gökçeada city

Genoese fortress in Kaleköy village on Gökçeada

15th, when it is visited by its former residents who come together to celebrate the feast of the Dormition of the Mother of God.

Sunbathing and windsurfing

The best sandy beach on the island is located on its southern side, in Aydıncık. It is situated right next to the small Salt Lake (tr. *Tuz Gölü*). It is possible to try windsurfing and kitesurfing, both on the waters of the Aegean Sea, and on the lake. On the same side of Gökçeada, you can find small beaches in the vicinity of Uğurlu and Kapıkaya.

VISITOR TIPS

Transportation on the island

BY PUBLIC TRANSPORT: the travellers arriving at the island by ferry can take advantage of buses and minibuses that connect the harbour of Kuzu Limanı with Gökçeada town (15 minutes) and Kaleköy (25 minutes). The buses depart every hour and are usually synchronized with the arrival of a ferry. You can also get a minibus to the villages of Yenibademli and Kaleköy from the town of Gökçeada.

BY TAXI: because the public transport is underdeveloped on the island, the travellers who do not have a car, need to hire a taxi.

BY CAR: a car can be transported to the island by ferry or rented at the car rental agency in the town of Gökçeada, on Atatürk Street.

Keep in mind that the distances on the island are not long, but the only petrol station is situated on the eastern side of Gökçeada town, by the road to the ferry terminal.

Accommodation

Accommodation can be easily found on Gökçeada, with the exception of August the 15th, when most of the hotels are occupied by the Greeks visiting the island for the religious holiday.

The most interesting accommodation options in the capital of the island – Gökçeada (Çınarlı) are:

- Kale Palace Hotel – in the center of the town, on Atatürk Street.
- Özbek Hotel – also located in the city center, at Republic Square (tr. *Cumhuriyet Meydanı*).
- Taşkın Hotel – just west of downtown, on Olive Street (tr. *Zeytinli Caddesi*).

In other towns and villages on the island, there are also many accommodation options of various standards, from simple guesthouses and boutique hotels to modern holiday resorts.

The best, but also the most expensive option in Kaleköy is Anemos boutique hotel, located on a hill, with a pool and very comfortable rooms. A more economical choice is a guesthouse with an unusual Greek-Turkish name Kalimerhaba, located on the waterfront.

In Aydıncık, right on the beach, there is a camping ground known as Şen. You can pitch a tent or rent simple rooms, breakfast is extra paid. Next door there is Gökçeada Surf Hotel, built, as its name suggests, for people interested in windsurfing.

Zeytinli village does not offer a great selection of places to stay, but Zeytindali Hotel is an exceptional boutique hotel. It operates in two renovated stone buildings, and each room is named after a different deity of the Greek pantheon. Please note that the hotel only operates from May to October.

The most famous place to stay in Tepeköy village is Barba Yorgo guesthouse, consisting, in fact, of many buildings scattered around the village. The owner – Yorgo – also runs a Greek tavern, but it only operates from May to September.

Restaurants

There is at least one restaurant in almost every village on the island, so getting a hot meal is not difficult. In the capital of the island, it is worth to visit Gül Hanım Mantı Evi on Atatürk Street. In this simple eatery both typical Turkish dishes – such as mantı dumplings, as well as Greek dishes, including an excellent moussaka, are served.

In Kaleköy, the most attractive restaurant is Yakamoz, located in the old quarter of the village, with a terrace offering panoramic views. In Tepeköy, you can enjoy Greek specialties at Yorgos Taverna. Among the dishes served there you can enjoy such rarities as wild boar stew, goat meat dishes, and typical Greek drink – retsina.

Shopping and services

Since Gökçeada is trying to promote itself on the tourism market as a place famous for organic products, it might be interesting to browse the shops offering local specialties, such as locally produced olive oil, dairy products, vegetables, and fruit. The easiest way to find them is to walk along the main streets of the capital of the island. Among them, the best-known are: an organic farm stand Elta-Ada at the Republic Square and Ekozey on Atatürk Street.

In the town of Gökçeada operates a post office and several banks with ATMs. The tourist information office is located at the Republic Square, but it opens only seasonally, from June to September, from 10 am to 8 pm.

Traditional soap from Gökçeada

GETTING THERE

BY FERRY FROM KABATEPE: the most frequent ferries connect the island of Gökçeada with Kapatepe harbour, located on the western coast of the Gallipoli Peninsula. During favourable weather conditions, ferries depart from Kabatepe at 10 am, 3 pm, and 7 pm, and return from Gökçeada to Kabatepe at 7 am, noon, and 5 pm. In summer, the frequency of ferries increases to six per day, and on weekends – up to eight per day. The trip takes, depending on a vessel and weather conditions, from 1.5 to 2.5 hours.

BY FERRY FROM ÇANAKKALE: less frequent ferries connect the island of Gökçeada with Çanakkale. They only set sail on Fridays and Sundays and return to Çanakkale on Saturdays and Sundays. The cruise lasts longer than the one from Kabatepe, and ticket prices are slightly higher.

Please note that the ferry schedules are often modified, and ferries are sometimes canceled due to the stormy weather. Check the connections on the website of the ferry operator – Gestaş – before setting out on a cruise.

Bozcaada

COORDINATES: 39.8346° N, 26.0727° E

Bozcaada Island is often mentioned together with the other Turk-ish island in the Aegean Sea – Gökçeada. In fact, there are many links between them – including a similar history and geographical proximity, but on the other hand, the islands are of a completely different nature. They are distinguished from each other by their terrain, and above all by that elusive trait called picturesqueness. Simply stated – Bozcaada is much prettier and more fun to visit than harsh and mountainous Gökçeada.

BRIEF HISTORY

Prehistory

Archaeological research has shown that the earliest settlements on the island of Bozcaada date back to the early Bronze Age, i.e. the period from 3000 to 2700 BCE. These findings suggest close ties of the local culture with north-western Asia Minor and the Cyclades – an archipelago of islands off the southeastern coast of Greece. The oldest settlements on Bozcaada were located on the eastern side of the island, where the numerous bays served as natural harbors. Some researchers speculate that the first inhabitants of the island belonged to the tribe of the Pelasgians, who arrived there from Asia Minor.

Mythical beginnings

Tenedos is mentioned for the first time in the Iliad. Homer informs us that the main deity of the island was Apollo, and to be more precise – his incarnation known as Smintheus or 'Lord of Mice,' who can both bring the plague upon people and save them from it. This incarnation was indeed worshiped in Asia Minor, in the famous temple of Apollon Smintheion located in the Southern Troad. The territory of the island was occupied during the Trojan War by Greek troops under the command of Achilles. In the Odyssey, Tenedos is the first stopover for the Greeks on the way back to their homeland.

Virgil, who was active much later, in the first century BCE, also wrote about Tenedos, in his epic Aeneid. According to the author, the Greek army moved to Tenedos, leaving the famous wooden horse with the warriors hidden inside under the walls of Troy. The snakes that killed the Trojan priest Laocoon and his sons also were supposed to come from Tenedos. It was an act of revenge for an attempted warning of the Trojans, trying to prevent them from bringing the horse into the city.

The mythical ruler of the island was Tenes, who appears in many, often conflicting, stories. According to one of them, he was the grandson of the god of the oceans – Poseidon. Wrongly accused of raping his stepmother, he was abandoned at sea by his father, Cygnus. The waves threw him on the shores of the island Leucophrys, where he was proclaimed a king. The name of this island was later changed in his honor to Tenedos. In another version of the myth, Tenes was the son of Apollo and was killed by Achilles, who stopped at Tenedos on the way to Troy. Achilles was not aware of the divine origin of Tenes, but that did not save him from the wrath of Apollo.

Ancient times

The first known coins with Greek inscriptions come from the islands of Lesbos and Tenedos. On these coins, there were bunches of grapes and vessels for wine storage – a reference to the main branch of the economy of the island, and double axes, which, according to Aristotle, were a reference to the capital punishment for adultery on Tenedos.

For many years, on the basis of the writings of ancient authors, it was assumed that Tenedos was colonized by the settlers from

Aeolis in Greece in the early Iron Age. However, archaeological research carried out so far has not confirmed these claims, on the contrary – the type of burial and everyday objects point out to the closer ties with Asia Minor than with Greece.

In the archaic and classical periods, Tenedos it was famous for its wine and olive trees, which were the main source of wealth for its inhabitants. An important activity was also a ferry service between the nearby islands and the mainland. The residents of Tenedos were famous for their dependability, as a saying 'a man of Tenedos' described a person of impeccable integrity and immutable moral principles.

Cleostratus, a famous astronomer, was born on the island around 520 BCE. He is known as the author of the poem, which introduced the concept of the signs of the Zodiac and the solar calendar to the Greeks. However, these were not his own ideas, but he merely borrowed them from the astronomers of Babylon.

In the year 493 BCE, Tenedos, along with other Aegean islands, was conquered by the Persians. Then, in the 5th and the 4th centuries BCE, the island was a naval base belonging to Athens. During the military campaign led by Alexander the Great in Asia Minor, the Persians took advantage of the opportunity and reconquered Tenedos, forcing severe conditions on its inhabitants. Soon afterward, the island was reconquered by the Macedonian army under the command of Hegelochus, and the Macedonian army was reinforced by 3,000 mercenaries and rowers from the island.

The Romans acquired Tenedos in 133 BCE, when the island, along with a considerable territory in Asia Minor, was offered to them in the will made by the last king of Pergamon. However, with the construction of a new harbour, located opposite the island on the mainland, in Alexandria Troas, the importance of Tenedos declined. The local harbour was abandoned, and the inhabitants – got much poorer. They even abandoned their vineyards, and olive oil production was limited to meet the local needs.

In 73 BCE, during the third Pontic War, a great battle was

fought between the forces led by the Roman commander Lucullus and Pontic fleet under the command of Neoptolemus, on the waters of the Aegean Sea near Tenedos. The Romans won the decisive victory. At the turn of the first century BCE and the first century CE, the harbour on Tenedos regained some importance, due to silting up of the harbor of Alexandria Troas. Local coins were minted again, according to old patterns.

Byzantine period

In Byzantine times, Tenedos served as an important trading post. Emperor Justinian ordered the erection of a huge granary on the island. The harbour was a safe heaven for vessels transporting grain from Egypt to Constantinople.

The strategic location of the island meant that it became a tasty morsel for many contemporary powers – Venice, Genoa, and later – the expanding Ottoman Empire. Tenedos was repeatedly passed down within the resolutions of peace treaties and diplomatic arrangements.

The most serious event in the history of the island was the Treaty of Turin between Genoa and Venice that ended the war waged in the period from 1378 to 1381. Under this Treaty, Venice had to destroy all castles, walls, and houses located on the island, so that they never could be rebuilt and the island was supposed to remain uninhabited. The Greek population of the island, then numbering about 8,000 people, had nothing to say, but received financial compensation for the forced resettlement to Crete and Evia. Venice continued to use the harbour on the island, but for many decades no one lived at Tenedos with the exception of this base.

Not much later, a new player – the Ottoman fleet – appeared on the waters of the Aegean Sea. The first sea battle, in 1416, was won by Venice. In 1419, under the peace treaty, Tenedos became a border zone of the spheres of Ottoman and Venetian influences, beyond which the Ottoman fleet had no right to maneuver. In 1437, the island was visited by the Spanish adventurer and explorer, Pedro Tafur, who described it later as the place deserted, mostly inhabited by rabbits, but with a well-maintained harbour. At this time, Tenedos was the target of frequent Ottoman attacks.

Ottoman times

Tenedos was captured by the Ottoman troops in 1455, two years after the conquest of Constantinople by the army of Sultan Mehmed II. Tenedos was the first island in the Aegean Sea controlled by the Ottoman Empire, although, in 1464, it was temporarily reconquered by the Venetian troops. In the Ottoman times, the fortress was rebuilt on the island, and settlers arrived, attracted by the promises of tax exemptions. Tenedos also served as a place of exile for the prisoners of the Ottoman state.

The next fight for Tenedos took place between Turkey and Venice in the years 1646-1657. After the Ottoman victory, Grand Vizier Köprülü Mehmed Pasha visited the island and personally oversaw its reconstruction, contributing to the erection of the mosque bearing his name, café, bakeries, shops, mills, schools, inns, and baths.

In 1807, during the Russian-Turkish War, Russian and British troops occupied Tenedos, which served as a military base for the attacks in the direction of the Dardanelles and the Athos Peninsula. Once again, Russian occupation led to the destruction of the infrastructure on the island – the city was burned, the harbour was almost completely filled up, and most of the buildings were demolished. The residents fled from Tenedos, and after the situation stabilized, the island was resettled, mostly by the Greeks.

During the Greek War of Independence in 1822, the insurgents under the leadership of Konstantinos Kanaris attacked the Ottoman fleet off the coast of Tenedos and destroyed one of its ships. As a result of the war, almost all the trees growing on the island were destroyed. During the period of temporary stabilization, the main source of income of the inhabitants was the production of wine and wool. In the early twentieth century, the island had a population of about two thousand people, of which one quarter were the Muslims.

Balkan Wars, the First World War and post-war period

During the First Balkan War, Tenedos was the first island in the northern Aegean Sea occupied by the Greeks. It remained under their control until 1922. During the First World War, the British used the island as a supply base, and also built a military airport. Finally, under the provisions of the Treaty of Lausanne, Tenedos, like Imbros, was granted to Turkey. Since then, these islands have been the only inhabited Aegean islands belonging to this country. The Greek population of Tenedos was excluded from the forced re-settlement after the war, and Article 14 of the Treaty acknowledged their special rights and privileges.

Despite these safeguards, political tensions between Greece and Turkey subjected the Greek population of Tenedos to considerable pressure, aiming to persuade the Greeks to leave the island. In 1927, the administration of the island was entrusted to the Turks, and Greek schools were closed. Harassment, confiscation of land, and the persecution had the effect desired by the Turkish government. Local Greeks gradually went into exile, both to Greece and to other countries.

Until the 90s of the twentieth century, foreigners were forbidden to visit Tenedos. Gradually, the tourism potential of the island was recognized. The government supported the development of vineyards and holiday resorts, making Tenedos an attractive place to spend summer holidays. In recent years, the situation has slightly improved for the Greeks who decided to stay on the island. After a visit of Recep Tayyip Erdogan, then the Prime Minister of Turkey, the government provided the funds for the restoration of the bell tower of the church, but it was only a small step towards mitigating the effects of many years of persecution of the local Greek community.

The name of the island

The current official name of the island is Bozcaada, derived from a combination of two Turkish words: boz – gray, faded, and ada – island. This name, however, is still used alternately with the

Greek term Tenedos, which comes from Greek mythology, and is associated with the Greek hero Tenes. He governed the island during the Trojan War and died at the hands of Achilles.

Moreover, in the historical sources, other names of the island are reported. Pliny the Elder mentions the names Calydna, Phoenice, and Lyrnessus, and Apollodorus of Athens adds the name Leocophrys to this collection.

The island nowadays

The island of Bozcaada is located in the north-eastern part of the Aegean Sea. It is the third largest island that belongs to Turkey, after Gökçeada and Marmara. Its surface is almost 40 square kilometers, and it is currently inhabited by about 2.5 thousand people. In the summer, the number of people on the island rises to 10,000. There is just one town on this triangular island – also bearing the name of Bozcaada. Interestingly, there are no villages, and the entire population is concentrated in just one settlement.

The island is relatively flat, and its hill elevation rises only 192 meters above sea level. Most of the land is not forested – a small pine grove is located on the south-western side. Much of the island is farmland, except for the sandy areas on the western side. At Bozcaada, there are several sources of drinking water, but they are insufficient for the needs of its residents, and the island is now connected to the mainland by a pipeline that supplies water.

Traditional activities of the local people are fishing and wine production. The wine produced here has a long tradition, but until recently this industry was controlled solely by the Greeks. Vineyards constitute about 80% of all arable land on Bozcaada. In addition, olive trees and wheat are grown. Tourism is a relatively new addition to the sources of income of the locals.

SIGHTSEEING

Most people reaching the island begin the tour in the town of Bozcaada. The first structure, clearly visible after the arrival, and also the biggest tourist attraction of the town, is an impressive fortress (tr. *kale*). It is true that the fortifications have stood in this place at least since the Byzantine times. However, most of the currently visible buildings of the castle were erected in the later periods, in the time of the Genoese, Venetian, and Ottoman rule. Inside the fortress, the remains of the mosque, ammunition depots, a hospital, barracks and a few pillars of the Roman period can be seen. The official opening hours of the fortress are from 10 am to 1 pm and from 2 pm to 6 pm.

Historically, the town was divided into two districts (tr. *mahalle*) – one Greek and one Turkish, with a distinct character and diverse architecture. Unfortunately, the Greek district, located on the northern side, burnt down in 1874, and although it was subsequently rebuilt, many historical buildings were irretrievably lost. Today, this part of the city, laid out on a grid of perpendicularly intersecting streets, is the place where most of the shops, restaurants, and hotels are situated. The most distinctive building in the district is the bell tower belonging to the church of the Dormition of Mary the Mother of Jesus. It was built in 1869, but the current appearance is the result of its rebuilding in 2009.

In the Greek district, near the church, operates the Museum of Local History of Bozcaada (tr. *Bozcaada Yerel Tarih Müzesi*). In its collections there are many objects testifying to the rich history of the island, including maps, old prints, photographs, and everyday objects. In the neighborhood, there is also a small gallery selling pictures and images of the island. The museum is open from 10 am to 7 pm, but only in the summer season, i.e. from the end of May to September.

The Turkish district – Alaybey – is located in the south. Because it was not destroyed by the fire, it boasts many old buildings. In its present form, this district was established in 1702. It consists mainly of residential houses, but the attention of tourists can be attracted to the grave of Halil Hamid Pasha, Grand Vizier exiled to Tenedos and then executed for participating in a conspiracy against the reigning sultan. The tomb stands in the courtyard of the historical Alaybey Mosque (tr. *Alaybey Cami*). Another old mosque in this neighbourhood is Köprülü Mehmet Paşa Mosque.

In this area, you can also find historical baths and fountains.

Outside the town, you can search for local beaches. The best of them are situated on the south-western coast. They are called: Ayazma, Ayana, Sulubahçe, and Habbele. On the hill above Ayazma Beach, there is a small chapel and a monastery, built at the holy spring as ayazma actually means a sacred spring in Turkish. Ayazma Beach is the best equipped of all the beaches on the island. There are bars and restaurants; you can also rent deck-chairs and umbrellas. A favourite point to watch the sunset over the Aegean Sea is near Polente lighthouse, on the westernmost tip of the island.

VISITOR TIPS

Transportation

The big advantage for the travellers planning to tour the island is its small area. It makes it relatively easy to explore is on foot or on a bike. If you do not have your own bike, you can rent one near the ferry terminal in İskele Sancak Café. The distance from the town center to Ayazma is 6.5 km, and to the westernmost promontory with a lighthouse – 10 km.

Public transport on the island consists of minibuses, connecting the town with Ayazma and Sulubahçe beaches.

Accommodation

Accommodation options are numerous in Bozcaada, and additionally – they enjoy the opinion of the best in the country. Beside luxury boutique hotels and simple B&Bs you can rent a room in a residential house. The offers of such accommodation await the tourists arriving by ferry, as the owners of rooms for rent wait at the terminal. You can also find them walking around the Greek district of the town. In addition to the numerous hotels in the city, a few guesthouses are located along the road leading along the eastern coast of the island, and near Ayazma beach. Note that some hotels and guesthouses are open only in the summer season.

In the center of Bozcaada you can consider the following accommodation options:

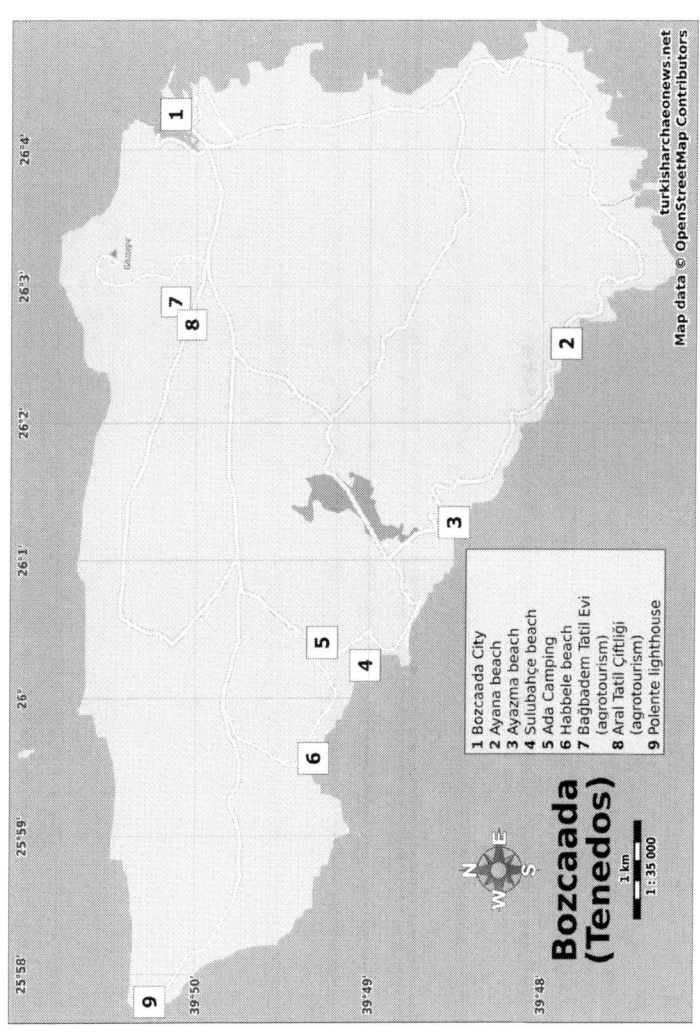

Map of Bozcaada (Tenedos) island

- Patalya Pansiyon – Boruzan Street No. 31, on a hill over-looking the sea, with a beautiful garden.
- Destina Hotel – on the same street, a little closer to the port. The hotel is famous for its rich breakfast buffet, served in the garden.
- Eftelya Hotel – Boruzan Street No. 7. It is a relatively cheap option, but beware as some of the rooms are located in the basement.
- Dokuz Oda Hotel – Eylül Street No. 43, at the church. These are actually two restored buildings. The hotel is owned by a local Greek called Kosta.
- Kale Pansiyon – Üstgeçit Street No. 20, on a high hill, with sweeping views of the town.
- Armagrandi Hotel – Dolapli Street No. 4-6. It is an unusual place as the hotel has been organized in the former wine factory. It offers spacious and stylish rooms and suites.

An interesting accommodation option in Bozcaada is a stay on a farm outside the town. Highly recommended places of this kind are Harmani Tatil Çiftliği and Aral Tatil Çiftliği, located close to each other, about 2.5 km west of the town. Both places offer accommodation in stone dwellings, located at the top of the highest hill on the island. The meals are prepared from locally manufactured products.

If you prefer camping, there is Ada Campsite, located at Sulu-bahçe Beach. Unfortunately it is very poorly equipped.

Restaurants

In the center of town, there are numerous tea houses, bars, and restaurants, but remember, as in the case of hotels, that some of them operate only during the summer season. The best place to sample local specialties is Ada Café, where the juice of poppies (tr. *gelincik şerbeti*) and biscuits with mastic (tr. *sakızlı kurabiye*) are served.

The lovers of Greek cuisine can choose from several taverns offering typical dishes of this country. The most notable ones are

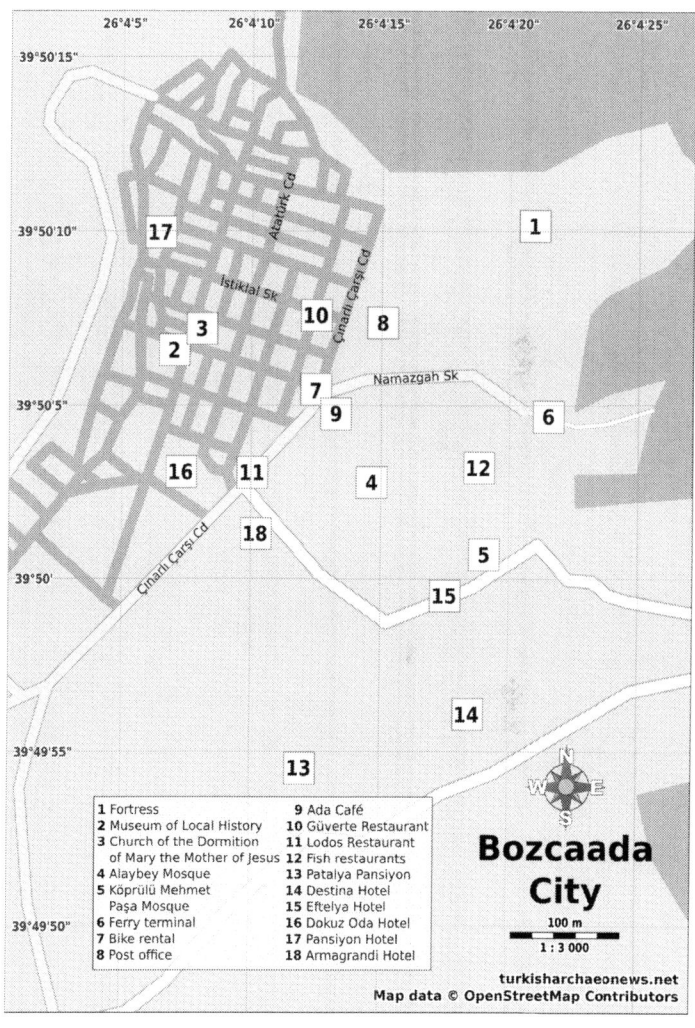

Plan of Bozcaada city

Lodos on Çınarlı Çarşı Street and Güverte on Istiklal Street. In the vicinity of the port, there are many fish restaurants, but you have to be very careful and check the prices of the meals.

Shopping and services

Most service points, including a post office, bank branches, and ATMs, are located at the intersection of Namazgah, Çınarlı Çarşı, and Çınar Çeşme streets, in the center of the town.

The most important product bought by tourists on the island is the locally produced wine from three grape varieties: Karasakız, Altınbaş, and Karalahna. Wine shops, run by major producers – Corvus, Talay, Amadeus, Güler, and Ada, are also located in the very center of Bozcaada town.

GETTING THERE

BY FERRY: the island of Bozcaada can be reached by the ferries departing from Geyikli İskelesi terminal (also known as Yükyeri İskelesi). The terminal is located on the coast of Asia Minor, 4 km west of the town of Geyikli and 19 km from Ezine. The harbour is connected to Ezine by coaches. Their timetable is synchronized with the ferries.

The number of ferry connections per day depends on the time of year and the weather, ranging from six a day in the middle of the summer season, three – in the winter, to zero – during storms. The cruise lasts just 30 minutes.

BY HYDROFOIL: you can also get to Bozcaada by a hydrofoil from the city of Çanakkale, although the cruises take place infrequently, and their timetables are subject to frequent changes. Typically, such a crossing is possible on Wednesdays, Saturdays, and Sundays.

Appendices

Before you come to Turkey

When you are planning the trip to Turkey, whether with the assistance of a travel agent or on your own, there are some issues worth remembering about that are discussed in this chapter. Following the advice will help you avoiding any unpleasant surprises and your holidays will be certainly a much more enjoyable experience.

PASSPORTS AND VISAS

This might sound obvious, but to enter the territory of Turkey you need a passport. European travellers, spoiled by the comforts of Schengen zone, sometimes forget about this obligation, as only the ID is necessary for visiting the area of the European Union. However, Turkey is not the member country of the EU, so remember to take your passport. What's more, the passport should be valid for at least eight months at the time of entry to Turkey.

Most Western nationalities do not need a visa, but it is best to make sure by visiting the official website the Ministry of Foreign Affairs of the Republic of Turkey (http://www.mfa.gov.tr/visa-information-for-foreigners.en.mfa). If you find out that the visa is required, purchase it online from Electronic Visa (e-Visa) Application System (https://www.evisa.gov.tr). Remember to obtain the visas for all members of your group or family as children are not exempt from this obligation. If you buy an electronic visa remember to have the printed copy of this document with you all the time during your journey.

TRAVEL INSURANCE

If you purchase a tour or a holiday package to Turkey, offered by a travel agency, in addition to the airfare, accommodation and meals you will get a basic travel insurance package. Read the terms of this coverage carefully, to avoid embarrassing situations in the case of any health problems. Basic travel insurance usually does not cover the accidents that occur while practicing many sports and it does not guarantee the reimbursement of the costs of treatment of chronic diseases.

Those traveling to Turkey on their own must purchase the right insurance package from an insurance company. Remember that the European Health Insurance Card (or EHIC) is not valid in Turkey.

DRIVING A CAR

If you are planning a tour of Turkey by car or are considering a quick trip from Bulgaria or Greece into Turkey, it is necessary to obtain International Motor Insurance Card, known simply as a Green Card – without this document, your vehicle will not be admitted to Turkey. Also remember that, in most of the cases, Comprehensive Cover and Assistance insurance packages do not include the territory of Turkey.

The matters get complicated when you try to enter Turkey with a car that is not your property as may be in the case of a rented car or a vehicle obtained through leasing. In this situation, you have to prepare well in advance and carefully read the list of documents required for entry.

Do you use car navigation? It is a very useful thing, but the territory of Turkey is often not included in these systems. Check this out before you go, and purchase/download additional maps, if necessary.

In Turkey, some motorways are paid, the fees also apply to the bridges crossing the Bosphorus in Istanbul. The fee is paid in the form of a sticker known as HGS, which must be purchased at a post office or selected petrol stations. Often it is not possible to obtain an HGS at the entrance to the toll motorway section, so obtain the sticker in advance.

SAFETY ISSUES

Before leaving, take a look at the messages on the current safety situation in Turkey. People going to the holiday resorts on the Aegean Sea and the Mediterranean Sea have no reason to worry, but if you plan a trip to the east of the country, be sure to check these messages on a regular basis.

Remember that when you travel you must have a passport with you, naturally not in the case of a walk from the hotel to the beach or a shop. In the case of any longer trips, the passport should not be left at the hotel.

Road safety is a separate issue – many travelers share blood-chilling tales of crazy Turkish drivers. In fact, the situation does not look that bad, although you have to prepare for an entirely different style of driving – indicators are not used, and pedestrians are ignored, even on crossings. If you do not feel up to the challenge, do not rent a car and use public transportation instead.

CURRENCY

The official currency in Turkey is the Turkish lira (tr. *Türk lirası*). In the holiday villages often there is a possibility to make a payment in euros or US dollars, but this is not always the case. In many places (e.g. discount stores), only Turkish liras are accepted.

You must also remember that despite numerous exchange offices, not every currency is easily exchanged into liras. Before leaving your country purchase an easily convertible currency (such as US dollars, euros, or British pounds). Credit cards are widely accepted as the form of payment, but always have some cash with you just in case.

CULTURAL DIFFERENCES

A trip to Turkey is not an opportunity to experience an enormous culture shock, especially if you go to the cities frequently visited by foreigners. However, be aware of some differences in the behaviour of the Turkish people, such as their body language, non-verbal communication and appropriate clothing (e.g. during the visit to the mosque). Also, note that the discussion about religious and political issues is not always a great idea.

In rural areas and in the east of the country you should wear clothing covering your arms and legs – it is not required by the law, but helps to avoid surprised or intrusive glances. Women should not look Turkish men directly into their eyes. That gesture, in many Western countries considered to be a sign of respect, in Turkey is understood as an incentive to flirt.

Weather in the Troad region

The area described in this guidebook belongs geographically to the Marmara Sea region. It is an area with a temperate climate, but also characterized by very changeable weather, because of the varied terrain. The average temperature in winter is 4 degrees Celsius (39 degrees Fahrenheit), and in summer it reaches 27 degrees Celsius (80 degrees Fahrenheit).

In winter, there are several days when the temperature falls below freezing. The lowest recorded temperature in the region was -25.7 degrees Celsius in 1929 in Istanbul, and the highest was 43.7 degrees Celsius in Balıkesir in 1958. The average annual precipitation ranges from 500 to 1000 mm, and in winter the snow covers the ground for about ten days only.

Currency, Prices and Payment Methods

Many tourists associate a visit to Turkey with a shopping spree. This association probably dates back to the eighties of the 20th century, when it was possible to buy in Turkey clothes, fur, and leather products as well as and famous sweaters with a distinctive design at bargain prices. Although the times have changed, along with the prices and the range of offered products, the tradition of making purchases in Turkey and strong conviction of great shopping opportunities have remained. Meanwhile, in recent years the prices of many products on the Turkish market caught up with European standards and sometimes even exceeded them.

The art of bargaining

Shopping in Turkey can cause a lot of emotions, both positive and negative. The joy of an occasional purchase can quickly be overshadowed by disappointment when, after the transaction, we realize that the price was overblown, and the prices are much lower on the adjacent stall. You should make shopping decisions, not on impulse, but as a result of research, comparison and bargaining till you drop.

Many tourists are afraid of the situations when they have to haggle. If you are one of them, the ideal solution is to shop at supermarkets and discount stores where the prices are fixed and non-negotiable. The same rule applies to pharmacies and grocery stores.

It would help if you haggled at the bazaars and souvenir shops, especially when buying leather products, carpets, ceramics, and jewelry. The basic principle of haggling is: do not start it at all if you do not intend to buy anything. Starting the price negotiations means that you are initially interested in buying. Of course, if the price does not suit you, you can always resign, explaining that the rate is too high, and walk away. Often this move helps to reduce the price that seemed to be the final offer. While bargaining, do not worry about offering the price that seems too low. Do not suggest the price that is just 5 or 10 per cent lower, but 50 per cent lower. By judging the reaction of the seller, you will find out how much the original price was overblown.

During haggling, it is also helpful to establish closer contact with the seller, so they no longer treat you as just another customer, but rather as a kindred spirit. Sellers often ask questions about your country of origin as the part of their standard approach. At that point, it is worth to bounce the ball back and inquire about their hometowns. If the vendor accidentally comes from the city that you have visited and gets the feeling that you liked it, you have just scored a point.

Payment methods

One of the endlessly repeated questions, asked by the people travelling to Turkey for the first time seems to be 'What kind of currency should I use in Turkey?'. The answer is obvious: the official currency of Turkey is the Turkish lira, and the prices quoted in this currency are usually the lowest. The abbreviations, indicating this currency, are TL and TRY. From 2012, the Turkish lira has its symbol (₺), which now can be often seen in shops and bazaars.

In the cities of the Turkish Riviera you can often also pay in foreign currency, most commonly accepted are euros, US dollars, and British pounds. The tales of the sellers offering the currency conversion scheme where 1 euro = 1 dollar are just a fairy tale. Traders do know current exchange rate very well, and meticulously recalculate the prices into other currencies. If in doubt, we recommend that you familiarise yourself with the current exchange rates, published on the Internet since the Turkish lira is not the most stable of the currencies in the world.

In many places, a reasonable alternative to cash payments is the use of debit or credit cards. The transactions with credit cards are not charged with a commission in Turkey. However, when taking the cash from an ATM using a bank card a fee is sometimes charged, and the amount depends on your agreement with the bank that issued the card.

PRICES

As mentioned above, Turkey is no longer the purchasing paradise, and the prices of many products do not differ significantly from the rates in European countries. Some products are even more expensive, including such essentials as fuel or some dairy products.

The products for infants and young children are also relatively expensive, and the choice is much smaller than in Europe. It is true that you can easily buy disposable diapers in Turkey, but the selection can be minimal. Infant formula is costly, and baby food is available in a small variety, with the tastes slightly different from those offered in other countries.

Many people are astonished at the high prices of some grocery products, including dairy products and meat. Also, alcohol is much more expensive in Turkey than in Europe. Naturally, you can still make some excellent deals while shopping, especially when it comes to Turkish spices, seasonal fruit and vegetables, and clothing.

Political system, population and geography

Finding basic information about Turkey is not difficult, and many websites and guidebooks repeat the same dry facts. However, sometimes it is helpful to add some details to the raw data, to get a better idea about the place you are going to visit. The confrontation of the imagination with the reality is a different story; after all, this is why we travel – to witness with our eyes how this imaginary world looks like in reality.

POLITICAL SYSTEM

Turkey is a democracy and its political system is described as a unitary presidential constitutional republic. The head of state is the president, and this function has been held, since 28 August 2014 by Recep Tayyip Erdoğan, a longtime leader of the Justice and Development Party, known by the acronym AKP (tr. *Adalet ve Kalkınma Partisi*). AKP is sometimes cleverly explained as Ak Parti or White Party, which suggests its purity and transparency. This image has been somewhat tarnished by a huge corruption scandal disclosed in 2013, which involved AKP government members and their families.

AKP is officially described as a moderately conservative group, but one should remember that the activity of religious parties is banned in Turkey. In the past, political parties that were accused of attempting to change the secular character of the state and were referred to as pro-islamic were repeatedly outlawed.

What does conservatism mean concerning AKP? Some illustration of the views of its leaders may be a statement of a former Deputy Prime Minister Bülent Arınç, who in harsh words criticised the women laughing in public areas. In 2007, Recep Tayyip Erdoğan, then holding the position of Istanbul mayor, in his speech quoted the words of the poem by Ziya Gökalp: 'The mosques are our barracks. The minarets are our bayonets. The domes are our helmets. The faithful are our soldiers.' This statement cost him the loss of the office and a few months in prison.

There are other political parties on the Turkish political scene. Among them, the worthy of special mention is the Republican People's Party (CHP or Cumhuriyet Halk Partisi), founded in 1919 by Mustafa Kemal Atatürk. For many years, until the introduction of a multiparty system in 1945, it was the only legally functioning party in Turkey.

The Turks are very patriotically inclined, and many foreigners are amazed by the familiar sight of Turkish flags and a considerable number of the monuments of Atatürk, the father of the Turkish Republic and its first president. Although currently many Turks cast some doubt on his achievements, any criticism of Atatürk from the mouth of a foreigner may be met with great indignation.

POPULATION

Turkey is home to approximately 80 million people, that is twice as much as in Poland, and only about 3 million less than in Germany. It also means that if Turkey were admitted to the European Union, it would become the second most populous state of the EU.

It is a country relatively homogeneous both ethnically and religiously. According to various estimates, from 70 to 75% of the population are the Turks and the most significant ethnic minority are the Kurds. They make up about 18% of the population, although this figure is highly approximate, and you can find both the information that there are only 10% or even 20% of them. Until recently, they represented a group officially unrecognised by the Turkish authorities, but when AKP first formed the government their situation started to improve gradually, e.g. in towns in the east of the country, where most Turkish Kurds live, signposts in Kurdish began to appear. The peace process was stopped in 2015, and the situation has been deteriorating since then, with the renewed activity of the Kurdistan Workers' Party (PKK), a Kurdish militant organisation fighting the Turkish forces in the east of the country.

Among other national-ethnic minorities living in Turkey, we should mention Circassians (2.5 million), Bosniaks (2 million), Albanians, Georgians, Arabs, and Pomaks (Muslim Slavs). Before the First World War, the Ottoman Empire was inhabited by numerous communities of Armenians and Greeks. However, due to political and ethnic conflicts, mass murders, and population displacements, these nationalities are represented in Turkey by tiny groups. A very interesting, from the ethnographic point of view, is an ethnic group living on the Black Sea coast – Laz people (80,000), who belong to the South Caucasian group.

Turkey is a secular country according to its constitution, with no official state religion. However, while travelling around the country one needs to remember, that according to official statistics, 99.8% of its population is Muslim. What's more, the confession of Turkish citizens is entered on their identity cards, and the idea of an atheist raises a genuine surprise. The remaining 0.2% of the population of Turkey are mainly Christians and Jews.

The dominant group of the Muslim citizens of Turkey are Sunni Muslims, the members of the world's most populous sect of Islam. Another Muslim group is the Alevis, representing 20 to 30% of the Muslims in the country. Alevis' religious beliefs, oficially belonging to the Islamic world, are actually a syncretic combination of Islam with elements of Christianity, Buddhism, and shamanism.

For many years, headscarves, traditionally worn by Muslim women, were banned in schools and government offices as a sign of Islamisation of public space. However, in recent years the ban has been gradually lifted – first at universities, then in offices and, in 2014, in schools. In the country there are numerous signs of religious revival and many new mosques are being erected. Several years ago a debate about the future of Hagia Sophia in Istanbul was revived – this Byzantine church was converted into a mosque in the 15th century, and in the early Republican era into a museum. Today, many influential politicians demand the restoration of the building's function into a mosque.

GEOGRAPHY

Largest cities

Over 70% of Turkish citizens live in cities, though many Turkish city dwellers cherish an enormous sentiment to the rural and pastoral lifestyle of their ancestors. There are eight cities in Turkey with a population of over 1 million. In these metropolitan areas lives 35% of the total population of the country. For comparison – in German cities with over 1 million inhabitants live only 10% of the country's citizens.

The largest city of Turkey is Istanbul, the former capital of the Ottoman Empire, and earlier, as Constantinople, the capital of Byzantine Empire. In this city, according to official data, there are approximately 15 million residents. Because 2/3 of the inhabitants are settled on the European shore, Istanbul is considered to be the largest urban agglomeration in Europe. It is also the sixth most populous city in the world. It grows by about half a million new inhabitants every year, as a result of births and migration.

Turkey's second largest city is its capital – Ankara – inhabited by 5.5 million people. In comparison to Istanbul, it seems to be a small town, but it's worth to realise that it is more populous than Los Angeles and comparable to Ireland. Moreover, as the new capital of the Republic of Turkey, in 1927 it only had 75,000 inhabitants.

Other metropolies of Turkey are Izmir (3 million), Bursa, and Adana, with 1.7 million inhabitants both, which means that each of them is the size of Polish capital city – Warsaw. To complete the list, one must mention Gaziantep, Konya, and Antalya, each with more than 1 million people.

Territory

The territory of Turkey lies on two continents: about 3% of the country is in Europe, in the area known as Eastern Thrace or

Rumelia. Turkey is bordered here with Greece and Bulgaria, and its Asian part is separated from Europe by two straits – the Bosporus and the Dardanelles, and the Sea of Marmara between them. On both banks of the Bosphorus, the largest Turkish metropolis – Istanbul – is situated, and the strategic importance of this location was already appreciated by the ancient Greeks and Romans, who called it Constantinople.

The Asian part of the country, representing 97% of its area, occupies the westernmost peninsula of the Asian continent, called Asia Minor or Anatolia. Turkey is bordered here with Georgia, Armenia, Iran, Iraq, Syria, and the Nakhchivan Autonomous Republic, the exclave of Azerbaijan. For political reasons and because of the current situation in the Middle East, it is now impossible for tourists to cross the borders with Armenia, Syria, and Iraq.

The area of Turkey is more than 780,000 square kilometres. Americans vividly write that it is slightly larger than Texas, but it is still two and a half times bigger than Poland. Remember this when planning to travel through Turkey – the distances to cover when going from the west to the east or from the north to the south of the country are enormous. For example, to reach Van in the east of Turkey from the city of Izmir situated on the Aegean coast one needs to travel 1800 km – that translates into 27 hours of non-stop driving. The distance from Istanbul to Van – 1750 km – is the same as from Istanbul to Krakow in Poland.

Also, in the case of so-called Anatolia tours you must take into account the considerable distances between the seaside resorts and popular destinations for such trips. To reach Pamukkale from Alanya you need to travel 370 km, and the distance from Side to Cappadocia is 470 km. Additionally, you should forget about the express pace of such a journey – a narrow strip of Mediterranean coast is separated from the central plateau by the mighty Taurus Mountains range. Many people dream of a quick getaway from the Mediterranean coast to Istanbul, but since the road distance from Antalya to Istanbul is 725 km, these trips are only possible by air, and thus are relatively expensive.

Terrain

The terrain of Turkey may prove to be problematic during longer journeys. Many people think of Turkey as a coastal state, but it is, in reality, a mountainous country. Nearly 85% of Turkey is situated at an altitude of over 450 meters above sea level, and the average elevation of the country is as high as 1332 meters above sea level. For comparison – this value for the United States is 760 meters and for the United Kingdom – 162 meters.

Along the northern Black Sea coast of Turkey extends the Pontic Mountains range, over a distance of 1000 km, and along 1500 km of the southern Mediterranean coast runs the Taurus Mountains range. On the east of the country, these mountain ranges converge in the Turkish part of the Armenian Highlands where the average altitude is more than 1,500 meters above sea level. On the territory of Turkey, near the border with Armenia, Azerbaijan, and Iran, the majestic massif of Mount Ararat, the highest peak in Turkey, known from the biblical story of Noah's Ark, rises to a height of 5137 meters above sea level.

The longest river flowing only through the territory of Turkey is Kızılırmak or Red River, joining the Black Sea after passing 1350 km. It is a river relatively little known outside Turkey, in contrast to the two rivers very well recognized by all those fascinated by ancient history, having their sources in Turkey. They are the Tigris (tr. *Dicle Nehri*) and the Euphrates (tr. *Fırat Nehri*) and between them, in the ancient times, existed the land known as Mesopotamia. While the most historically significant part of Mesopotamia is situated in present-day Iraq, but it is worth remembering that we can also visit the area of Mesopotamia during the trip to Turkey. Lovers of geological sciences should be intrigued by the fact the Meander River (tr. *Büyük Menderes Nehri*), whose numerous bends gave the name to a particular shape of a riverbed, flows in the western part of Turkey.

In Turkey, there are 51 natural lakes with an area larger than 1 square km and plenty of smaller lakes. The biggest and the deepest lake in Turkey is Lake Van (3755 square km), located in the east of the country. The famous Hungarian Lake Balaton is over six times smaller. Van is a saline lake with no outlet and only one endemic species of fish from the carp family lives there. On its shores, the famous Turkish Van cats dwell, characterised by white fur, two-coloured eyes and legendary penchant for swimming in the lake. The second largest Turkish lake is Tuz Gölü or Salt Lake (1665 square km), situated in Central Anatolia. Its salinity is as high as 33% – which is 5% more than the famous Dead Sea. Lake Tuz is the source of salt on an industrial scale as 2/3 of the salt consumed in Turkey is obtained from this lake.

In addition to the natural lakes of great importance for the economy of the country are artificial lakes, created by the construction of dams on many Turkish rivers. The largest of these reservoirs – at Atatürk Dam and Keban Dam – are located on the Euphrates and contribute to the irrigation of central Anatolian steppes. Atatürk Reservoir has an area of 817 square km, which means that the largest Polish lake – Sniardwy (113 square kilometres), could fit into it over seven times. The construction of dams in Turkey is very controversial, especially among archaeologists, who mourn the loss of many valuable sites that provided relevant information about the prehistory of Asia Minor.

There is an excellent reason why Turkey is called 'the country of the Four Seas'. In addition to the most widely-known coasts of the Mediterranean Sea and the Aegean Sea, Turkey is surrounded by the Sea of Marmara and the Black Sea. The longest stretch of the Turkish coast is in the west, in the Aegean region. The length of this section is 2805 km, which in no small extent is the result of the shape the coastline, with numerous bays and peninsulas. The second longest coast is the Black Sea (1695 km) and the third – the Mediterranean (1577 km). The shortest coastline belongs to the internal sea of Marmara (927 km). If you add to these values the coasts of the islands belonging to Turkey, the total length of the coastline of the country will be over 8000 km.

Cuisine

For many travellers, an opportunity to taste new dishes is the essence of exploring and learning about the local culture. These gourmets will not be disappointed in Turkey. The cuisine of this country is exotic enough to surprise, and yet close enough to Western taste buds so that everyone can find something for themselves.

Historically, Turkish cuisine is the result of the turbulent history of Asia Minor. In local dishes, we can find the traces of Chinese, Central Asian, Russian, Greek, Arabic, and French influences. Due to the geographical diversity of the country there are many regional dishes, but some recipes can safely be considered as generally Turkish. Turkish cuisine is characterised by the overall simplicity and the use of fresh, local ingredients.

The Turks are very proud, both of their regional dishes, as well as of the fact that Turkey is one of the few countries in the world that can feed itself. It is facilitated by the climate so that the crops can be harvested up to three times a year.

BREAKFAST

The most important meal of the day is often included in the price of accommodation, in hotels, guesthouses, and Teachers' Houses. However, this is not the rule, so you should make sure if breakfast is provided when choosing accommodation, as sometimes you have to pay extra.

Standard Turkish breakfast (tr. *Türk kahvaltı*) in its basic version consists of bread, salty white cheese, tomatoes, cucumbers, olives, butter, and hard boiled eggs. The extended version can additionally include sausages, cheese, honey, and yoghurt. The main drink served with breakfast (and all other meals) is strong black tea, while coffee is rare and is usually served in its instant version.

If the hotel does not provide breakfast, travellers can choose from these options: look for a restaurant serving typical breakfast, go to lokanta (small restaurant) to eat some soup or visit a bakery. In the morning, many restaurants serve famous Turkish scrambled eggs with vegetables known as menemen. The lentil soup (tr. *mercimek çorbası*) is a traditional breakfast dish in Turkey, as it is tasty, nutritious, and cheap.

In the bakery, you can buy various pastries, including börek – rolls of thin dough, stuffed with meat or cheese. A popular breakfast choice is also pogača, a distant relative of Italian focaccia, sold plain or with a filling, which may include cheese, herbs, and various vegetables, even potatoes.

Lunch, dinner and supper

The choice of restaurants in Turkey can give you a headache. The traditional venues specialise in a small variety of dishes. Some serve meat dishes: kebabs and köfte or minced meat, while others offer a local variant of pizza (pide) or various soups (tr. *çorba*).

Foreigners are usually surprised by the wide variety of kebabs as they associate this dish with thin slices of meat served in a bun with vegetables and sauces, as typical fast-food. The closest to that image is the original Turkish döner kebab, although it is prepared without sauce, in a flatbread called lavaş.

In Turkish, the word kebap encompasses all kinds of roast meat dishes, often served on a plate, accompanied by a salad and rice. The most popular varieties of kebabs are Adana and Urfa – minced meat, spicy seasoned and roasted in the form of cylinders on the skewer over the fire. Also, Iskender kebab (frequently called Bursa kebab) is often served. These are thin slices of meat on pide-type bread with yoghurt and tomato sauce, sprinkled with melted butter. An interesting variation of kebab is patlican kebap – the meat is grilled on the skewers, accompanied by eggplant slices. Obviously, there are many more kinds of kebabs in Turkey.

Köfte are all kinds of meatballs. Sometimes, paradoxically, they are even served in a vegetarian variation as çiğ köfte – prepared from bulgur (wheat cereal) with spicy seasoning. Köfte are also made by the combination of meat and bulgur with herbs, vegetables, bread crumbs, or eggs. The resulting mass is formed into various shapes and then boiled, fried, or baked. The most common varieties in Turkey include: İnegöl köfte – a combination of beef ribs, lamb and onions, Tekirdağ köfte – minced meat mixed with garlic, cumin, flakes of red chili, and black pepper, and Izmir köfte – lamb mixed with stale bread, onion, parsley, salt, pepper, dried mint, and cumin.

Turkish pizza or pide takes the shape of boats of dough filled with cheese or meat in various configurations, but without tomatoes typical to Italian pizza. The cheapest variant is called lahmacun – a round, thin cake with minced meat filling. Other exciting dishes in Turkey are: mantı – small dumplings with meat filling, topped with yoghurt sauce, güveç – meat, mushrooms, or seafood baked in a clay pot with vegetables and cheese, and kuzu pirzola – lamb chops.

In so-called lokantas that is restaurants where the dishes are displayed to the customers on the heaters, you can compose your meal from the ingredients such as rice, bulgur, pasta, stews, casseroles with eggplant and other vegetables and meats, referred to collectively as sulu yemek. In larger eateries, there are so-called family rooms (tr. *aile salonu*). They are designed not only for families with children but also for women who might feel self-conscious eating in the same room with men.

The waiter serving a meal can wish you 'Bon appetit' or 'Afiyet olsun!' When you are served it is customary to thank the cook or the host by saying 'elinize sağlık' which means 'health to your hands' and is a praise of culinary abilities.

SNACKS ON THE ROAD

When travelling there is not always enough time for a proper meal in the restaurant. In Turkey, it is easy to satisfy your hunger quickly by choosing from a variety of snacks sold by street vendors and in small eateries.

Basic snacks of this kind in Turkey are: a bagel sprinkled with sesame seeds (tr. *simit*), boiled corn (tr. *mısır*), mussels (tr. *midye*) with lemon juice, and seasonal fruit from the market.

Fans of sandwiches will be satisfied by: Ayvalık toast – a toast with cheese and ham, kumru – a rye flour bun sprinkled with sesame seeds, layered with grilled sausage (tr. *sucuk*), beef salami (tr. *salam*) and yellow cheese (tr. *kaşar*), or balık ekmek – half of bread with roasted fish, accompanied by fresh vegetables.

A slightly more sophisticated snack is gözleme – a dish similar to pancakes, made with thin dough known as yufka, stuffed with cheese, parsley and green onion, spinach, or minced meat. The appetite for meat will be quickly satisfied with the dürüm version of many dishes. It means that our selection of kebab or köfte will be prepared in takeout from, wrapped in flatbread.

SWEETS

Turkish sweets are famous all over the world. Those with a sweet tooth should try the following specialties:

- Baklava – prepared from French dough. It consists of layers of cake, sandwiched with chopped walnuts, almonds, or pistachio nuts and honey or şöbiyet syrup (made from butter and sugar). The top is usually glazed with icing or syrup and sprinkled with unsalted pistachios.
- Halva – has two basic varieties. The first one is made on the basis of semolina (coarse flour obtained from durum wheat). It has a jelly-like consistency and is somewhat transparent. The second variant is prepared on the basis of tahini (a paste obtained from sesame seeds). It is dry, hard, and brittle. Halva, which can be bought in Turkey, is available in many flavours, of which the most popular are vanilla, pistachio, and cocoa.
- Lokum – also known as Turkish delight, is a variety of hard jelly produced from sugar and starch wheat or corn flour, often coloured with rose water. To this base different ingredients are added: nuts, raisins, and coconut.

- Pişmaniye – resembling cotton candy in appearance and texture, but made from different ingredients. Pişmaniye is prepared from wheat flour, butter, and sugar, with the addition of vanilla, and sometimes pistachios or cocoa.
- Dondurma – traditional Turkish ice cream. It differs significantly in taste and consistency from its European counterparts. The consistency is compact, dense, and flexible, and it melts much more slowly. Dondurma owes its properties to the addition of two specific components. The first one is salep and the second – mastic. Salep is an extraordinary kind of flour that is produced from the tubers of wild orchids. This flour contains a special starch, called bassorin. Mastic is a resin with a distinctive flavor, obtained from a bush growing in the Aegean region.

NON-ALCOHOLIC BEVERAGES

The primary drink while travelling in Turkey should be water (tr. *su*). Especially on hot days you always need to have its supply. The cheapest bottled water can be purchased at discount stores and supermarkets which offer a large number of brands and volumes. The price of water sold right next to the biggest tourist attractions tends to be heavily overblown. In restaurants, bottled water is typically served with the meal (at an additional fee) or in the jug (for free). In this second form, it is sometimes ordinary tap water, so people with sensitive stomachs must remain vigilant. In the mountainous regions, tap water is sometimes delicious, but in the coastal areas the water quality can leave much to be desired.

In addition to water, the thirst is best quenched by ayran – a refreshing soft drink, made from yoghurt blended with water and a pinch of salt. Ayran is also famous for its soothing effect on the digestive system.

The most popular hot drink in Turkey is tea (tr. *çay*). It is here drunk by gallons. Traditionally it is served very strong and aromatic in little tulip-shaped glasses with plenty of sugar. It is a beverage widely available and inexpensive. Customarily, tea is served after each meal in the restaurants, often for free. In the version prepared for tourists, it is sometimes very weak or replaced by instant apple tea.

Surprisingly, it is challenging to get a good cup of coffee in Turkey, and most common are instant coffees known here as neskafe, regardless of their manufacturer. True Türk Kahvesi or Turkish coffee is drunk on special occasions and relatively expensive. It is prepared in a small pan-shaped vessel with a long handle, called cezve. Most frequently it is prepared with sugar right away, so when placing an order, indicate if you wish to get your coffee without it (tr. *sade*).

While in Turkey, try local fruit juice of different variations. We especially recommend peach juice (tr. *şeftali suyu*) and apricot juice (tr. *kayısı suyu*). On the other hand, beware of the dispensers with coloured drinks that have little in common with fruit.

The seekers of new taste sensations should try şalgam, a drink that is based on fermented black carrot juice. Its Turkish name means turnip, which is actually merely an addition to the drink. The other ingredients are salt and bulgur. Şalgam is touted as an extremely healthy product. Its positive effects include: facilitating digestion, calming, strengthening bones and teeth. It is also good for the cardiovascular system, eyes, stomach, and liver.

ALCOHOLIC BEVERAGES

Although Turkey is inhabited mainly by Muslims, access to alcoholic beverages is relatively easy. They are sold in supermarkets and small buffets. However, it is hard to buy alcohol at local discount stores. There are also many restaurants that do not serve alcoholic beverages. In many cities operate special the beer halls (tr. *birahane*), frequented exclusively by male clientele.

Turkey's most famous beer brand is Efes. This beer also has its light version with lower alcohol content, as well as dark beer and extra beer with increased alcohol content. There are other local brands, including Marmara, and imported or licensed products, with Tuborg being the most popular one.

Although Turkey is rarely mentioned among the countries where the vines are grown, it is worth trying out local varieties of wine (tr. *şarap*). The most famous Turkish wines are produced in Cappadocia, where there are right soil conditions for the cultivation, but, unfortunately, less favourable climate – hot summers and cold winters. Two most well-known Turkish companies selling wine are Doluca and Kavaklıdere. The wines of these brands tend to be quite tasty, although in the mouth of a gourmet they are far from world class. Şirince village, located near Selcuk, is famous for its production of fruit wines.

The strongest alcohol drunk in Turkey is rakı. The basis for the production of rakı are grapes, and anise is used for flavouring. Typically, the strength of this drink is from 40 to 50%. For this reason, few people in Turkey drink it undiluted. Chilled rakı is mixed with water or ice, resulting in a beverage of a colour similar to milk (its pure version is transparent). The comparison to milk is the source of the popular description of rakı as the 'lion's milk' (tr. *aslan sütü*).

Drinking raki is associated with the entire ceremony, centred around the so-called rakı table (tr. *rakı sofrası*), with plenty of hot and cold appetisers. The most common of these are roasted chickpeas (tr. *leblebi*), hard white cheese, and pieces of melon. Traditional toast is Şerefinize! (Good luck!).

REGIONAL CUISINE OF TURKISH AEGEAN COAST

Of all culinary regions of Turkey, the Aegean coast can boast the cuisine closest to the Greek one. Because of the climatic conditions, mainly olives, citrus fruit, and stone fruit such as peaches or plums are grown on the coast. It is worth knowing that over 80% of fig trees in Turkey grow in the Aegean region. Turkey is also the world's fourth largest producer of olives, mainly cultivated in this region of the country.

Local dishes are prepared primarily on the basis of olive oil. A typical dish of the area is seafood, rarely served in other regions of the country. Meat and fish dishes are delicately seasoned, to bring out their natural flavor and the most commonly used spices are mint, oregano, dill, and allspice.

In the Aegean region, instead of the traditional Turkish breakfast consisting of bread, olives, white cheese, cucumbers, and toma-toes, it is worth trying a dish called menemen. It resembles scram-bled eggs but contains many more ingredients, of which the most common are onions, peppers, and tomatoes. There are also vari-eties with sucuk, i.e. local sausage or pastırma – smoked beef slices. Aydın çemen, a spicy paste prepared from tomatoes and paprika with the addition of olive oil, black pepper, and cumin, is a perfect seasoning to sandwiches and many other dishes.

For dinner, you may enjoy the dish called kırlı kızartması, pre-pared from eggplants, with the addition of onions, peppers, and garlic, and later topped with yoghurt. If you prefer meat dishes, then try the speciality from Söke – çöp şiş. These are small cubes of lamb meat, skewered on sticks, and roasted over a fire.

The most interesting regional dishes include kabak tatlısı – a dessert prepared from a pumpkin. Cooked and peeled pumpkin is cut into pieces and sprinkled with sugar. After adding walnuts, the dish is cooked and served with honey dressing. The traditional regional dessert is also kar helvası, literally meaning 'snow halvah'. In the old days, it was prepared from snow obtained in the moun-tains, combined with fruit syrup. Currently, snow is often replaced with crushed ice, served with cherry or cranberry juice. Another of local desserts are figs cooked in milk with sugar.

The best addition to dining out in the evening are meze – the Turkish version of appetisers or Spanish tapas. In the Aegean region, there is a great number of meze varieties, primarily based on vegetables, including peas, beans, artichokes, and zucchini. These snacks are prepared by cooking vegetables in olive oil but are usually served after cooling down. You might also want to try locally produced wines. Admittedly, they are inferior to French or Spanish ones but should please even the palates of the connoisseurs.

Brief history of Greek colonization in Asia Minor

The history of Greek colonisation in Asia Minor is an epic that lasted from the beginning of the Iron Age to modern times. Here we will focus on the colonisation of ancient Anatolia by the Greeks, therefore, for greater clarity and to distinguish this wave of settlement from later movements, we will call them Hellenes.

The beginnings of the Hellenic colonisation of Asia Minor date back to the 10th century BCE when the Aegean Sea coast and nearby islands were settled. The most intensive phase of this process was the so-called Archaic Period, between 700 and 500 BCE. During that time, the Hellenistic settlements on the shores of the Black Sea and the Mediterranean developed. Of course, the territorial scope of Hellenic colonisation was not limited to Asia Minor and covered the areas of the Iberian Peninsula, the Apennine Peninsula, the northern coast of the Black Sea, and North Africa.

The main reason for mass migration from the area of mainland Greece was overcrowding, and the consequent lack of arable land. Through the process of migration, political tensions and conflicts between aristocrats and farmers were relieved. Sometimes the motivation was the development of trade relations, which resulted in the establishment of so-called emporia, i.e. trading colonies. Hellenic trading stations exported timber for shipbuilding, grain, as well as olive oil, wine, honey, and dried fish. Simultaneously they imported papyrus, earthenware, glass, ivory, and purple.

The cities established during the colonisation maintained ties with their native poleis (city-states). However, with time these links were weakened and became more of a symbolic nature. Over time, the cities that began their existence as colonies started further expansion, establishing their colonies. This was, for example, the case of Miletus.

Based on the identity of the tribe that founded the colony, these cities were divided into Ionian, Doric, and Aeolian groups. Ionian settlements in Asia Minor formed the union of twelve cities (so-called Ionian League). This confederation consisted of Miletus, Myus, Priene, Ephesus, Colophon, Lebedos, Teos, Erythrae, Klazomenai, and Phocaea, as well as the colonies on two islands – Samos and Chios. With time, they were joined by Smyrna, initially counted as the Aeolian colony. Ionian cities were located in the central part of the Aegean coast.

The Dorians founded their colonies on islands off the coast of Asia Minor, including Kos, Knidos, and Rhodes. They also settled two cities on the shores of the Bosphorus – Chalcedon and Byzántion. These two colonies turned out to be crucial from a historical perspective as they are now parts of a metropolis of Istanbul.

Aeolian colonies had their federation, just like the Ionian ones. Twelve Aeolian cities in Asia Minor were: Kyme, Larissae, Neonteichos, Temnus, Cilla, Notion, Aegiroessa, Pitane, Aigai, Myrina, Gryneia, and Smyrna.

Hellenic colonies in Asia Minor made a tremendous impact on the history of science because just at that time, the Hellenic researchers started inquiries about the nature of the world, based on scientific research, not on religion or mythology. The best-known Ionian philosophers were: Thales, Anaximander, and Anaximenes – all coming from Miletus, Anaxagoras of Klazomenai, and Heraclitus of Ephesus.

Thales is known for his accurate predictions concerning the date of the solar eclipse. He is the first known individual to apply deductive reasoning to geometry. Thales also thought that the beginning of all things is water. His discussion was continued by Anaximander, Anaximenes, Heraclitus, and Anaxagoras, who all dealt with deductions on the originating principle of nature. They claimed, successively, that this principle was apeiron (immensity), air, fire, and the germs ordered by reason. Heraclitus was also the father of the thought concerning the volatility of the world and became famous for saying that everything flows (panta rhei).

Colonisation movement began to wane from the mid-sixth century BCE. This was due to several reasons: the saturation of the colonies with the settlers, the stabilisation of the economic and political situation in Greece, and most of all – the establishment of the power of Persia and the expansion of Carthage.

Namık Kemal – freedom and homeland

Namık Kemal (b. 1840 – d. 1888) was a pioneer and chief representative of the literary movement, which changed the face of the Turkish literature in the second half of the 19th century. The main feature of the new literature was drawing on the works produced in France and a departure from the traditional Ottoman form and content.

Short biography

Namık Kemal was born in Tekirdağ, to an aristocratic family. His father served as an astronomer at the court of the sultan, and his mother, a native Albanian, was a daughter of the governor of the province. Kemal was educated at home, where he mastered many languages, including French, Arabic, and Persian. As was normally the case for young people from well-to-do families, he entered the career in civil service at the age of 17. He was employed at the Customs Office of Translation, and then in the Sublime Porte, i.e. the Ottoman government.

He soon teamed up with Ibrahim Şinasi, a poet, playwright, and journalist, 14 years his senior. Ibrahim participated in the 1848 revolution in Paris and was a protégé of the Grand Vizier Reşid Pasha. Their friendship resulted in the acquisition by Kemal of the role of editor of daily Tasvir-i Efkâr, after Şinasi fled to France in 1865. This newspaper played a significant role in shaping the opinions of the intellectual elite of the Ottoman Empire.

Initially, Namık Kemal dealt only with the translations of texts for the newspaper but eventually started writing his articles. The subjects covered included the January Uprising in Poland and the Civil War in the United States. His essays on Ottoman issues landed Namık in trouble with the authorities and forced him to emigrate to Europe in 1867.

For the next three years, Namık Kemal moved between European capitals – London, Paris, and Vienna, where he earned his living by writing articles for opposition newspapers owned by the Young Ottomans movement. Simultaneously, he began studying law and economics and translated texts from Turkish to French.

After returning to Turkey in 1871, he renewed his editorial activities. He also created his most important work of literature – a patriotic drama 'Homeland' (tr. *Vatan*). A powerful response to this publication resulted in the imprisonment of the writer in Cyprus, where he remained for more than three years.

After the loss of power by the Sultan Abdülaziz in 1876, Kemal was allowed to return to Istanbul. There he took an active part in the preparation of the constitution. However, soon he fell out of favour of Sultan Abdülhamid II and spent the rest of his life in exile. He died on the island of Chios in 1888, and his tomb can be visited in Bolayır, on the Gallipoli Peninsula.

SIGNIFICANCE

In Turkey Namık Kemal is best known as a preacher of two innovative phrases: freedom and homeland. In his articles, essays, plays, and poems he explained to his compatriots these ideas that had been popular in Europe since the French Revolution, in a form adapted to the perceptions and traditions of Muslim readers.

Despite the revolutionary message of his works, he remained loyal to the Islamic religion. When writing about the motherland, he instead meant a common territory and not a national community. He believed that the ideas imported from Europe should be adapted to local conditions. He even mentioned the pan-Islamic community, which could arise under the leadership of the Ottoman dynasty.

Although the achievements of Western civilisation made a colossal impression on Namık Kemal, he maintained that the backwardness of the Islamic world was not the result of congenital defects of this religion, but rather the dominance of Western countries. It prevented the countries of the East to develop and modernise. As a result, he claimed that the acquisition of the achievements of European civilisation by the Ottoman Empire would be, in fact, returning to the sources of the Muslim tradition.

The works of Montesquieu and Rousseau inspired Namık Kemal's political theories, and his suggestions for their practical implementation were modelled on the parliamentary systems of England and France. He identified with the ideas of Montesquieu and tried to fit them into the requirements of Islamic religious law (the Shari'ah). In his eyes, the religious rules were in fact identical with natural law, as described by the French philosopher.

The far-reaching effects of this reasoning became apparent during the opening meeting of the session of the Ottoman parliament in 1909 when the Sultan himself began his speech by referring to 'a parliamentary form of government prescribed by the Shari'ah.'

The works of Namık Kemal also became a source of inspiration and a topic of discussion for the Cadets of Harbiye Military School in Istanbul. It was read secretly. One of the attentive readers was a young cadet called Mustafa Kemal, the future Father of the Turks.

The curious case of Ottoman minelayer Nusret

On March 18, 2015, there was the centenary of the naval battle of the Dardanelles, fought during the First World War. From the outbreak of this war, the Allied forces were planning to cross this narrow strait that connects the Aegean Sea with the Sea of Marmara and therefore is an essential section of the sea route from the Mediterranean to Istanbul. Their primary goal was to capture to this city which was, at that time, the capital of the Ottoman Empire. The naval operations of the fleet, which consisted mainly of ships from the Royal Navy, were led by Rear Admiral John de Robeck. He had taken over the command of the operations in the mid-March 1915.

However, De Robeck did not realise that the outcome of the naval battle had already been decided by the events that had taken place before he took up the command of the Allied fleet. On the night of March 8, 1915, captain Hakki Bey of the Ottoman minelayer Nusret, secretly directed his ship to the waters of Erenköy Bay, located near the Asian shore of the Dardanelles. The crew spent that night laying 26 mines parallel to the shoreline. The Allies knew about the other mines protecting the Dardanelles from their attack, but Erenköy Bay area was considered safe for manoeuvres. This way, the trap had been prepared for the flotilla of British and French ships.

On the 18th of March 1915, the grand flotilla of Allied vessels began a concentrated attack in the Dardanelles. The French battleship Bouvet struck a mine while manoeuvring in Erenköy Bay. It sank quickly, taking 639 crew members to the bottom of the Dardanelles. The British thought that the ship was hit by a torpedo or a missile which caused an explosion on board but did not suspect that in reality, Bouvet sank because of a naval mine.

Around 4 pm, a British battlecruiser HMS Inflexible ran into a mine near the place where Bouvet sank. This time, 30 people were killed, but the cruiser remained on the surface and eventually made it as far as the island of Bozcaada (Tenedos) where it was beached. Another ship that fell into the same trap was a Formidable-class pre-dreadnought battleship, HMS Irresistible. As a result, another 150 lives were lost. The surviving members of the crew were taken from the deck of the sinking ship by HMS Ocean. This Canopus-class battleship was sent to tow away the severely damaged Irresistible. However, during the manoeuvres carried out in the shallow waters the Bay, HMS Ocean also hit a mine. Several destroyers rescued the crews of both ships, but HMS Ocean drifted into Morto Bay and sank there.

Heavy losses forced de Robeck to order the withdrawal of the remaining ships from the Dardanelles. The 18th of March 1915 turned out to be a day of great victory of the Ottoman Empire and one of the few triumphs its army could claim during the First World War. The Allies began to prepare for the land invasion of the Gallipoli peninsula, which began on the 25th of April 1915.

Since these events, Nusret has been regarded as a hero of the Dardanelles campaign. However, the fate of the ship does not reflect its role in the Ottoman victory in March of 1915. After the end of the First World War, Nusret was moored in Istanbul until 1927, when it was refitted in a shipyard in Gölcük, where one of the Turkish Navy bases is located. For a short period, from 1937 to 1939, the ship, renamed as Yardım, served as a diving vessel. Then, in 1955, again as Nusret, it was decommissioned, and the plans were made to convert it to a museum ship. However, unexpectedly, in 1962, the vessel was sold to private entrepreneurs who turned it into a merchant vessel known as Kaptan Nusret. The end to Nusret's long service in the merchant navy came in 1989 when it sank near Mersin harbour.

However, this is not the end of the story – after almost ten years under the waters of the Mediterranean, Nusret was pulled out of the sea and acquired by the Municipality of Tarsus. After extensive reconstruction ashore, Nusret was finally transformed into a museum ship and is now the main attraction of Tarsus Çanakkale Park opened in 2008. In the meantime, or more precisely, in 1982, a replica of Nusret was built by the Gölcük Naval Shipyard to be displayed in Çanakkale Military Museum. On board of this replica, some photos and plans showing the history of the ship are displayed. However, to see the real Nusret it is necessary to travel to Tarsus, located on the Mediterranean coast, far to the southeast of the Dardanelles.

The Battle of Gallipoli

In 1914, the authorities of the Ottoman Empire took the disastrous decision, which turned out to be the final nail in the coffin for 'the Sick Man of Europe' as the Ottoman Empire was called in the last years of its existence. The Committee of Union and Progress (tr. *Ittihat ve Terakki Cemiyeti*), actually exercising power on behalf of the powerless Sultan Mehmed V, decided to take part in the First World War. They supported the side of the Central Powers; that is the German Empire, the Austro-Hungarian Empire, and the Tsardom of Bulgaria. The direct responsibility for this decision rests with three leaders of CUP: Talaat Pasha, Enver Pasha, and Jemal Pasha.

From the very beginning of the war, the Ottoman army suffered severe defeats. On the eastern front, in the Caucasus mountains, the Russians defeated the army led by Enver Pasha, and in the Battle of the Suez Canal, the British army quickly repelled Jemal Pasha's troops. However, the biggest threat to the very existence of the empire was much closer to its capital – Istanbul. The route for the Allied Navy (i.e. an alliance of Great Britain, France, and Russia) to Istanbul led through the Dardanelles Strait, from the Aegean Sea to the Sea of Marmara. If the forces of the Entente had gotten through this strait and the Gallipoli Peninsula, nothing would have prevented them from taking the Ottoman capital. This situation would have been tantamount to the final defeat of the Ottoman Empire.

Initially, the Allied forces attempted to break through to Istanbul by sea. In February 1915, there were 18 warships, under the British, French and Russian flags, in the waters of the Aegean Sea just off the Gallipoli Peninsula. However, an attempt to break out through the Strait failed as the long-range guns and naval mines heavily protected the peninsula and the waterway. The Allies retreated after the loss of three ships and decided to initiate the land campaign. The person responsible for its preparation was Winston Churchill, better known from his later achievements as the Prime Minister of the United Kingdom.

Pessimistic sentiments prevailed in Istanbul. The city was preparing for evacuation and the gold and archives of the Ottoman sultans were transported to Asia Minor. The command of the defence of the Gallipoli Peninsula was given to the German General – Liman von Sanders – who had predicted that there would be fighting for the land section of this front. He asked for a new division, which would become a part of the Fifth Army, and his request was granted.

At this point, let us travel back in time, to January of 1915. At that moment, Colonel Mustafa Kemal took command of the 19th Division, which had been stationed on the European shore of the Marmara Sea. At the time the division existed mainly in official documents. When von Sanders asked for reinforcements, he was assigned to this unit. Mustafa Kemal had two months to organise his troops and prepare them for fighting on the crucial military front.

Von Sanders and Mustafa Kemal disliked each other from the very beginning. During their first meeting, von Sanders asked Kemal why the Bulgarians had not joined the fighting yet. Kemal replied that they were not convinced of the German victory. When von Sanders wanted to know the opinion of Mustafa Kemal, he said that he had agreed with the Bulgarians.

Colonel Kemal knew the terrain that he was supposed to defend from his practical experiences gained during the Balkan Wars. He developed strong convictions about the strategy which should have been adopted: the control of mountain ridges, that would be stormed by the Allies after landing on the peninsula was of the utmost importance.

The land campaign began on the 25th of April 1915. The French troops attacked the area on the Asian shore, in the vicinity of Kumkale, and the British forces landed on the Gallipoli Peninsula. This manoeuvre was intended to outflank the Dardanelles. Additional Allied forces, comprised of soldiers from Australia and New Zealand, collectively referred to as the ANZAC, were supposed to land on the peninsula in the vicinity of Kabatepe. Surprisingly, due to the strong sea currents, they disembarked 2 km away, in Arıburnu. No one expected such a turn of events. The narrow beach was walled off from the plateau by a 70-meter-high wall of rock. Natural conditions of this location prompted the Turks to ignore the necessity of defending this area because no sensible commander would have planned the attack from this point.

In the morning of the 25th of April, the division under the command of Mustafa Kemal was holding the manoeuvres in the vicinity of Arıburnu. Suddenly, excited scouts appeared in front of the commander, shouting something about approaching Englishmen. Mustafa Kemal made a snap decision to transform a military exercise into a regular battle. In this way, the element of surprise unexpectedly worked to the benefit of the Turkish forces. Colonel Kemal took a considerable risk, judging that the enemy forces were of significant size, despite the report of the scouts, describing 'small units of the enemy.' Exceeding his authority, Mustafa Kemal ordered his best regiment to occupy strategic positions on the ridge of Koja Chemen. If he had been wrong, that would have meant the weakening of the forces defending other potential points of the Allied landing. However, no mistake was made, and a moment of hesitation of the ANZAC forces at the sight of the Turkish troops, let the whole 57th regiment reach the battlefield. During the fight, Mustafa Kemal uttered these famous words 'Men, I am not ordering you to attack. I am ordering you to die.' And so, exactly this happened: while almost the entire 57th regiment was killed during the battle, but the Allies were detained.

Over the next three months, Mustafa Kemal resisted the relentless attacks of hostile forces, often exceeding his authority as a commander of just one division. After the first unsuccessful attack of the Allies, both parties turned to entrenched warfare, punctuated by sudden attacks aimed at breaking the Turkish resistance.

On the 18th of May, another great battle took place, this time planned by Liman von Sanders. The lack of imagination and proper planning resulted in a massacre of the Turkish troops. The losses on both sides were so high that a truce was announced to bury the dead.

The brilliant leadership of Mustafa Kemal was recognised, and he was honoured by the Iron Cross. Nevertheless, he asked for a transfer to another front. The reason was the impossibility of cooperation with Liman von Sanders. Enver Pasha did not fulfil the request of Colonel Kemal who resigned to this fate and threw himself into the fray of the Gallipoli Campaign. During the conversation with the corps commander Essad Pasha, he mentioned the possibility of another attack of the Allies in the vicinity of Suvla Bay. Essad advised him not to worry because the opponent could not do this. Kemal summed up the conversation by saying 'Let's hope you're right.'

However, the right was on Kemal's side. In August 1915, the British planned another offensive on the Gallipoli Peninsula. It began with an attack on Suvla Bay, located in the vicinity of two villages bearing the names of Great and Small Anafarta. The terrain was so difficult that it was counted as an indispensable element of surprise. This bold plan of the Allies was again thwarted by Mustafa Kemal. Upon learning about the movements of the British troops, he took the risky decision to transfer two companies to the area of Suvla Bay. By this ruling, he weakened the main front of fighting where an Australian offensive was in progress. By the decision of von Sanders, Mustafa Kemal was appointed as the commander of all Turkish troops located in the vicinity of Anafarta. During the fighting, he virtually stopped sleeping and was further weakened by the bouts of malaria.

On the third day of the battle, Mustafa Kemal personally led the attack and narrowly escaped death. Shrapnel hit him in the chest and destroyed a commemorative watch. On the same day, the fight on the Anafarta section was finally over, and the Turks captured the British positions. The famous, damaged watch was donated to Liman von Sanders, in exchange for a chronometer with the coat of arms of the German commander.

It was not yet the end of the campaign on the Dardanelles. It lasted until February 1916. Vast numbers of people lost their lives: more than 120,000 soldiers died, including 80,000 Turks. Among the British citizens, 8.5 thousand Australians and 2.7 thousand New Zealanders were killed. Mustafa Kemal left the Gallipoli Peninsula just before the withdrawal of the Allied troops. He moved to Istanbul to improve his health.

The merits of Mustafa Kemal in the Gallipoli Campaign are hard to overestimate. It is true that he was not responsible for the whole front and that other commanders also contributed to the success of the Turkish army. However, undoubtedly his contribution to the ultimate success and repulsion of the enemy was significant. Istanbul was saved, at least temporarily, but nobody greeted Mustafa Kemal as a war hero. For a long time, his fame was limited to military circles, mainly because of Enver Pasha. He did not want a competitor to the role of the heroic leader. He was so effective at overshadowing Mustafa Kemal, that in 1919, during the occupation of Istanbul by the British army, the main translator at the British Embassy, and also an expert on local issues, Andrew Ryan, did not remember the name of Mustafa Kemal. This way Mustafa Kemal successfully became the inspector of the 9th Army. From that moment another struggle of Mustafa Kemal began, this time for the liberation of Asia Minor from the occupation of the Allied forces.

References

- Akurgal, Ekrem, Ancient Civilizations and Ruins of Turkey, NET Turistik Yayinlar, Istanbul, Turkey, 2011.
- Bossert, Helmut T., Asia, Universite Matbaasi Komandit Sti., Istanbul, Turkey, 1946.
- Bryce, Trevor, The Kingdom of the Hittites, Oxford University Press, Oxford, UK, 2010.
- Freely, John, The Western Shores of Turkey, Tauris Parke Paperbacks, London, UK, 2004.
- Grimal, Pierre, Słownik mitologii greckiej i rzymskiej, Ossolineum, Wrocław, Poland, 1990.
- Jablonka, Peter, Troy in Regional and International Context, [in:] The Oxford Handbook of Ancient Anatolia pod red. Steadman, Sharon S., McMahon, Gregory, Oxford University Press, Oxford, UK, 2011.
- Jevakhoff, Alexandre, Kemal Atatürk, Dialog, Warsaw, Poland, 2004 (in Polish).
- Jevakhoff, Alexandre, Kemal Atatürk : les chemins de l'Occident, Jules Tallandier, Frace, 1989 (in French).
- Jewett, Robert, Mapping the Route of Paul's 'Second Missionary Journey' from Dorylaeum to Troas, Tyndale Bulletin, 48.1 (1997).
- Kinross, Patrick, Atatürk. The Rebirth of a Nation, Phoenix, London, UK, 2001.
- Kiyak, N.G. et al., Luminescence Dating of Prehistoric Site of Smintheion (Gulpinar) in NW Turkey, Mediterranean Archaeology and Archaeometry, Vol. 10, No. 4 (2010).
- Korfman, Manfred O., Mannsperger, Dietrich P.,

Troia/Wilusa Guidebook, Çanakkale-Tübingen Troia Vakfı, Turkey, 2010.

— Lewis, Bernard, The Emergence of Modern Turkey, Oxford University Press, Oxford, UK, 2002.

— Mango, Andrew, Atatürk, John Murray, London, UK, 2004.

— Oliphant, Margaret, Antyczny Świat, Muza S.A., Warszawa, 1993 (in Polish).

— Starke, Frank, Troia im Kontext des historisch-politischen und sprachlichen Umfeldes Kleinasiens im 2. Jahrtausend, Studia Troica, 7 (1997) (in German).

— Winter, Frederick E., Notes on Neandria, American Journal of Archaeology, Vol. 89, No. 4 (1985).

— Wolski, Józef, Historia Powszechna - Starożytność, PWN, Warsaw, Poland, 2002 (in Polish).

— Wolski, Józef (red.), Atlas Historyczny Świata, PPWK, Warsaw-Wroclaw, Poland, 1992 (in Polish).

— Wróblewski, Andrzej K., Historia Fizyki, PWN, Warsaw, Poland, 2007 (in Polish).

Printed by Amazon Italia Logistica S.r.l.
Torrazza Piemonte (TO), Italy

11198959R00185